Daring to be myself

Daring to be myself

A case study in
rational-emotive therapy

Windy Dryden and
Joseph Yankura

Open University Press
Buckingham · *Philadelphia*

Open University Press
Celtic Court
22 Ballmoor
Buckingham
MK18 1XW

and
1900 Frost Road, Suite 101
Bristol, PA 19007, USA

First Published 1992

British Library Cataloguing-in-Publication Data

Dryden, Windy
  Daring to be myself: a case study in
  rational-emotive therapy.
  I. Title   II. Yankura, Joseph
  616.89

  ISBN 0–335–09341–8

Library of Congress Cataloging-in-Publication Data

Dryden, Windy.
    Daring to be myself: a case study in rational-emotive therapy/
  Windy Dryden, Joseph Yankura.
      p.   cm.
  Includes bibliographical references and index.
    ISBN 0–335–09341–8 (paper)
    1. Rational-emotive psychotherapy—Case studies.   I. Yankura,
  Joseph.   II. Title.
  RC489.R3D785 1992
  616.89'14—dc20   91–33610
                                                         CIP

Typeset by Inforum Typesetting, Portsmouth
Printed in Great Britain by Biddles Limited, Guildford and Kings Lynn

To Sarah,
in recognition of
her willingness to share an
intensely personal experience
with others

Contents

Foreword

This is a remarkably good and quite unique book on rational-emotive therapy (RET). The authors show in unusual detail how RET can be adapted to the specific style of an experienced therapist, how it can be democratically taught to an unsophisticated and hesitant client, and how it can be effective in a limited number of sessions over a brief period of time.

Windy Dryden beautifully reveals himself, as well as his client, in the verbatim protocols in this book; and while sticking closely to rational-emotive theory, creatively adapts it in his own inimitable way. He succeeds incredibly well with the client, Sarah, but he and his collaborator, Joseph Yankura, also courageously display Windy's limitations and lapses, and thereby come up with a rare, exceptionally honest book showing how therapy is actually done and what its restrictions are. Few therapists have ever so clearly revealed the details of what they have actually done with their clients, nor have they revealed these details in an uncensored, warts and all manner. In doing so, Drs Dryden and Yankura have published an outstanding document that is rare in the entire annals of psychotherapy.

Does Windy Dryden, in these protocols, truly practice RET? Indeed he does, because almost any rational-emotive therapist would tackle his client's, Sarah's, main problems and try to help her work on her self-denigration and her low frustration tolerance and would therefore cover the most important points that Dr Dryden covers. His uses of vivid, dramatic techniques is uniquely and marvellously done; but this is often an essential part of RET along with its heavy cognitive or philosophic procedures. His use of humour is also a normal part of RET sessions, though his particular way of employing it is his own original and creative adaptation. None of the methods that he uses in the sessions with Sarah are foreign to RET; and, as shown by his coauthor, Joe Yankura and himself, his relating to Sarah very amiably but still not with excessive sympathy and warmth, is also typical of RET. Other rational-emotive therapists might have chosen to be even warmer to Sarah but many, like myself, would have chosen pretty much to treat her in the manner that Windy did.

If I had seen Sarah myself is there anything that I would have done with her that Windy did not do? Yes, I would have done a few additional things that are often employed in RET and that Windy sometimes uses himself today even though he did not get around to doing them in the course of his ten sessions with Sarah.

First, I would have given Sarah reading or listening assignments, such as reading RET pamphlets and books, because such bibliotherapy assignments might have helped her understand and use some of the RET philosophy quicker and better. Windy's own recent book with Jack Gordon, *Think Your Way to Happiness* (London: Sheldon Press, 1990) or some of the pamphlets we routinely give to the clients at the Psychological Clinic of the Institute for Rational-Emotive Therapy in New York might well be used in this connection.

Second, I would probably have worked with Sarah on her smoking, as Windy did, but when she still kept smoking too much, I would have used reinforcement principles as is often done in RET. Thus, I would have encouraged her to reward herself every time she kept to her smoking goals and possibly penalize herself whenever she did not do so.

Third, I would have used regular self-help report forms with Sarah, to help her zero in on her specific irrational beliefs when she upset herself and to work out disputations for them.

All of the above RET additions to what Windy did with Sarah, however, are hardly necessary, as long as the basic principles and practice of rational-emotive therapy, which he did beautifully employ, were included in the course of his sessions with her. Because Windy Dryden did such an excellent job with Sarah and because he and Joe Yankura detail exactly what he did (and did not do), I think that *Daring to be Myself* had better be required reading for anyone who wants to practice RET – as well as for those who choose to use it to help themselves with their own problems.

Albert Ellis, Ph.D., President, Institute for Rational-Emotive Therapy

Preface

We believe that this is a unique book. While there are now numerous clinically oriented texts on rational-emotive therapy (RET), there is none that takes an in-depth look at a single case as it unfolds over time. Indeed, there are very few books in the entire field of psychotherapy that detail a single case and draw upon extensive actual dialogue to show therapy in action.

This book closely traces the developing therapeutic work between Sarah and Dr Windy Dryden and uses substantial transcript material to illustrate the therapist's interventions and the client's response. We want to stress that apart from minor cosmetic changes to enable the dialogue material to flow better, the exchanges between Sarah and Dr Dryden are reported here as they actually happened.

A further unique aspect of the book is that the second author (Dr Joe Yankura) conducted interviews with both Sarah and Dr Dryden eight years after the end of their therapeutic work together.

We wish to stress that this book was undertaken with the full support of Sarah and her family. To protect her and their confidentiality all names and identifying material have been changed.

Windy Dryden, London   June 1991
Joe Yankura, New York

1 Background information: therapist and client

In order to facilitate the reader's appreciation and understanding of the therapy session transcripts and commentary contained within this book, the present chapter will provide some basic factual information on the therapist, Dr Windy Dryden, and the client, Sarah. Dr Dryden's material will emphasize aspects of his training and experience which are relevant to his treatment of Sarah; her material will provide an outline of her educational, employment and family background. Her material is purposely somewhat non-specific in order to preserve her right to remain anonymous.

Dr Dryden

Windy Dryden received his PhD in Social Psychology in 1974. The topic of his thesis was 'self-disclosure' and as a result of carrying out his research he became interested in counselling and psychotherapy. His first training in the field was on the one-year full-time postgraduate Diploma in Counselling in Educational Settings run at Aston University which was rooted in the person-centred tradition of counselling. Dr Dryden was appointed as a lecturer in counselling at Aston University as soon as he completed his studies there in 1975.

As a result of his initial experience as a counsellor in the mid-1970s, Dr Dryden came to believe that the core conditions of empathy, warmth and genuineness were important but neither necessary nor sufficient for good client outcome. Thus, he sought further training in the field. After a brief but unsatisfying 'flirtation' with psychodynamic psychotherapy, Dr Dryden became interested in rational-emotive therapy because it seemed to offer the practical help that his clients were seeking. He began his training in RET in July 1978 at the Institute for RET in New York and continued his training over several years achieving Associate Fellow and Supervisory status in RET.

In order to broaden his experience Dr Dryden took a Masters degree in Psychotherapy at the University of Warwick, which he was awarded in 1980. This was an eclectic course and provided Dr Dryden with a broad framework in which to practise RET. Additionally, in 1981, he took a sabbatical from his post at Aston University and spent six months at the Center for Cognitive Therapy in Philadelphia and thus became one of the few people at that time who were trained in both RET and cognitive therapy.

Up until he saw Sarah, Dr Dryden's clinical experience was in a university counselling service, a general medical practice, where he worked part-time as a counselling psychologist, and in the Mood Clinic at the Center for Cognitive Therapy.

His varying training and practical experience as a psychotherapist is evident in his work with Sarah that forms the basis of this book.

Sarah

Sarah was born into a family of seven children; she has five sisters and one brother. Her mother (now deceased) was English, and her father is Pakistani. While she was raised to be a Moslem, she presently has no formal affiliation with any particular religious group or church. Sarah believes that her mother would have liked to have borne more than one son in order to please her husband, and that she was chronically critical and demanding of her daughters because they weren't boys.

Sarah first married at age 17, against the wishes of her parents. Her son, Peter, was a product of this union. She subsequently divorced her first husband, and is currently married to Art. Art's family is Catholic; at the time her therapy began, Sarah believed that they disapproved of her because she was non-Catholic, previously divorced, and had an ethnically mixed heritage.

Sarah never went to college, and considers herself to have a working-class background. She has held a variety of part-time jobs during her marriage to Art; these jobs served to supplement the family's income while not significantly interfering with her role as a homemaker. Sarah is proud of her ability to run a household and budget the family finances; she, however, tended, before seeking therapy to be perfectionistic with regard to her home and personal appearance.

At the time of Sarah's therapy, her son, Peter, was attempting to pursue a university education. Sarah fully supported him in this endeavour, but was quite worried about the possibility that his efforts might fail. In addition, she was experiencing frequent anxious and depressed moods in relation to a number of other issues, most of which revolved around her relationships with family members. She consulted her general practitioner, hoping that he would provide her with some medication to relieve her upsets. Noting that much of her distress appeared to be psychological in origin, he instead recommended that she seek counselling. He referred her to Dr Dryden, with whom he had a professional affiliation. Sarah, now in her late 30s, subsequently decided to act on her physician's advice, and contacted Dr Dryden to arrange her first therapy session.

Having gained some familiarity with the players who will hold centre stage throughout most of this volume, the reader is now advised to become acquainted with the technical features of the treatment that Dr Dryden provides to Sarah. The following chapter provides this information by reviewing the origins, theory and techniques of rational-emotive therapy.

2 The basic theory and techniques of rational-emotive therapy

As noted in the Preface, the present volume intends to provide an annotated explication of the manner in which RET was applied to the problems presented by a particular client in Dr Windy Dryden's psychotherapy practice. The authors recognize, however, that potential readers of the transcript material which follows in subsequent chapters will possess varying degrees of sophistication and knowledge concerning the rational-emotive approach. As such, this chapter will attempt to provide a brief introduction to the basic theory and techniques of RET.

Readers who have received approved training in RET (through the Institute for Rational-Emotive Therapy) or have previously researched this approach to psychotherapy may reasonably choose to omit the first part of this chapter, which provides basic background material. Readers with little or no knowledge of RET are strongly encouraged to take the time to study it, as it will serve to provide a context for understanding Dr Dryden's choice of strategies and interventions with his client. Without such a context, it is possible that many of his therapeutic activities may be misinterpreted and misunderstood.

The authors recommend that almost all readers complete the second, briefer portion of this chapter, which provides details on a number of technical innovations and variations employed by Dr Dryden. This material is considered important, as it will serve to underscore the manner in which his approach differs from that of the premier practitioner and creator of RET, Dr Albert Ellis. It is here noted, however, that while Dr Dryden makes use of certain innovations, he consistently operates from a rational-emotive theoretical base. Hopefully, it will be apparent to the reader that his innovations tend to flow naturally from this conceptual foundation.

The basic theoretical concepts of RET

Few 'new' ideas are completely original, as almost all thinkers and theorists are heavily influenced by the work of individuals who preceded them. While Dr

Albert Ellis correctly maintains that his formulation of RET represents a unique contribution to the field of psychotherapy, he has also been quite specific in identifying and describing the ideas and experiences which influenced it. In this regard, he has credited a number of the concepts contained within the writings of certain ancient and contemporary philosophers as being instrumental in his creation of RET. Consequently, unlike most other schools of psychotherapy, RET can be seen to have an explicit and strong philosophical heritage.

The ancient Greek and Roman Stoic philosophers (such as Epictetus and Marcus Aurelius) stressed the notion that human happiness and misery were largely philosophically based. This view can be summarized in Epictetus's statement that 'People are disturbed not by things, but by the view which they take of them' (Epictetus 1956). With respect to more contemporary philosophical influences, Ellis has been influenced by such individuals as Kant, Popper and Russell. Kant is here considered to be representative of philosophers who wrote on the power (and limitations) of human cognition. Popper and others emphasized that humans are always forming hypotheses about the nature of the world, and that it is important to test the validity of these hypotheses. Russell was representative of a philosophical cadre which opposed the deification and devil-ification of humans. Ellis has also indicated that he was influenced by the work of the existential philosophers (such as Heidegger and Tillich) and the general semanticists (such as Korzybski).

In addition to these philosophical ancestors and relatives, Ellis's formulation of RET was also influenced by the work of a number of other psychologists. Horney (1950) introduced the concept of the 'tyranny of the shoulds', while Adler's (1927) Individual Psychology stressed the importance of humans' goals, purposes, values and meanings. Some of the early behaviourists, such as Jones (1924) and Watson and Rayner (1920), espoused techniques which involved active, *in vivo* exposure to feared stimuli.

Ellis's creation of RET was also heavily influenced by his own life experiences. In this vein, he has made reference to what he regards as his own inborn temperament, as well as his early professional experiences as a practising psychoanalyst (Dryden and Ellis 1989). With regard to the former, he has described how he tended – from a very early age – to resolve to make the best of unfortunate circumstances by applying an active problem-solving approach. With regard to the latter, he has detailed his gradual dissatisfaction with the results he obtained with clients by utilizing the relatively passive techniques of psychoanalysis, and how he came to experiment with a more active-directive, confrontative approach. This experimentation led him to conclude that such an approach was both more effective and efficient, and led to his earliest publications on his new method (Ellis 1957; 1962).

Ellis's formulation of RET can be viewed as representing a grand synthesis of all of the influences cited above. It is noted, however, that the whole can be regarded as greater than the sum of its parts, as Ellis has added his own particular emphases and invented his own terminology in his expositions of RET. The reader will now be introduced to some of these emphases and terminological inventions in the subsequent presentation on RET's basic theoretical concepts. The section immediately below describes the role played by cognition in producing either psychological health or disturbance.

Rational and irrational beliefs

Many currently practised forms of psychotherapy emphasize the role played by environmental circumstances in promoting or compromising psychological health. Psychoanalytic therapists, for example, tend to stress the impact of early childhood experiences, while behaviour therapists may highlight the importance of the individual's conditioning history. While RET acknowledges that prior history and present circumstances certainly contribute to the level of psychological adjustment attained by a human being, it emphasizes the role played by current *internal* events in the genesis and maintenance of psychological disturbance. Here, the term 'internal events' is used to refer to the cognitions which affect and influence an individual's emotions and behaviour.

With respect to such cognitions, rational-emotive theory makes a distinction between *rational* and *irrational* beliefs. Rational beliefs are described as promoting our basic welfare and happiness, while irrational beliefs are viewed as strongly contributing to emotional distress and dysfunctional behaviour. Ellis (1976; 1979) hypothesizes that the tendency to create and subscribe to irrational beliefs is biologically based, as such beliefs appear to be so numerous, pervasive and difficult to eradicate in human thinking.

It is relatively easy to distinguish between rational and irrational beliefs, as they can be contrasted on the following dimensions: verifiability, demandingness, emotional consequences, behavioural consequences and goal attainment.

Verifiability Rational beliefs are largely based upon observable data, while irrational beliefs are not. Thus, it is possible to cite sound evidence to support the validity of rational beliefs. Irrational beliefs, on the other hand, cannot be supported by the facts. They aie not based in reality. As an example, consider the following statement: 'It is good to have the approval of other people; therefore, I *must* have this approval.' The initial part of this belief would be considered rational, as we can find ample evidence to support the notion that it is beneficial to have the approval of others. The second part is clearly irrational, since there is no evidence to support the contention that one *must* have that which is desirable.

Demandingness Irrational beliefs have a demanding, rigid, absolutistic quality to them, while rational beliefs have a more probabilistic flavour and most often merely reflect our preferences, desires and wishes. Irrational thinking is frequently reflected in sentences which contain words and phrases such as *should*, *must*, *ought to* and *need*, when these idioms are employed in a fashion which reflects a philosophy of absolutism and dogmatism. Such a philosophy refuses to accept the reality of circumstances as they actually exist. To illustrate, the phrase, 'I wish it would stop raining', would be considered rational, since it merely states what an individual's preference might be. 'It *must* stop raining' is irrational, because it is absolutistic and in conflict with reality.

Emotional consequences Both rational and irrational beliefs can lead to negative emotions; however, irrational beliefs result in the types of negative emotions that will most often have a debilitating effect upon an individual's functioning. The negative emotions produced by rational beliefs, on the other hand, are most often less extreme and can actually facilitate effective functioning in so far as they provide the individual with an impetus for attempting to change modifiable aspects of a given situation. Within RET, debilitating negative emotions are referred to as *inappropriate* feelings, while facilitative negative emotions are labelled *appropriate* feelings (Ellis 1973; 1977; 1980). Emotional states such as anger, anxiety, depression, guilt and shame fall into the inappropriate category; feelings such as concern, regret, disappointment and sadness are considered to be appropriate emotions.

Behavioural consequences As stated above, irrational beliefs can lead to debilitating emotional states. These states are debilitating not only because they are strongly dysphoric, but also because they often contribute to a variety of associated behavioural problems. Thus, the individual plagued by guilt might engage in a number of self-punishing, self-destructive behaviours, the anxious person might behave in an avoidant fashion, and the individual who frequently becomes angry may act in an accusing and aggressive manner. Rational beliefs result in feelings that, although possibly still negative, enhance the probability of engaging in constructive problem-solving behaviours.

Goal attainment Most people want to have good interpersonal relationships, to fill their lives with a maximum of pleasure, and to make optimal use of their skills and talents. Because irrational beliefs produce inappropriate negative emotions and contribute to self-defeating behaviours they will often create significant obstacles to the attainment of these goals. Rational beliefs increase the probability of attaining such goals, as they usually result in self-enhancing feelings and behaviours.

In addition to the distinctions described above, rational beliefs differ from irrational beliefs in terms of the latter's contribution to the forming of erroneous evaluative conclusions about one's self, other people, or conditions as they exist in the world. These erroneous evaluations are viewed as comprising three major categories, which in RET's lexicon are termed awfulizing, person-rating, and 'I-can't-stand-it-itis' (Dryden and Ellis 1987). They can be described as follows.

Awfulizing When individuals rigidly believe that certain conditions in the world *must not* exist, they are likely to conclude that these conditions are *awful* (i.e. much more than merely unfortunate or inconvenient). Awfulizing has the potential to cause humans to make themselves anxious with respect to anticipated future events that they believe *must not* occur, and depressed with respect to past events that they believe *should not* have happened.

Person-rating When individuals apply absolutistic shoulds and musts to themselves (e.g. 'I *must* always be competent on my job') they may be prone to engage in global negative self-evaluations when they perceive that they have failed to meet these self-imposed demands ('I made a significant error at work; that makes me a total loser!'). When they direct such absolutistic demands to other people's behaviour (e.g. 'You *must* always treat me fairly and considerately'), they will likely rate these individuals in a totally negative and condemning manner ('You treated me unfairly; therefore, you are the lowest life form on earth!'). Global negative *self*-evaluations can bring on affective states such as guilt and depression; global negative evaluations of others contribute to angry, rageful feelings.

I-can't-stand-it-itis   When individuals subscribe to the beliefs that they *must not* experience pain, discomfort or inconvenience, and *must* always have what they want when they want it, they will be likely to conclude that they *can't stand it* when unpleasant or unfortunate events occur. I-can't-stand-it-itis contributes to low frustration tolerance (LFT), which in turn may result in avoidance of activities which involve discomfort, as well as needless emotional misery when such activities are finally faced.

The irrational beliefs to which individuals subscribe can produce two major types of emotional disturbances, which rational-emotive theory terms *ego disturbance* and *discomfort disturbance*. The former results when one's irrational beliefs lead to total self-condemnation and the idea that one is worthless; the latter occurs when one's absolutistic demands for comfort, safety and convenience are perceived as violated. The rational-emotive solution to ego disturbance is to approach a state of self-acceptance wherein one is able to fully acknowledge personal faults as well as assets, without attempting to rate one's self in either a negative or positive fashion. Developing greater tolerance for frustration is considered the main means for remedying discomfort disturbance.

RET places an emphasis upon helping clients to identify and replace their upset-producing irrational beliefs with more rational ones. As a preliminary step in this process, however, it is deemed beneficial to provide clients with a means for understanding the interrelationships between their external circumstances, beliefs, emotions and behaviours. RET provides a succinct and readily comprehensible model for facilitating such understanding, described below.

The ABC model of emotions and behaviour

When clients first enter psychotherapy, they may be in considerable confusion regarding the nature and origin of their emotional and behavioural disturbance. They may lack adequate terminology for labelling their upsets, and may experience anxiety and negative self-rating with respect to their perceived inability to understand and control their symptoms. Rational-emotive therapists are able to help such clients quickly gain important insights regarding their presenting problems by teaching them Ellis's famous ABC model of emotions and behaviour. The components of this model can be defined as follows.

A denotes *Activating Events*, a term which is used to refer to perceived events and circumstances which precede and appear (to the client) to trigger emotional upsets. Such events may be regarded as external (such as the loss of a job or a love relationship) or largely internal (such as thoughts regarding an anticipated unfortunate future event). In addition, the client's recognition that a psychological problem exists can also serve as an activating event.

B stands for *Beliefs*, which as detailed above can fall into either the rational or irrational category. Typically, an emotionally distressed individual will have both types of beliefs in operation with respect to a given activating event. Thus, for example, an individual may recognize that 'It is desirable to make competent decisions at work' (a rational belief), and then escalate this belief into the absolutistic demand that 'Therefore, I *must* always make competent decisions' (an irrational belief). As per rational-emotive theory, the latter belief will contribute to significant emotional upsets and behavioural dysfunction when the individual is required to make an important decision, or is confronted with evidence of personal responsibility for a poor decision.

C is used to refer to *Consequent Emotions and Behaviours*, which are here viewed as the products of applying one's belief system to a given activating event. If this belief system is mainly rational, it will lead to the types of emotional and behavioural consequences which facilitate effective problem-solving and goal-attainment. If these beliefs are mainly irrational, however, they will lead to a variety of dysfunctional emotions and behaviours which serve as obstacles to psychological adjustment.

In order to illustrate the interrelationships between these components of the ABC model, consider the case of a young male client who enters therapy in part because of self-described 'shyness'. When confronted with a social situation (such as an office party), this individual tends to fade into the background, approaching few people and initiating even fewer conversations. This behavioural deficit stems from the anxiety he experiences when he thinks about the possibility of being rejected when he makes a social overture. Thus, the anticipation of a rejection experience serves as an (internal) activating event, while his anxiety and avoidance behaviour are viewed as dysfunctional consequent emotions and behaviours. These undesirable consequences could conceivably stem from his irrational belief that 'I *must* gain the approval of people I consider significant; to be rejected by them would be *awful!*' If he instead only subscribed to the rational belief that 'It is merely *desirable* to gain the approval of important others, and only *unfortunate* if I am rejected', then he would likely have a much easier time in getting himself to approach and speak to co-workers at social functions. His rational-emotive therapist would attempt to help him see the relationship between his beliefs and consequent emotions and behaviours, and would (over the course of treatment) teach him how to identify and replace his dysfunctional irrational beliefs.

With respect to the ABC model it is important to note that thoughts, feelings and behaviours are interactive (Ellis 1985a), and can influence each other to a significant degree. In the brief example outlined above, for instance, it is likely that the client's social anxiety contributed to his acting in an avoidant fashion (an emotion influencing a behaviour). In addition, his experience of social anxiety could serve for him as 'proof' that the possibility of rejection is indeed *awful* (an emotion reinforcing an irrational belief). RET places a special emphasis upon treating clients' *secondary symptoms*, which are generally viewed as representing 'upsets about upsets'. A given client could, for example, engage in negative self-rating in response to her perception that she has a particular emotional disturbance ('I *shouldn't* be anxious; the fact that I am means I'm a *weak person*'). Alleviation of secondary symptoms is regarded as important because it allows the client more readily to address primary symptoms.

The interactive quality of thoughts, feelings and behaviours can function to keep clients stuck in the psychological mire; on the plus side, it provides the rational-emotive therapist with an array of intervention points and techniques. Thus, irrational beliefs can be countered through cognitive, emotive and/or behavioural means. The multi-modal nature of rational-emotive interventions will be further described in the forthcoming section on therapeutic techniques utilized within RET.

As alluded to earlier, rational-emotive theory describes two categories of negative emotional consequences, and uses the adjectives *appropriate* and *inappropriate* to distinguish between them. Appropriate negative emotions include affective states such as sadness, regret, concern and annoyance, and tend to be experienced when rational beliefs are brought to bear upon particular activating events. It is noted that although such feelings are negative in tone, they are less likely to result in very serious disruptions to an individual's functioning and may actually serve to motivate effective problem-solving. Inappropriate negative emotions include depression, guilt, anxiety and anger, and usually follow when irrational beliefs are applied to the activating events which are experienced. Inappropriate negative emotions usually compromise sound problem-solving, are frequently experienced as more intensely dysphoric by the individual, and generally present obstacles to happiness and goal-attainment. RET generally attempts to help clients to decrease the frequency and duration of inappropriate negative emotional episodes, rather than trying to reach the probably unattainable (and perhaps impractical) goal of eliminating negative emotions altogether. It is important for clients to understand this distinction; otherwise, they might conceivably view their periodic experiences of sadness, concern or annoyance as evidence that RET is failing to work for them.

With many clients, it may make good therapeutic sense to teach the ABC model explicitly through verbal description and visual presentation (i.e. diagrams). With others, however, the model can be conveyed in implied form. Thus, bright or highly motivated clients may be able to learn to analyse and understand their upsets according to the ABC format simply by having their therapist utilize it repeatedly over the course of their therapy.

By now, it may be obvious to the reader that RET can be viewed as a psychoeducational approach to psychotherapy. Rational-emotive therapists attempt to teach their clients to utilize the ABC model, discriminate between rational and irrational beliefs, recognize the differences between appropriate and inappropriate negative emotions, and employ means for replacing irrational beliefs with rational ones. With respect to this last teaching task, therapists expand the ABC model to include 'D', which stands for *Disputing*. Disputing is the process by which clients learn to challenge their irrational beliefs with a variety of logical and/or empirical arguments. By so doing, they are able to demonstrate to themselves that their irrational beliefs represent invalid and dysfunctional hypotheses, which will help to weaken the degree to which they subscribe to them. As clients work at surrendering their irrational beliefs, they can construct rational beliefs with which to replace them. The variety of means by which disputing can be accomplished is described below.

Therapeutic techniques utilized in RET

The armamentarium of therapeutic techniques utilized within RET can be considered to fall into two broad categories. The first category is comprised of the various techniques employed to dispute clients' irrational beliefs; these techniques can be classified according to whether they mainly employ the cognitive, behavioural or emotive modality. The second category contains various skills-training approaches, which are used when clients present skills deficits in important areas of their functioning. This section will detail these categories, and will conclude with a discussion of the importance of homework assignments within RET.

Cognitive disputing

This intervention represents the process of utilizing the therapist's and the client's verbal reasoning skills in order to construct arguments which challenge the validity of the client's irrational beliefs. In the earlier stages of therapy the therapist takes the lead in actively applying these arguments to the client's operative irrational beliefs; later in therapy, the client is encouraged to engage in this task on a more independent basis. Cognitive disputes can be categorized according to the *type* of argument that they utilize (DiGiuseppe 1991). Thus, client and therapist might engage in logical disputing, reality testing of irrational beliefs, or in heuristic disputing. In addition, disputes can be further distinguished on the basis of whether the therapist employs a didactic or Socratic mode of presentation. Each of these dimensions is described below.

Logical disputing   As noted earlier, irrational beliefs are illogical in nature, and this feature can be demonstrated to clients through logical disputing. When clients are clearly able to see the illogical aspects of their irrational beliefs, they may be more readily able to surrender them.

To provide an example, a given client might subscribe to the following belief: 'Because it is desirable to have the love and approval of my spouse, I *must* have it.' This belief is clearly irrational, as it escalates that which is desirable to the level of an absolutistic demand. With such a belief in operation, this client would probably be prone to experience anxiety and depression when it is perceived they are unloved by their partner. The therapist can help the client to avoid (or overcome) these inappropriate negative emotions by logically disputing the irrational belief in this manner: 'Just because it is desirable for your spouse to love you, does that then mean that he *must*?' By employing this question, the therapist can show the client that her irrational belief represents an illogical *non sequitur*, as that which is desirable does not *have to be*.

Reality testing of irrational beliefs   Clients can be shown that their irrational beliefs are not consistent with reality. By putting their irrational beliefs to an 'empirical test', it is possible to weaken further the degree to which they subscribe to them.

As an example, consider a client who stoutly maintains that 'My employer *must* treat me fairly'. If this belief were true, then it would follow that the client would always be treated in an exemplary manner by her boss. By citing instances of unfair treatment as evidence, the therapist can demonstrate to the client that this belief is simply not in consonance with reality as it currently exists.

Heuristic disputing   Rational beliefs will generally help individuals to approach their desired goals, while irrational beliefs will often create obstacles to such progress. Hence, a given irrational belief can be evaluated in terms of its functional value: is holding the belief helpful to the client in terms of facilitating goal attainment? By highlighting the manner in which clients' irrational beliefs can present obstacles to their happiness and satisfaction in life, therapists can further erode the degree to which they are maintained. A specific client, for example, might be shown that the consequences of believing, 'I *must* always excel in my work', are frequently anxiety and poorer performance.

Didactic vs Socratic disputing   In presenting various types of disputing arguments to clients, therapists may employ either a didactic or Socratic style. A didactic style involves direct teaching and explanation, wherein clients are plainly told the reasons why their irrational beliefs are illogical, anti-empirical and lacking in functional value. A Socratic approach, on the other hand, requires the therapist to employ skilfully phrased and sequenced questions in order to stimulate the client to ponder and eventually see for herself the untenable nature of her irrational beliefs. Rational-emotive therapists are advised to utilize both of these approaches with clients, as this will introduce a balance to sessions which both maintains client interest and facilitates therapeutic efficiency (Walen, Di-Giuseppe and Wessler 1980). The Socratic questioning approach, however, may offer special advantages, as it can serve to model for clients the manner in which they can independently ask themselves the sorts of disputing questions which will lead to more rational thinking.

To assist clients in the process of learning to dispute their irrational beliefs independently, the Institute for Rational-Emotive Therapy publishes a homework Self-Help Form (Sichel and Ellis 1984). This form provides a structured format wherein clients identify their activating events, consequent emotions and behaviours, and irrational beliefs, and then go through the process of disputation. This form not only allows clients to practise their disputation skills, but also provides a means for obtaining relief from distressing emotional states.

Behavioural disputing

With behavioural disputing, clients engage in activity-oriented exercises which have the goal of helping them to recognize their irrational beliefs as invalid hypotheses. Such exercises can be viewed as data-gathering forays, as they are able to provide clients with 'concrete' evidence which runs counter to their irrational beliefs.

Shame-attacking exercises (Ellis 1969) represent one category of behavioural disputing exercises. When clients undertake shame-attacking exercises, they agree to engage in some form of foolish (though non-harmful) behaviour in public. By doing so (and monitoring the responses of other individuals who are present at the time), they are able to show themselves that the actual consequences of such behaviour are not awful, and that the disapproval of others often has no significant or enduring negative effects. Thus, such exercises assist individuals in becoming less vulnerable to guiding their lives and choosing their actions on the basis of an approval-needing philosophy.

Ellis frequently employs shame-attacking exercises with his clients, particularly in group therapy (Yankura and Dryden 1990). Some of the ones he most frequently suggests include the following:

1 Announcing the stops along a subway route in a voice loud enough for fellow passengers to hear.
2 Requesting to purchase a gross of condoms at the chemist's shop, and loudly insisting on a discounted price because one uses so many.
3 Stopping a stranger on the street and saying, 'Excuse me, I've just gotten out of the loony bin – can you tell me what year it is?'

Rational-emotive therapists will attempt to explain carefully the rationale for shame-attacking exercises to clients, and when appropriate, may encourage particular individuals to try them. In addition, therapists may encourage clients to implement shame-attacking exercises of their own design. In this way, they can attack a problem area which might be of particular relevance to them.

Risk-taking exercises (Walen, DiGiuseppe and Wessler 1980) represent another vehicle for accomplishing behavioural disputing. In these exercises, clients are encouraged to engage in an activity which they erroneously regard as dangerous or frightful. Ellis himself often describes the manner in which, as a young adult, he managed to overcome one of his fears by giving himself the assignment of starting conversations and asking for dates with women he met in a local park. As he tells the story, he was able to conquer his anxiety in this area despite the fact that out of one hundred women approached, only one assented to go out with him – and she subsequently failed to show up for the date! Further illustrations of risk-taking exercises could include the client with public-speaking anxiety who takes on the assignment of giving a lecture to a potentially critical audience, or the non-assertive client who decides to request of her employer a long-desired rise in pay. Risk-taking exercises can have the capacity to show clients that many of their most extreme fears and anxieties are founded upon irrational beliefs. This insight can help them to overcome their specific anxiety, as well as enable them to become more generally able to engage in feared (though in reality, non-dangerous) activities in the future. Such exercises can also have positive side-effects in some instances: the anxious client cited above may receive positive recognition for the lecture he delivers, while the non-assertive client may actually receive the pay rise she desires.

Behavioural disputing exercises can also be directed at assisting clients to raise their level of frustration tolerance. Individuals who procrastinate on certain tasks because of the discomfort involved, for example, can be helped to design assignments which will show them that they can accomplish these activities *uncomfortably*, and still survive quite well. Here, an example can be given of a young male client who puts off cleaning his flat because it is inconvenient (in a short-term sense) and boring. By forcing himself to take on the assignment of housecleaning prior to a particular day of the week, he can prove to himself that he can 'stand' the discomfort involved in doing so.

The nature of behavioural disputing exercises need be limited only by the joint creativity of therapist and client. Enacting such exercises can help clients to engage in long-avoided activities and approach valued personal goals and achievements. Most important from the RET perspective, however, implementation of these exercises can provide clients with strong evidence concerning the

illogical, dysfunctional and empirically untenable nature of their irrational beliefs. By *doing*, they can prove to themselves that nothing is awful (in the sense of
being 101 per cent bad), that they don't *need* the approval of others, and that they
can stand discomfort for the sake of long-term gain.

Emotive disputing

Within RET, emotive disputing refers to the process of teaching the client to
employ mental images of negative activating events in order to trigger the irrational beliefs and subsequent emotional upsets associated with them. Triggering
an upset in this fashion provides an immediate opportunity to deal with it
through rational thinking.

The procedure usually espoused by Ellis for accomplishing emotive disputing is
termed *rational-emotive imagery* (REI). Ellis (Maultsby and Ellis 1974) describes two
variations of this technique, which he refers to as the negative imagery version
and the positive imagery version. In the negative imagery version (which is the
one he most often uses), the client is instructed to imagine herself vividly in a
situation usually associated with an inappropriate negative emotion, and to signal to the therapist when she is actually experiencing this typical upset. The
therapist then encourages the client to change the inappropriate feeling to an
appropriate feeling, and to indicate when this change has occurred. Once the
client provides this second signal, the therapist makes an inquiry as to the manner in which the client managed to effect the change in feeling. Ideally, clients'
responses to this inquiry will indicate that they modified some aspect of their
thinking regarding the activating event. Hopefully, this modification represents a
shift from irrational to rational thinking; if not, the therapist can address and
correct any potentially self-defeating messages the client may be giving herself.
This approach to emotive disputing provides a particular therapeutic advantage
in that it requires clients to employ their own creativity and idiosyncratic self-talk
(which may be more personally meaningful to them) in the service of countering
irrational beliefs and affecting beneficial changes in their emotions.

In the positive imagery version, clients use mental imagery to place themselves
in a difficult situation, but then attempt to picture themselves acting and feeling
in a more adaptive fashion than is typical for them. Once they signal that they
have been able to muster a coping image, the therapist asks them questions
intended to elicit and underscore the self-talk used to produce it.

Aside from REI, an emotive dimension can be added to cognitive disputing
when it is conducted with especially strong, forceful language (Ellis 1985b). Clients can, for example, increase the impact of their disputes by employing profanity, or by 'turning up the volume' of their rational self-talk.

Skills-training techniques

Clients in psychotherapy often present behavioural excesses and deficits which
create obstacles to important personal goals and result in self-defeating consequences. On occasion, such clients may possess the practical skills required to

counter these behavioural problems, but are blocked from employing them by their self-created emotional disturbance. From the RET perspective, helping clients to overcome these emotional obstacles through disputation is likely to enable them to utilize the skills they already possess in their behavioural repertoires.

Quite frequently, however, clients in therapy present both emotional disturbance *and* significant skills deficits. In certain cases, for example, long-standing emotional disturbance may have contributed to avoidance of particular types of situations (as with the shy client who assiduously avoids social activities), such that opportunities to develop particular types of skills were rarely encountered. With clients who fit this type of profile, rational-emotive therapists would usually attempt to remediate *both* the emotional disturbance and the skills deficit. Therapists may often choose first to address a client's emotional problems, as progress in this area may clear the way for successful practice of new skills.

Clients may sometimes benefit from training in social skills, such that they become better able to initiate and maintain satisfying interpersonal relationships. As such, rational-emotive therapists might teach them the components of conversational skills (see, for example, Garner 1981), and allow time for within-session modelling and practice of these skills. Other individuals might require assistance in developing assertiveness skills, in order to increase their ability to appropriately obtain preferred outcomes in various types of social situations. As with conversational skills, assertiveness skills can be modelled and practised within therapy sessions.

As the above types of skills are probably best practised with a variety of people and situations, the Institute for Rational-Emotive Therapy in New York City offers separate group training workshops in both conversational and assertiveness skills. These workshops typically meet for approximately six weekly ninety-minute-long sessions, and utilize a structured format wherein particular skills are introduced and participants are allowed an opportunity to try them. Skills practice is often suggested as a homework assignment to both individual therapy clients and workshop participants, such that they can report on and refine their skills implementation during the following week's session.

Training in conversational and assertiveness skills can be viewed as a means for addressing particular types of behavioural deficits. Skills training can also be directed at behavioural excesses, such as cigarette smoking, problem drinking and over-eating. Rational-emotive therapists can help clients with such problems by teaching them how to recognize and deal with high-risk situations (wherein stimuli present in the environment may prompt an episode of indulging the behavioural excess), self-monitor target behaviours, engage in reasonable goal-setting, and employ various other strategies and techniques for overcoming the self-defeating habit. Here, the rational-emotive approach for addressing emotional disturbance represents an especially important component of treatment, as behavioural excesses such as those mentioned above may often follow closely on the heels of an emotional upset.

Use of homework assignments within RET

Homework assignments occupy a place of central importance in the rational-emotive approach to the treatment of emotional and behavioural problems.

Here, the term 'homework assignments' is used to refer to therapeutic activities enacted independently by the client between therapy sessions. They are viewed as facilitating the change process in therapy in a number of significant ways.

Review of the prior week's homework assignment can serve to provide continuity between sessions and help to establish an agenda for the current session. As an example, a client with a significant anger problem might have agreed to practise his disputing skills whenever he recognized that he was feeling and acting angrily towards his spouse. At his next session, his rational-emotive therapist would ask him to report on his experiences in this regard. If it became apparent that the client had experienced difficulty in implementing his disputing skills, a portion of the session could be devoted to troubleshooting. Thus, the homework assignment becomes a vehicle for structuring the session in a therapeutically useful fashion.

Homework assignments also represent a means for extending treatment time, as they enable clients to continue working on their problem areas outside of the therapist's office. Further, such assignments may help clients to attribute positive changes to their own, as opposed to their therapist's efforts. This is a feature of special significance, as it mitigates against client dependency. Finally, homework assignments can enhance the transfer of any learning that occurs during clients' therapy sessions to their natural environments. It is, after all, one thing to dispute one's irrational beliefs within the comfortable confines of the consultation room; it is quite another thing to employ such skills in the face of an emotional upset in the outside world.

Rational-emotive homework assignments can take many different forms, depending largely upon the problem area they are intended to address. In addition, they may be mainly cognitive, behavioural or emotive in nature. As a cognitive homework assignment to deal with evaluative anxiety, for instance, a client might take on the assignment of completing several homework Self-Help Forms (Sichel and Ellis 1984) in the days preceding an important examination. A behavioural homework assignment directed at overcoming shyness could have a client attempting to start a conversation at an upcoming party. An emotive homework assignment to deal with anger could involve a client's practising REI, or utilizing forceful, evocative rational self-statements to counter his other-directed musts.

In order to increase the likelihood of homework implementation, Ellis advocates the use of what he refers to as operant conditioning techniques. In his public demonstrations of RET with volunteer 'clients', for example, he almost always makes inquiries regarding activities that these individuals very much like and dislike, respectively. He then suggests that the favoured activity be utilized as 'reinforcement' for completing a previously discussed homework assignment (which, at his public demonstrations, is usually independent practice of REI), while the disliked activity be used as a penalty for failing to do it. He emphasizes to his volunteers that if they adhere to these self-assumed contingencies, they will be encouraged to carry out their intentions regarding the homework assignment.

Variations and innovations employed by Dr Dryden

In his formulation of RET, Ellis created an approach to psychotherapy which most trainees are probably capable of learning and applying in a relatively short span of time. Many observers have noted, however, that Ellis possesses a very distinctive style in terms of his application of RET to clients' problems (Johnson 1980; Walen, DiGiuseppe and Wessler 1980). This style is marked by a no non-sense emphasis upon cognitive disputing, a very high degree of verbal activity, and frequent confrontation.

Novice rational-emotive therapists often seem to attempt to increase their therapeutic efficacy by mimicking certain aspects of Ellis's style. More experienced therapists, however, generally understand that one does not have to be Ellis to practise RET effectively. As such, although they still operate from a rational-emotive theoretical base and emphasize the importance of modifying irrational beliefs, they may feel freer to introduce technical innovations and are more likely to allow their therapeutic style to be in congruence with their personality style.

As a result of his advanced training in RET, Dryden is well acquainted with the manner in which Ellis practises psychotherapy. Dryden has, however, also been influenced by his readings and training in other therapeutic approaches. In addition, he has utilized his own experiences as a psychotherapist to modify and refine his application of the principles and techniques of RET. Consequently, his practice of RET has evolved in a fashion which differs from Ellis's in certain important regards.

The present section of this chapter will attempt to introduce the reader to the technical innovations and variations Dryden has incorporated into his practice of RET. Particular aspects of these modifications will be presented and described in the subsections that follow, and will be compared with Ellis's approach. It is important to note, however, that it is not the authors' intention to provide here a complete picture of Ellis's therapeutic style. Rather, the emphasis will be placed upon highlighting divergences and differences between Ellis and Dryden, such that readers will be better able to understand and interpret the transcript material contained in subsequent chapers. Readers who are interested in pursuing more detailed study of Ellis's therapeutic style and approach are referred to the book *Doing RET: Albert Ellis in Action* (Yankura and Dryden 1990). Like the present volume, this work also employs transcript material for purposes of illustration, and provides samples of client responses to Ellis's therapy.

The client–therapist relationship

It is almost universally acknowledged that the relationship that exists between client and therapist is a significant variable in determining the process and outcome of psychotherapy. In his practice of RET, Dryden employs Bordin's (1979) formulation of the working alliance as a means for understanding and facilitating this relationship. Within Bordin's model, the therapeutic relationship is conceptualized as having three separate but interrelated components: bonds, goals and tasks.

The *bond* between client and therapist refers to the nature and quality of the interpersonal relationship that exists between these two individuals. If an effective bond fails to form between client and therapist, therapeutic failure may become more likely. While Ellis generally appears to base his relationships with clients upon his status as an expert in the field of psychotherapy (Yankura and Dryden 1990), Dryden tends to emphasize adopting an interactional style which 'fits' the preferences and expectations of the client. Thus, he may act in a very formal manner with certain individuals (thus emphasizing his role as a professional), while with others he may behave in a more informal, friendly manner (Dryden 1987a). It is noted, however, that his willingness to modify his interactional style applies only in so far as it does not prove to be counter-therapeutic. With a client who has apparent difficulties with expressing feelings, for instance, he would be far less likely to adopt a very formal, professionally aloof style, as this might feed into the client's problem (Dryden 1987a).

In the sessions which form the basis for this book, Dr Dryden adopts what can be characterized as a relatively friendly, informal style. While he retains the aura of a professional with expertise in his given field, he relates to his client in an open, relaxed and non-authoritarian manner. He utilizes very informal language (with a minimum of professional jargon), and can at various times be heard employing humorous comments and self-disclosure. It becomes evident as the therapy progresses that Sarah responds well to this approach, as she at several points makes reference to her eagerness to attend her sessions and her trust in Dr Dryden.

Goals refer to the changes the client would like to see result from participation in therapy. It is highly important that client and therapist mainly agree about the goals for therapy, as misunderstandings and lack of agreement on this dimension can also contribute to client resistance and therapeutic failure. Ellis and Dryden employ somewhat similar means for dealing with this issue by keeping a focus upon problems which clients present as having the greatest (or most immediate) importance for them. Both therapists will also suggest to clients, however, that they attempt to address other issues initially not perceived to have particular therapeutic relevance. This is a point of significance, as clients often enter therapy with an impoverished awareness and understanding of the psychological factors which create and maintain their symptoms. Thus, Dryden and Ellis utilize pacing (here defined as the strategy of first responding to the client's self-perceived problems) and leading (the process of influencing the client to address problems perceived by the therapist as significant).

In addition to the above-described general strategy, Dryden also employs other techniques – typically not utilized by Ellis – in order to ensure that client–therapist congruence exists within the goal domain. He begins his initial session with Sarah, for instance, by attempting to assess her attitudes about entering therapy. This can be viewed as a vehicle for addressing what could be referred to as a meta-goal: does the client view therapy as a legitimate means for addressing personal problems? He also begins each session (following the initial contact) by allowing time for *agenda-setting*. By directly asking his client what she would like to work on (as well as advancing his own suggestions for agenda items), he increases the likelihood that goal agreement will exist for the present session. Finally, Dryden sometimes requests that clients write a *problem list* as an initial homework assignment. He does this with Sarah, and it provides another vehicle by which he is able to ascertain that he is working in congruence with her goals. This problem list serves another useful function as well, as it helps to establish an overall structure for the therapy. These techniques – assessing client attitudes about therapy, agenda-setting, and utilization of a problem list – are advocated by Beck and associates in their approach to cognitive-behaviour therapy (see Beck *et al.* 1979).

Tasks are the final component of Bordin's conceptualization of the therapeutic alliance, and refer to the actual activities carried out by both client and therapist in the service of the former's goals. As with goals, it is important for both of these individuals to be in agreement as to the nature of therapeutic tasks. As per the standard RET approach, Dryden and Ellis are both quite verbally active from the very start of therapy, and thus convey to their clients that their role as therapist is not that of passive listener. Unlike Ellis, however, Dryden will often make direct statements to clients concerning the manner in which he believes he might be of assistance to them. Thus he attempts to clarify, in a general sense, the overall tasks he will take responsibility for as therapist.

As an additional important means for monitoring the client–therapist bond and ensuring that agreement on goals and tasks is maintained, Dryden directly asks his clients to provide him with feedback regarding their reactions to present and prior sessions. At the conclusion of a particular therapeutic contact, he will inquire as to what clients found helpful and unhelpful about the session. Also, at the start of the next session, he will check to see if clients had any additional thoughts about their last meeting. In this way, he is able to monitor both clients' immediate responses to his ministrations as well as the reactions they may have had after some time has passed (see Beck *et al.* 1979). He is thus enabled to keep track of interventions and communications experienced as particularly helpful, as well as being able to correct misunderstandings and modify his approach as appropriate.

The use of vivid methods

Dryden (1984a) has written about the desirability of employing especially vivid methods in RET as a means of gaining clients' full attention and making therapy a more memorable experience for them. When clients are fully engaged and interested in the process of therapy, they are likely to make swifter and more lasting changes.

In his use of strong language, slogans, profanity and humour, Ellis can be viewed as a pioneer in employing vivid methods in RET. Dryden (1984a) recognizes the value of these particular vehicles for increasing the therapist's impact on the client, and has described a number of others which he has employed. Here, it is noted that he refrains from utilizing such techniques with clients until he has gained a sense that a sound working alliance has been established. With particular relevance to his sessions with Sarah, Dr Dryden's vivid methods include the following: rational-emotive problem solving, flamboyant therapist actions, using visual models, exaggeration, and therapist self-disclosure.

Rational-emotive problem solving   Originally described by Knaus and Wessler (1976), this technique requires the therapist to structure conditions in the therapy session such that they mimic problematic situations (i.e. those that serve to trigger emotional and behavioural problems) that the client encounters in daily life. As an example, a therapist might make an unreasonable request of a non-assertive client, without initially explaining the rationale for doing so. Time can then be devoted within the session to processing the client's cognitive, behavioural and emotional reactions to this simulation.

Flamboyant therapist actions   During the course of a therapy session, it will often become evident to the therapist that the client is basing a global negative rating of self upon some discrete aspect of their behaviour or personality (e.g. 'Because I acted stupidly in this situation, I am a stupid person'). A typical therapeutic response to such a fallacious conclusion is to employ verbal disputes to show the client that it is illogical and dysfunctional to engage in negative self-rating. As an alternative means for making this point, the therapist might engage in some form of outlandish behaviour (such as dropping to all fours and barking like a dog), and then ask the client to evaluate this action. Usually, clients will indicate that they viewed the behaviour as silly or stupid. The therapist can then ask if that stupid action truly makes him or her a stupid person, ideally communicating that while it is possible to rate behaviours positively or negatively, it is incorrect to apply global ratings to human beings.

Using visual models   In order to enhance client understanding and recall of key rational-emotive concepts, it is sometimes helpful for the therapist to employ a visual model or diagram. Dryden (1984a), for example, has described the use of a model which he terms the 'LFT Splash'. In this model, he presents an illustration of a young man positioned at the crest of a roller coaster with a young woman standing at the bottom. He tells his clients that the young man fails to move because he is telling himself that he can't stand the splash, and asks them to imagine what this figure would have to tell himself in order to reach the woman. This particular model can be useful for teaching clients that it is possible to tolerate acute time-limited discomfort, and that such tolerance will often help them to reach their goals.

Exaggeration   Clients will sometimes predict that the consequences of behaving foolishly or otherwise poorly in public will be awful, without taking the time to think through as to what these consequences will actually be like. The therapist can humorously escalate these anticipated awful outcomes to the extreme, thus helping clients to reach a point where they are able to recognize the faulty nature of their thinking. As an example, a given client might believe that it would be terrible to 'say the wrong thing' at an upcoming office party. The therapist might respond to this by saying, 'You're absolutely right – that would be awful! No doubt we'll be hearing about your *faux pas* on the eleven o'clock news that evening!' When employing such exaggeration, it is essential that therapists manage to convey that they are poking fun at the client's beliefs, rather than at the client him or herself.

Therapist self-disclosure   Therapists can have a significant impact on some clients by sharing their experiences in dealing with particular problems. Like other vivid techniques, however, self-disclosure is best utilized in a discretionary manner, as not all clients will have a positive response to it. In addition, it appears advisable that when self-disclosing, therapists present themselves as coping, as opposed to mastery models.

It is hoped that this chapter has provided the reader with a basic knowledge of the principles and techniques of RET, as well as an appreciation of the manner in which the approaches of Ellis and Dryden differ from each other. With this background material in place, the reader is now prepared to enter Dr Dryden's office and participate in his sessions with Sarah as an educated (albeit silent) observer. The chapter that follows takes us into the first session, wherein the client's initial complaints are addressed and the tone for subsequent sessions is established.

3 The initial session

Within most approaches to psychotherapy, the therapist's initial sesion with a client represents an important vehicle for accomplishing a number of tasks germane to the therapeutic process. Therapists are generally interested in attempting to engage the client in therapy (such that a subsequent session will be scheduled), establishing a working therapeutic relationship (wherein the respective roles of therapist and client are made somewhat clear), and gaining a sense as to the types of problems which have led the client to seek treatment at the present time. In addition, therapists who practise active-directive forms of therapy may try to apply some initial therapeutic interventions, in the hope that the client will leave the session feeling somewhat relieved and hopeful.

In his first session with Sarah, Dr Dryden wastes no time in implementing the active-directive approach which is typical of RET. He begins the session by immediately assessing her attitudes about seeking therapy, and then quickly moves to an inquiry regarding her main presenting problems. After a problem area is identified, he begins the process of intervention. It is noted that he devotes a minimum of time to assessing the fine details and parameters of this problem area; as per the rational-emotive approach, the client's response to the therapist's ministrations is deemed to be the most efficient means of gauging the accuracy and effectiveness of attempted interventions.

Frequently, new psychotherapy clients are not sure what to expect from their therapist when they first enter the office. As such, Dr Dryden utilizes his first session with Sarah as an opportunity for setting a number of therapeutically important precedents. He is quite verbally active during the session, thus demonstrating that his role is not that of passive listener. Through his behaviour, he makes it clear that he will be confrontative and authoritative (though not authoritarian) in the service of helping Sarah to recognize, challenge and modify her dysfunctional belief systems. In addition, he obtains feedback from her regarding her response to the session, and suggests homework assignments relevant to the problem areas discussed. As will be seen in subsequent sessions, these activities represent regular features of Dr Dryden's approach to practising rational-emotive therapy. The feedback he requests enables him to identify and correct any misunderstandings the client may have formed during the session, and allows him to modify his approach, as needed. Homework assignments assist the client in carrying therapy outside of the consultation room, and have the potential to speed and enhance therapeutic progress.

As noted earlier, the session begins with Dr Dryden's inquiry regarding Sarah's thoughts and feelings about beginning therapy:

Dr Dryden: So – when did your doctor suggest that you come to see me?

Sarah: (very soft-spoken, as if shy) The last time I went to see him, which was about three or four weeks ago.

Dr Dryden: And what was your reaction when he suggested that?

Sarah: I told him I would, because I'm hoping that some good will come out of it and that I'll be a better person to live with. Hopefully.

Dr Dryden: Okay – but what was your initial reaction?

Sarah: I wasn't shocked.

Dr Dryden: Did he explain anything about what I do?

Sarah: Not really – he didn't go into too much detail. He said that you were involved in some sort of research at the time, and that it might be a few weeks before I could see you.

Dr Dryden: And in the interim – the period between then and now – did you have further thoughts about coming to see me?

Sarah: Yes, I thought about it quite often when I found myself becoming upset and irritable and doing all of the nasty things I do.

Dr Dryden: What did you think at those times?

Sarah: That I should get some help.

Dr Dryden: Right – so is it correct to say that in a sense, you've been looking forward to coming to see me?

Sarah: (very quietly) Yes.

Here, Dr Dryden has established that Sarah seems to have generally positive feelings about beginning therapy. This is important information for him to possess, as he now has a sense that his client will probably be fairly co-operative and receptive with respect to his attempts at intervention. Following his inquiry regarding Sarah's pre-therapy attitudes, he begins to assess problem areas which are of relevance to her:

Dr Dryden: Okay. Well, the main thing I'd like to do today is to give you an opportunity to tell me what your concerns are. Then, I'll try to outline how I might be of help to you, and we'll make some decisions concerning how often we need to meet. Okay? So – why don't you tell me what concerns you have.

Sarah: Well, I think I worry too much about Peter.

Dr Dryden: Mm-hm. Your son.

Sarah: I suppose it's not a perfect world for him, and it's not going to be, is it?

Dr Dryden: Well, not as far as we know! But you want a perfect world for him – in what sense?

Sarah: (sighs) Well, I want him to be educated properly. He's gone on to college, which I'm very glad about . . .

Dr Dryden: Mm-hm.

Sarah: . . . but then he frightened me to death when he told me he was going on a course that would take two years. It frightens me because he gets so upset if he doesn't achieve what he wants.

Dr Dryden: He gets upset . . .?

Sarah: Yeah – if he doesn't achieve what he wants. And he just barely got the A levels that got him into college and got him this course, anyway.

He seems fairly happy and confident – but then, like all kids, he wants to go out and miss homework. (More animated now) And I never know whether I should – this is what *really* upsets me – I never know whether I should say to him, 'Now look, Peter, you've got to stop in and do homework!' I mean, he's 17 years old – and besides that, I don't want to come on as the domineering mother! But then I know there'll be hell to pay, because I saw it in the first year – he failed his exams! He didn't get the grades he wanted, which meant he had to spend another year at school – and I saw how upset he was!

I said to him, 'If you're really upset and you're determined to go to college, stay on another year and have another go. But you must work! You must learn by your mistakes!' Well, he was better this year because he got the A levels – but he just got what he needed – nothing more, he just scraped through. But there were times during the year when he did what I realize is normal – wanting to go out with girls and such – you know what they want to do . . .

Dr Dryden: (humorously) Yes, a dim memory from my past . . .

Sarah: But then I sat thinking, '*Now* what do I do?' This is what really upsets me – I never know what decision to make! I don't know whether I should say to him, 'Now look, Peter, forget about going out! You told me you've got an essay to do, and you know that if you don't do it, there's a chance you're going to fail your exam' – or whether to think, 'Well, let him go – he'll have to learn the hard way!' But when the hard way came and I saw him so upset the first year, I felt guilty that I hadn't been firm enough with him. This year when I was stricter, he at least achieved the standard he needed for college. But I felt that I had dominated him, and perhaps took a lot of fun away from him. I must admit, though – seeing how happy he is about going to college, I don't feel too guilty about it now. But when it's actually happening, I don't know what to think! I just wish I'd never had any kids – I don't know why we have them!

Dr Dryden: Because . . .?

Sarah: Because everything that you do, every word that comes out of your mouth – except for the odd occasion when it's just sheer temper – is because you love them! You only want to show them what you *honestly* believe to be right for them!

Dr Dryden: For them to follow.

Sarah: For them to follow – to hopefully guide them in the *very best* way that you know how!

Dr Dryden: Yes, but I'm hearing this – you correct me if I'm wrong: your major desire is for your son to get on and do well.

Sarah: Yes, I'd be lying if I said I didn't have that desire – I do.

Dr Dryden: So, your dilemma is, 'What sort of stance do I take with him in order to best help him achieve this?'

Sarah: Yes.

Dr Dryden: I'm also hearing, 'I *have to* make the right decision in this regard!'

Less than fifteen minutes into the session, Dr Dryden has defined and restated the practical problem of most immediate concern to his client. In addition, he has advanced a hypothesis regarding a particular irrational belief to which the client appears to subscribe.

Sarah: Well, yes – I would hate to think that I'd steered him wrong. When he first told me he was doing two A levels, my inward reaction was, 'My God, I can't stand the thought that he'll have to do all that hard work and still might fail anyway'; but then I thought, 'Keep your mouth shut – it's *his* decision – let him do it and support him all the way.'

Dr Dryden: What's so terrifying about the prospect that he might fail and become upset?

Sarah: I feel as if it's me! I'd know how hurt he would be and . . .

Dr Dryden: Would he recover?

Sarah: Well, I suppose he'd have to recover!

Dr Dryden: He could kill himself!

Sarah: (somewhat humorously) *I* should probably end up doing that if he fails, not him.

Dr Dryden: Because . . . how come *you* would kill yourself?

Sarah: Because I can't stand seeing him so upset!

Dr Dryden: Ahh – because . . .?

Sarah: Because I feel that . . . well, I can't really say that it would be my fault! But I know a lot will depend on how I advise him – because he definitely does need a stern hand.

Dr Dryden: Okay – but what is your ultimate goal? Is your ultimate goal to have him stand on his own two feet, or to rely on you?

Sarah: I want him to stand on his own two feet! But I believe that it's part of my duty to set standards for him, until he eventually becomes able to do it himself. But I don't feel that . . . well, maybe I've made him rely on me a bit too much – and he *does* take me for a bit of a fool.

Dr Dryden: Right – and therefore, how is that going to help him stand on his own two feet?

Sarah: Well, I was hoping that college would make him feel more independent. The tutors will make demands of him, and it *won't* be me making demands of him. He'll just have to carry out what the tutors say.

Dr Dryden: Or not!

Sarah: Right, or not.

Dr Dryden: What I'm hearing you say is, 'I want him to stand on his own two feet, and this is my hypothesis: he'll probably learn to stand on his own two feet better when he's upset and has to rely on his own resources, than if he relies on *me*.' But if when he gets upset you come to his aid, he'll be stopped from doing that– and you'll be likely to jump in and rescue him if you're telling yourself, 'Oh, I can't stand to see my son so upset – it's like I'm losing my right arm!'

In this portion of the session, Dr Dryden has more specifically identified the dilemma Sarah faces with respect to her son: she wants him to become an independently functioning adult, but believes that she *can't stand* to see him suffer the frustrations which usually accompany one's passage into adulthood. He has begun the process of showing her how this belief will interfere with her ultimate goal. Sarah responds to his statement.

Sarah: All of that is true – I mean, I *hate* to see him upset.

Dr Dryden: But – if you really want him to stand on his own two feet and deal with his problems *himself,* hadn't you better put up with seeing him upset? Because, isn't it only when he has to deal with his own upsets himself – without continually running to you – that he'll gain that goal? You see, I'm hearing that you want him to gain the goal *painlessly*! Now, how likely is that?

Sarah: I believe he wants all of the things he says he wants. But throughout his school years, each of his teachers told me that if he didn't develop greater discipline with respect to his homework, he would fail. That's all I've heard from teachers since he started school!

Dr Dryden: And if he fails . . . what?

Sarah: Well, they drummed it into me that it's my responsibility to see that he does his homework.

Dr Dryden: (humorously) Well, I think I've got the picture now! He's 36, and you're *still* forcing him to do the right thing! Isn't that the most likely outcome if you keep on forcing him? Think about it!

   You see, there are two courses of action here: one is that you really keep on forcing him, making him do his homework, and the second is that you say, 'Well son, you're 17 now – you're quite old enough to discipline yourself. I can be of assistance to you, but I'm *not* going to discipline you!' Now, what are the likely outcomes of these two courses of action? Let's take the first one – that you keep chasing up after him. What's likely to happen there?

Sarah: Well, he just *pretends* to take notice – but I don't believe he *really* takes notice of me.

Dr Dryden: How do you feel about that?

Sarah: In some ways, I'm glad he doesn't do everything I say – because I don't want to be a dominating mother!

Dr Dryden: Okay – if you keep on chasing up, you think he's not going to listen anyway . . .

Sarah: Right. But it clears my conscience that at least I *tried* to tell him what was right – and if he does wrong now, it's just going to be hard luck, you know.

Dr Dryden: Yes – but hard luck on whom?

Sarah: On him, really.

Dr Dryden: But what if he whines and screams about it and gets very upset?

Sarah: Well, he did over the A levels in the first year, and even though it broke my heart I said to him, 'Well, you were told what you had to do, you knew the amount of work that was involved – and you didn't do it.' And I didn't show that I was upset for him; to his face, I pretended to be quite hard. But of course, I was as upset as he was.

Dr Dryden: Because you were telling yourself *what* about his upset? What were you saying to yourself?

Here, Dr Dryden asks a question which is intended to prompt the client to examine her belief system. Such questions, which require the client to engage in 'thinking about one's thinking', are frequently utilized within RET.

Sarah: Well, I was saying he must really be hurt . . .

Dr Dryden: And . . .? He's hurt, and then what?

Sarah: Well, if he's hurt, I'm hurt.

Dr Dryden: Yes – but do you *want* to feel hurt? And – is it your *goal* to feel hurt? Do you *want* to be hurt if he's hurt?

Sarah: (pause) Well, I never thought of it like that – but I'd prefer to say I'll feel hurt if my son gets hurt – rather than saying I don't care if my son gets hurt.

Dr Dryden: Right . . .

Sarah: I *do* care – but I know of people that can say, 'Well, if they get hurt, they get hurt' . . . and I wonder if they really mean that.

Dr Dryden: Yes, but there's a middle course there. Your hurt is really saying, 'Isn't it *terrible* that my son is hurt!' The opposite to that is, 'I don't give a damn whether my son is hurt!' Now, is there a middle ground?

Sarah: Yes, I suppose there is . . .

Dr Dryden: What is it, then?

Sarah: (laughing) I never thought about it!

Dr Dryden: That's right! What is the middle ground? What comes between, 'I don't care' and 'It's terrible'?

Sarah: I don't know what it is! I suppose I could just sit there and *pretend* I didn't care! Or pretend that I . . .

Dr Dryden: But you've been doing that – and inside, you *do* care . . .

Sarah: Yeah, but nobody knows, though – nobody *knows* I get upset.

Dr Dryden: Right. But I'm implying that the middle ground is to show yourself that it *is* sad that your son is hurt – but how is it *terrible*? 'Cause you know what 'terrible' means?

Sarah: I think so . . .

Dr Dryden: What does it mean?

Sarah: 'Terrible' is something you just don't want to feel.

Dr Dryden: 'Terrible', really, is the worst thing that could ever happen. (Pause) Isn't it?

Sarah: Yes, I suppose.

Dr Dryden: Is your son being hurt the worst thing that could ever happen? (Pause) You know it's *bad*; I'm not saying that it's not *bad* – but is it the worst thing that could ever happen?

Sarah: No – but to be honest, I feel it's one of the worst things that could happen. If he gets hurt during these A levels and so forth, it will affect his ability to get the kind of job he wants – and his life depends on his job, within reason. It's okay to say, 'Well, it doesn't matter if you get a job, but . . .'

Dr Dryden: But let's assume that's so. His life depends – as you say, to some extent but not to all extent – on his job. Let's imagine that he doesn't get a very good job – do you think he could still be happy, even if he doesn't get a very good job?

Sarah: No, I don't! I honestly believe that! Probably my fault again, but . . . For normal working-class people, he's doing very, very well, and he enjoys the best of what we can give him . . .

Dr Dryden: Yes . . .

Sarah: . . . which is, I'd say, above average with respect to the kids around here – and he's not going to like it when he can't afford these things himself! He's going to have to earn a good living to keep up the standard of living he's got at home.

Dr Dryden: Or, he can take a different attitude toward a lesser living! And really stop being a baby by giving up the belief that, 'I *must* have this standard of living – I can't stand it – it's terrible, it's terrible!' But really, is it *that* terrible if he has to put up with a lower standard of living?

Sarah: I'm not saying that he's said that – this is what I believe.

Dr Dryden: But let's even assume that he *does* whine and scream about not having the things he's really come to expect – doesn't he have the option of really *showing* himself, 'Well, I'd better *put up* with not getting what I want – because after all the world doesn't revolve around *me* – and I'll try to get as much happiness as I can, even though I *don't* have what I want!' Now, doesn't he have that option?

Sarah: Yes, he has that option.

During this portion of the session, Dr Dryden attempts to accomplish several tasks of particular relevance to Sarah's worries about her son. First, he introduces the notion that there is a 'middle ground' between caring too much (and acting in an overprotective manner) and 'not giving a damn'. In this way, he tries to show the client that there are alternatives to her current approach to parenting. Second, he redefines 'terrible' as meaning 'the worst thing that could ever happen', and disputes Sarah's belief that her son's having to endure a lesser standard of living falls into this category. Just as the interventions he directs to Sarah emphasize that there are alternative, more rational ways of thinking about these issues, he also emphasizes that Peter has choices with regard to the attitudes by which he guides his life.

Dr Dryden: Right! But you see, you're really saying you're responsible for the option he chooses! You're really treating him like a puppet!

Sarah: Mm.

Dr Dryden: Now, is he a puppet?

Sarah: No – far from it!

Dr Dryden: What is he?

Sarah: He's a young man . . .

Dr Dryden: . . . Who has choices! Doesn't he?

Sarah: Yes.

Dr Dryden: What sort of choices does he have? Let's suppose he doesn't get the type of job he'd like, and he starts to whine and scream about it. Now, what choices does he have?

Sarah: He'll have to take another job.

Dr Dryden: A *lesser* job! And put up with it, right? Or – he can continue to whine and scream about it, which is *sad* – and there's no way you're going to be happy about it – but does it make sense for you to not only see *him* being upset, but to needlessly upset yourself as well? Is your upset going to help him?

Sarah: Not really, no – it's not going to help, is it?

Dr Dryden: That's right! You're probably going to be very *sad* about it, but *hurt* is really saying, 'Oh, isn't it *terrible* that it's like this!' Right? He may not be very happy, but is it *terrible* if he's not very happy? We know it's *bad*, but is it *terrible*?

Sarah: (pause) I just want him to be happy.

Dr Dryden: Do you think that *you* have to be miserable if he's miserable?

Sarah: No, but I find most of my happiness from him!

Dr Dryden: Because you've set it up that way! Do you see that? You're really saying, 'He's my whole world, and my happiness depends on his being happy!'

Sarah: Yes, I suppose that's true.

Dr Dryden: Where's that going to get you?

Sarah: (pause) Happier by seeing him happy.

Dr Dryden: But if he's not happy?

Sarah: (humorously) He'd better be!

Dr Dryden: But you're really saying, 'As long as I make him my *all*, my whole world, my universe, my happiness is dependent upon his happiness.' It's no wonder you're going crazy to make him be so-called happy, because if he's unhappy the way you've set things up, you don't have any choice but to be unhappy.

Sarah: Mm.

Dr Dryden: Now, do you want to let him be *important* to you, but *not* be your universe?

Sarah: Well, yes . . .

Dr Dryden: Why do you want to do that?

It will be noted that at various points throughout his sessions with Sarah, Dr Dryden utilizes questions similar to the one above. These questions serve two major functions: first, they help to ensure that the client is genuinely giving thought to the issues being discussed and not merely providing responses that the therapist might want to hear; second, they provide the therapist with the opportunity to learn the client's rationale for providing a particular type of response. Thus, it becomes possible to make sure that the client isn't giving 'right answers' for wrong (i.e. irrational) reasons.

Sarah: Well, it's going to be better for him in the long run, isn't it?

Dr Dryden: But let's say it's *not* – would it be better for you? You see, you're still coming back to *him* – you're really saying, 'I have to find a way that's better for *him*!'

Sarah: But isn't that my duty as a mother?

Dr Dryden: To make him your *universe*?

Sarah: Well . . . well really, what else is there?

Dr Dryden: That's a good question – you don't see a lot else! What do other mothers do who have 17-year-old kids? Do they make them their universe . . . ?

Sarah: I don't really know because I don't mix that much. I've only got sisters – who've got younger children . . .

Dr Dryden: But if you *did* mix, what do you think you would expect to find?

Sarah: I'd expect other mothers– within reason – to feel more or less the same.

Dr Dryden: But then statistically, you'd be wrong – because there *would* be people like you who would make their son the centre of their universe, and focus all of their attention on him – but there'd be other people who wouldn't give a damn about their 17 year old. And you don't want to be like that – right?

Sarah: It's not that I don't want to be like that – it's just that I'd not be being myself if I acted that other way. I'd be forcing myself to act.

Dr Dryden: That would be right. I'm also hearing that you don't want to be disinterested in him – you couldn't be!

Sarah: No, I couldn't be . . .

Dr Dryden: At the moment you've got what we would call a *need*: you're saying, 'I *must* have him happy'. But you've also got a desire – 'I *want* to see him happy' – and there are certainly many women who allow their sons to be important to them, without making them the be all and end all of their existence. Aren't there?

Sarah: There must be.

Dr Dryden: There must be – and how do they get on?

Sarah: I don't know – I never thought about it.

Dr Dryden: Okay, but what sort of mother do you want to be? Do you want to be the sort of mother who's really disinterested, the sort of mother who puts her son at the centre of the universe – or, do you want to be the kind of mother who acknowledges that her son's happiness is very important, but not the only thing that's ever been invented?

Sarah: Well, obviously I'd prefer to be that last one.

Dr Dryden: Why?

Sarah: Because it sounds more sane and sensible.

Dr Dryden: For whom?

Sarah: For me, there.

Dr Dryden: Right! And aren't we really coming back to this – that in making your son the centre of your universe, whom do you *sacrifice*?

Sarah: Me.

Dr Dryden: That's right! Now, do you want to sacrifice yourself?

Sarah: If I have to, yes. But if I don't have to, no. (Laughs)

Dr Dryden: But do you have to?

Sarah: Well, no – I mean, I don't suppose I have to.

Dr Dryden: Do you *want* to?

Sarah: No, I don't *want* to!

Dr Dryden: That's right – because if you wanted to be the next martyr – we could call you Saint Sarah – I'd say, 'Sacrifice yourself, take a hair shirt and lie on it and whip yourself, because you're not doing a very good job of making *yourself* suffer if he's suffering.'

Sarah: Mm.

Dr Dryden: That would really be doing a better job! But if you want to take the middle course, you're right about one thing: it wouldn't be natural to you. Right? Just as when you were a baby, before you walked, was walking natural to you?

Sarah: No.

Dr Dryden: (chuckles) You walked though, didn't you?

Sarah: Yes.

In this segment of the transcript, Dr Dryden places an emphasis upon enlightened self-interest, one of the key tenets of psychological health as posited by rational-emotive theory. He shows Sarah that she can maintain her desire for her son's happiness without sacrificing her own emotional well-being. By employing an analogy concerning the process of learning to walk, he also makes the point that it is possible for her to adopt a new, healthier attitude.

Dr Dryden: That's right! So, I'm asking you what your goal is – is your goal to keep him the centre of your universe, or is your goal to make him very important, but to really show yourself that *you* can get happiness even if he's unhappy. You can advise him the best you can – given that your goal is to see him stand on his own two feet – and if he suffers, it's sad, but that's the way it is. He's choosing . . .

Sarah: That would help *him* as well, really – wouldn't it?

Dr Dryden: We don't know! The point is, do you want to *sacrifice* yourself in order for him to have the best – or do you want to acknowledge that you can also pursue your own happiness? Which do you want?

Sarah: Well obviously, I want some happiness myself.

Dr Dryden: Why 'obviously'?

Sarah: I don't know. I don't see myself being full of the joys of Spring, anyway.

Dr Dryden: Because there are other things on your mind?

Sarah: Yeah – Peter's not the only thing I worry about, you know.

Dr Dryden: All right – let's look at some of these other things. What else do you worry about?

Sarah: (pause) I don't find it very easy to mix . . .

Noting that Sarah appears to agree with the points he had made concerning enlightened self-interest, Dr Dryden allows the discussion to shift to another problem area.

Dr Dryden: Yes . . .

Sarah: So – unless you've got friends, you can't start being jolly. You can't be jolly all on your own. I mean, I love playing records, and I love taking care of the housework . . .

Dr Dryden: Do you *want* to mix?

Sarah: Well, I'm reluctant to say 'yes', because . . . I worked for four years with a group of middle-aged women, and to be honest, I found them very two-faced, very nasty. They didn't want to do their fair share of the job, and they couldn't wait to condemn anybody who wasn't in the room with them.

Dr Dryden: And they were like that all the time?

Sarah: Yes!

Dr Dryden: They didn't have good qualities, as well?

Sarah: They had good points in that they would have a laugh and a joke about anything. But the person who might have made us laugh and have a good day – as soon as that person left the room, they'd pull her apart about something. Now, I can't sit with somebody and be friendly and happy – and then condemn them to hell the moment they've walked out the door!

Dr Dryden: You didn't join in this . . .

Sarah: No, I did not! And I know I was disliked for it.

Dr Dryden: So they probably pulled *you* apart when you weren't there.

Sarah: I'm 100 per cent sure of that!

Dr Dryden: Right. But are you saying that because these particular people were like this, *all* people are going to be like this?

Sarah: Well, I had another job where I found all the girls to be very pleasant. They were smart and polite, and they all did nice work.

Dr Dryden: So they were more for you.

Sarah: Yes! I *could've* made friends with them.

Dr Dryden: Well, what stops you from *now* seeking out the sort of person who's for you?

Sarah: Well, I'm looking for work now . . .

Dr Dryden: But even outside of work!

Sarah: I don't know anybody!

Dr Dryden: Well, how does one get to know people?

Sarah: (pause) Well, with my other jobs, everybody would just get their coats on at the end of the day and go home ... .

Dr Dryden: (humorously) And of course, you invited them all back to your place for coffee one night!

Sarah: Well, I didn't feel I could approach them.

Dr Dryden: Because . . .?

Sarah: Because I couldn't see them wanting to come!

Dr Dryden: Ah! That may have been true, but do you also see that it may *not* have been true?

Sarah: It's a possibility, I suppose.

Dr Dryden: That's right! But other than *asking*, how are you going to test it out?

Sarah: But if they said 'no' . . .

Dr Dryden: Yes . . . if they said 'no', what?

Sarah: Well, I'd hate that!

Dr Dryden: Because . . .?

Sarah: Because I'd think, 'Even the nice people don't want to know me . . .'

Dr Dryden: Ohh! 'They don't want to know *me*!'

Sarah: (half laughing) Because I'm the sort of person . . . (Pause) My own sister tells me, 'You're the sort of person people won't approach.' We've joked about men actually, and I've said, 'God, I never get chatted up', and she said, 'No – because you're so unapproachable.'

Dr Dryden: Because – interestingly enough – aren't you somewhat *scared* of these people?

Sarah: Yes . . .

Dr Dryden: And in being scared, is it very likely that you'll give off signals that say, 'I want to meet you – come and approach me?' You see, we often find that people who are socially scared will hide in a corner and make themselves look unapproachable. Other people *think* they're unfriendly and don't want to know them!

Sarah: Yes – that makes sense.

Dr Dryden: Right. So, I'm hearing that you make certain predictions about how other people won't want to know you, and that you don't really test them out. Also, I'm hearing that if they *did* say 'no', you would perhaps take it personally and put yourself down for it. Do you know what I mean by 'put yourself down'?

Sarah: Yes.

Dr Dryden: Now these are things that I can help you with. You see, we've really been talking about your attitudes today: your attitudes toward your son, your attitudes toward what other people are going to think of you, and your attitudes about yourself. Can you see that?

Sarah: Yes.

Dr Dryden: Okay. Now, would you like to come for a course of treatment with me of about ten sessions – to see if we can really get to grips with these problems?

Sarah: Is this why I get so depressed and all that – because of these things?

Dr Dryden: What do you think?

Sarah: Yes, I suppose that's it – what else could it be?

Dr Dryden: That's right. So, would you like to take that offer up?

Sarah: Oh yes, definitely!

Dr Dryden: Okay – what I'd like you to do for next week is to write down on a piece of paper all the problems you'd like to deal with in therapy with me.

Sarah: Yes.

Dr Dryden: Just a list. Also, see if you can think of a number of places where you might start meeting other people. What do you think of that idea?

Sarah: Would it be just as well if I phoned Social Services and asked if I could do some sort of voluntary work?

Dr Dryden: Well, would that help *you*?

Sarah: It's meeting people, isn't it?

Dr Dryden: If you think that's going to be of assistance to you, then go do it. Okay? Now, what did you think of this, our first session? What's your reaction to it? Was it what you expected?

Sarah: I don't really know *what* I expected.

Dr Dryden: How have you found it?

Sarah: Well, I thought you were right to say that I mustn't centre my life around one particular thing, which has been my son.

Dr Dryden: You can choose to, but you're going to suffer!

Sarah: I don't want to suffer – I wouldn't be here if I wanted to suffer.

Dr Dryden: That's right!

Sarah: So I've got to start trying to change that bit. And I've got to start mixing more – and find pleasure in other things.

Dr Dryden: Our task is to find out those attitudes you have that are going to stop you from being happy. This was our introductory session – we'll start next week on session one, and I'll see you for ten sessions. Okay?

Sarah: Yes.

Dr Dryden: And you're going to bring the list of problems, and perhaps a list of places to go socially.

Sarah: Yes – thank you very much.

(End of recording)

In a relatively brief exchange, Dr Dryden begins to explore the parameters of Sarah's social reticence. It appears that her experiences in socializing with others have been somewhat limited, that she fails to extend social invitations to others, and that she expects to be rejected if she were to extend herself. Dr Dryden points out to her that she is operating on the basis of untested hypotheses, and notes that she would probably engage in negative self-rating in the face of rejection. Due to time constraints he chooses not to give further discussion to these issues; rather, he begins the work of drawing this first session to a close.

In concluding the session, Dr Dryden engages in a number of therapeutic activities in a short span of time:

1 he highlights the fact that much of the session's discussion focused upon *attitudes*
2 he obtains agreement from the client as to the duration of treatment
3 he suggests relevant homework
4 he assesses the client's reaction to the session.

It appears that Sarah has had a fairly positive response to the specific content of the session, as well as to the active-directive stance employed by Dr Dryden. If a client's reactions to the first session of therapy have any prognostic value, then it might be predicted that Sarah will benefit from her course of RET.

4 The early sessions

As described in Chapter 2, rational-emotive theory posits that human beings create upsets for themselves when they direct absolutistic demands (i.e. irrational beliefs) at themselves, other people, or circumstances as they exist in the world. The dysfunctional emotional and behavioural consequences of subscribing to such demands can take numerous forms, and it is often the case that clients begin therapy with a 'full plate' of presenting complaints. In actual practice it is relatively rare for therapists to encounter clients with well-circumscribed symptomatology, as problem areas can frequently overlap and secondary symptoms (e.g. becoming depressed about one's panic attacks) are often a part of the clinical picture. In addition, long-standing disturbance can often contribute to 'problems in living', such as employment and relationship difficulties. Fortunately, RET's ABC model provides a useful conceptual framework for identifying and understanding specific problem areas and their interrelationships.

In his initial session with Sarah, Dr Dryden suggested that she make a problem list prior to her next scheduled appointment. This problem list serves as a vehicle for organizing the content of her early sessions, and serves as a jumping-off point for identifying and dealing with her various issues and complaints. As will be seen, her difficulties include the following:

1 negative self-rating with concomitant depressed moods
2 guilt and shame
3 non-assertiveness
4 feelings of anger and hurt, with displacement of angry feelings
5 low frustration tolerance and discomfort disturbance.

In addressing these various problem areas with Sarah, Dr Dryden avoids using overly technical terminology. Non-assertiveness, for example, is framed as difficulty with 'saying "no" to people', while displacement of anger is described as 'kicking the cat'. By employing the language of the layperson, Dr Dryden advances rapport with his client and is able to begin teaching her the tenets of rational-emotive philosophy.

It is here noted that the titles given to the early sessions (e.g. 'The second session: teaching self-acceptance') are not entirely representative of their content, as a variety of issues and problems were raised and discussed during each one. In Sarah's therapy, however, it conveniently turned out to be the case that the three major loci to which irrational beliefs can be applied – self, other people, and external circumstances – each received treatment in successive order during sessions two through four. It is, of course, usually the case that things do not work out quite so neatly in psychotherapy, even with the structure that RET can provide. A given problem area might, for example, remain a focus across several sessions; alternatively, a given client may rapidly jump from one problem area to another within a single session. Nevertheless, the current organizational scheme provides advantages for the student of RET, as it serves to illustrate the broad applications of a philosophy of acceptance and non-demandingness.

The second session: teaching self-acceptance

Sarah's second session of therapy begins with the routine of agenda-setting, which becomes *de rigueur* across the entire course of treatment. Agenda-setting serves as a means for organizing and focusing the content of a session. In addition, in the manner in which it is conducted by Dr Dryden, it serves as a vehicle for promoting a collaborative relationship within therapy.

Dr Dryden: What I usually like to do at the beginning of every interview is to set up an agenda with you. I'll make suggestions about any items I might want to bring up, but it's mainly for any items that you want to talk about. This way, we can actually get the sense that we're working together on the same agenda. Okay?

Today, I'd like to discuss the problem list you were going to do – did you bring it with you?

Sarah: I did it very quickly last night.

Dr Dryden: Okay. Also, did you do any research on places to go?

Sarah: Well, I phoned up Social Services.

Dr Dryden: Okay – we'll go into that in a minute. But first, what would you like to spend the bulk of today's session talking about? What particular issue or problem?

Sarah: Well, to put it in a nutshell, I'd like to talk about why I'm sort of frightened to get on with people.

Dr Dryden: So it's mainly your fear with other people?

Sarah: Mostly people I know, funny enough.

Dr Dryden: Okay. (Writing) 'People I know . . .' Do you think that will take up the whole of the session?

Sarah: Well, I could go on forever about it, I suppose.

Dr Dryden: (chuckles) Yeah, but I won't let you go on forever about it!

Sarah: Well, I'll leave it up to how you feel as we go along.

Dr Dryden: Okay, we'll take a look at that, and we'll also review the problem list you made. But first, how did you feel about last week's session? How did you feel it went?

Sarah: Well, I feel you were right to tell me that my whole life can't be surrounded by Peter.

Dr Dryden: I didn't exactly say *that* – I said that you could choose to live your life that way . . .

Sarah: But I'm not going to be happy.

Dr Dryden: That's the consequence – right!

Sarah: Exactly. I think one of the reasons I tend to do that is because I feel safe with Peter. As I've said, I'm not very keen with people.

Dr Dryden: Right.

Sarah: But with Peter I tend to feel that even if we disagree, he's my son and we can get over it. I don't feel that way with other people.

Dr Dryden: So part of the reason you make him your life is because you feel safe with him. But do you feel that if you *did* get on better with other people you wouldn't then be so tempted to make Peter your life?

Sarah: Definitely, yes.

Dr Dryden: Okay – that's a good hypothesis that we can test out.
   Was there anything I said to you last week that sort of upset you or rubbed you the wrong way?

Sarah: Well, I think people often don't like to hear the truth – and I realized that I *am* being overpossessive with Peter. No mother likes to think that they're doing something wrong, and I suppose it *is* wrong for me to assume that Peter wants me to be like this with him – he obviously doesn't! As I've said, he's quite an independent young man – and I could be doing him more harm than good by wanting to take up his life. I think it's unfair – for both of us, really! More so for Peter . . .

Dr Dryden: If your being that way was wrong, would you then sort of blame yourself for it?

Sarah: I would, yes. Thinking about what you've said, and thinking about myself more, I'm pretty sure that I make so much of Peter because I don't have any outside contact.

Dr Dryden: Do you regard blaming yourself as being a good thing? Does blaming yourself make you happy?

Sarah: Well, no . . . no. I'm not happy about blaming myself – but I'm glad to think that I might have come to a solution that will be good for both myself and my son.

Dr Dryden: Can we put 'blaming yourself' as another problem on this list?

Sarah: Well, yeah – I suppose.

Dr Dryden: Okay. So, I'm hearing you say that our session last week was a bit like a bitter pill. I confronted you with what you were doing, and you weren't exactly in love with the fact (chuckles) that I did so. But was it harmful to you in any way?

Sarah: No, I found it useful.

Dr Dryden: Okay. Has it changed anything between last week and this in relationship to your son?

Sarah: Yes, because now I stop and think. For instance, on our way out to my sister's on Saturday night, I caught myself about to tell Peter to be careful crossing the road. I thought to myself, 'You idiot – he's 17 years old! If he can't watch the road now, he never will!'

Dr Dryden: Right. You have this tendency to be overprotective toward Peter, but now you can recognize that tendency and do something about it. You see, the tendency isn't going to go away overnight . . .

Sarah: Yes, I remember that's what you said last week. It probably won't all go away – but I can learn to control it and be sensible about it.

Dr Dryden: Right – you can learn to recognize it, and learn to change it.

Dr Dryden has worked with Sarah to establish an agenda for the session, and she has added her own agenda item: discussion of her interpersonal anxiety. In addition, Dr Dryden has made an inquiry regarding Sarah's response to the prior week's meeting. Such inquiry is considered important, as it allows the therapist to

1 determine which interventions are experienced as helpful or unhelpful by the client
2 identify and correct misunderstandings
3 track the client's progress in therapy.

In response to Dr Dryden's questions regarding their last session, Sarah reveals that she was made aware of her overprotective posture with her son, and states her insight that her overinvolvement in this relationship might stem from her lack of other interpersonal contacts. Dr Dryden determines that Sarah may be rating herself negatively on this count, and also learns that she is already making attempts to modify her usual pattern of relating to Peter. The session continues with a review of the problem list which Dr Dryden asked Sarah to make. Review of previously assigned homework is important, as it serves to underscore for the client the significance of homework within therapy and may function to enhance compliance with subsequent assignments.

Dr Dryden: Okay, let's go through the problem list – I'll read it out loud. The first problem written here is, 'Having to say "no" to people'. The second is, 'Having to change plans'. You find that difficult, do you?

Sarah: Oh, yes – terrible.

Dr Dryden: The third problem is 'Rowing – I don't know how to make up or give in'. With whom?

Sarah: I can sort of flare up about something with my husband. He's very good – he'll usually just say, 'Okay, I won't do that again', or, 'I'll make sure I do that job'. But I tend to carry it on, and then I can't sort of relax and pal up again. Do you know what I mean?

Dr Dryden: Right – and you'd like to?

Sarah: (laughs) Oh, yes!

Dr Dryden: Number four is, 'I hate having to go to see mum, even though I do it every week.'

Sarah: Yeah, I hate that – absolutely hate it! She really makes you feel like a second-class citizen.

Dr Dryden: Because of the way she treats you?

Sarah: Mainly because I wasn't a boy, and secondly because I wasn't fully Pakistani. I'm half Asian, and she wanted all beautiful Paki girls – and she never got them.

Dr Dryden: But your mother is English?

Sarah: Yes.

Dr Dryden: So you feel that she really wanted a boy . . .

Sarah: She tells you straight out – there's no beating around the bush!

Dr Dryden: Okay – she wanted a boy, and she also tells you that she wished you were fully Asian?

Sarah: Yeah – she believes they're more clever and respectable, and that they'd never dream of divorcing.

Dr Dryden: Right – and how do you feel when she speaks this way?

Sarah: Well, she makes me feel absolutely guilty – as if I'd committed a big crime.

Dr Dryden: Okay – we'll go over that. Problem number five is that, 'My husband Art's family makes me feel like an outcast. Even if I *am* half-caste, they don't have to show it.' How do they treat you?

Sarah: Well, there's a few problems involved there. First, they weren't very happy that Art was marrying a divorced woman. They're Catholics, you see.

Dr Dryden: Right.

Sarah: I've tried changing my religion – I was brought up to be a Moslem – but would you believe that they want your mummy to sign the form even when you're 37 years old! Mummy wouldn't sign the form, so that fell through. I've never really stuck to any religion, but I wanted to change to please them. Art's what I would consider to be a good Catholic – he doesn't believe he's got his ticket to heaven, but he does the best he can for what he knows.

Dr Dryden: (chuckles) Well, he's going to roast in hell for marrying you, isn't he?

Sarah: Exactly, yeah! That's what I love about him – he's so honest! He's said that you don't believe you're going to fall in love with somebody who's been divorced and has a child – but since that's where his feelings were, he was prepared to risk losing his ticket! And he can say that he's sorry to God, but he's not sorry that he married me – and God will have to put up with that! He's so honest about it!

Dr Dryden: And you respect him for that.

Sarah: Very much so, yes.

Dr Dryden: Okay. Now, as we go along we may add or subtract things, but I find that having a problem list will really help to keep up us on track – and that's important, because we've got a limited number of sessions within which to work.

Review of Sarah's problem list indicates that she experiences particular difficulty in dealing with situations in which others may act disapprovingly toward her. From the RET perspective, it can be hypothesized that this difficulty stems from a lack of self-acceptance, which leads Sarah to experience upsets when confronted by people and interactions in which censure is a possibility. Thus, she finds it hard to refuse requests, and is greatly troubled by family members' non-accepting behaviours. The problem list also indicates that Sarah finds it difficult to disengage from conflicts with her husband, and that she upsets herself when it is necessary to modify plans.

Dr Dryden continues with further inquiry regarding prior homework:

Dr Dryden Before we start to get into the list, let me just check with you on the 'places to go' issue. You said that you went to . . .

Sarah: I phoned Social Services and asked if there was any volunteer work, and they sent me to the Citizen's Advice Bureau. *They* sent me down to another office, where they offered me two types of jobs. One involved working with children in a nursery where the mothers attend as well, because they're a little slow on cooking and handling the housekeeping. Cooking and housework are fields that I feel pretty confident in – (humorously) I would probably get A levels in those!

Dr Dryden: (laughs) A levels in housework!

Sarah: Yeah! I know it's not considered work, but I *do* run a home quite efficiently.

Dr Dryden: What was the other job they offered you?

Sarah: Well, I told them that I hoped to be employed soon, so that I couldn't tell them exactly what sort of times I'd be available to help. They told me that they had positions where I could go to visit people in the evenings – which would suit me if I was working, you see. They would give me certain cases that the social worker found were okay, but not quite ready to take off the list. I would just sort of pop in and befriend them, but should I find out that Tommy hasn't been going to school, I would just give the office a ring. They'd take it up and do the necessary follow-up.

Dr Dryden: And what have you decided to do about it?

Sarah: I've decided I'd like to take the second position. It's people that I don't really know, so I think I'd be able to befriend them in a sensible way without getting too involved – and I might be able to help them, which would be nice.

Dr Dryden: Right – and when you brought up the notion of being afraid with people, you mainly had in mind your family, or people that you didn't know?

Sarah: Mainly the family.

Dr Dryden: Last week I had the picture that because you were scared to be around others, you might sort of keep yourself in the background with them – and that could contribute to their thinking that you don't want to know them.

Sarah: You're right in that respect. It's a bit of a cheat, really, what I did last night. I went to the meeting . . .

Dr Dryden: Which meeting was that?

Sarah: I had to go to this probation meeting to have these positions explained to me. I had to meet people that were educated and know what they're doing, but I wasn't frightened of that because they know that as a volunteer I'm *not* actually educated and I'm not supposed to know everything. And as a volunteer, they're not going to shout at me, either!

Dr Dryden: So you thought they'd look objectively at what you have to offer, and wouldn't expect too much from you.

Sarah: Yeah.

Dr Dryden: And as a result, you don't feel that they're placing any demands on you?

Sarah: Yeah, yeah. I could slowly prove to be a responsible person – I wouldn't have to do it immediately like you do when you go for a job interview. Plus, as I said, it's a bit of a cheat that the people I'm going to help have got problems! They're not superior people, and they've got problems that are probably a lot worse than I've got.

Dr Dryden: I'm struck by how you see certain people as being superior to you, and how you view yourself as being an outcast and inferior. That seems to be something that's recurred – has it ever struck *you* that way?

Sarah: Well, yeah – you're told you're inferior by your parents. I've got one parent that's not satisfied with me because I'm not fully Pakistani, and the other parent not fully satisfied with me because I'm not fully English.

Dr Dryden: Okay – and therefore, you have come to believe what?

Sarah: (pause) That I don't really please anybody.

Dr Dryden: And therefore . . .?

Sarah: Well, if you don't really please anybody, you're not coming up to standard, are you?

Dr Dryden: Okay – we'll come back to that, because that might be one of the things that runs through some of these problems. But let's go now to the major item on the agenda – you put it in terms of being *afraid* with people – and it's with people that you know?

Sarah: Yes.

Dr Dryden: Okay. Now, I find it quite helpful to discuss problems in terms of specific incidents in which you were scared with people. Can you recall a recent episode that could serve as a typical example of this particular issue?

Sarah: Mm . . . I can think of lots, yeah.

Dr Dryden: Why don't you start with one that comes to mind first.

Sarah: Well, the last time me and Art went to visit mum I didn't bring her anything – and she sat sort of waiting, as if to say, 'So what have you called for? You've come empty-handed!' See, my oldest sister married a Pakistani, and mum's always praising this guy up . . .

Dr Dryden: And she was doing that on this occasion when you visited her?

Sarah: She was already a bit moody because I hadn't presented her with anything, and as my husband and I were sitting there she was praising this brother-in-law of mine to the hills: 'Oh, he's got his ticket to heaven – he's adopted a baby, he's given your sister a good home, he's fully Pakistani, and he reads the Koran.'

I felt like saying, 'Don't annoy me with this anymore, because I'm sick of coming down here and listening to what a tin god he is.' Little does mum know that when I was 13 years old, he tried to sexually molest me! And if I ever told her about it, I'd get the blame!

Dr Dryden: Because she'd think that you'd led him on or something?

Sarah: Oh, yes! It would've been my fault!

Dr Dryden: Right. So you get the feeling that she sees him as a shining example of Moslem-hood, and that there's nothing you could say to bring him down – and if you *did* say anything, it would be reinterpreted.

Sarah: That I was to blame.

Dr Dryden: I'm also hearing that you'd like to tell her that you find her behaviour annoying.

Sarah: I'd like to say to her, 'If that's your opinion of what a decent bloke is, you sure are wrong – you've got it *all* mixed up!'

Dr Dryden: And what would your purpose be in saying that to her? Would you be trying to get her to change her mind?

Sarah: My purpose would be to try and stop her from going on about how superior he is!

Dr Dryden: Okay – but I'm also hearing that you're angry with her.

Sarah: I *am* angry with her, yeah!

Dr Dryden: And you want to stay angry with her?

Sarah: I'd rather not see her – but I can't bring myself to do that.

Dr Dryden: Because . . .?

Sarah: I'd feel guilty!

Dr Dryden: Okay. So on the one hand, when you go, you feel angry and you really want to tell her exactly what's what about your brother-in-law – in order that she might change her mind . . .

Sarah: In order for her to see that it's best to judge a person by what they are, and what you *really* know about them – and accept them with and without their faults. I wouldn't expect her to act badly toward this man, firstly because it's her son-in-law . . .

Dr Dryden: Okay. So – you're angry, and your purpose in telling her is to get her to change her mind. The alternative is not to go and visit her, but you predict that if you didn't go, you would feel rather guilty.

Sarah: Yeah, I would.

Dr Dryden: Okay. Now, with respect to the first alternative, some people choose to speak up because they want to put across their point of view – not necessarily to change the other person's mind, although that would be nice. Is it correct to say that even if you predicted that your mum would never change her mind, you would still like to speak up to her?

Sarah: Yes, I still want to speak up.

Dr Dryden: Right. So, what would you like to work on first? Would you like to work on the goal of going and speaking up, or would you prefer to work on *not* going, and not feeling guilty?

Sarah: I couldn't not go.

Dr Dryden: Because you'd feel guilty.

Sarah: Yes.

Dr Dryden: But if I were able to help you to not feel guilty – providing that's what you wanted – would you then choose not to go?

Sarah: (pause) I could never see myself . . . I just can't imagine that I'd not go – I just can't see that.

Dr Dryden: Right – because you've got this guilt thing. But just imagine you're not feeling guilty . . .

Sarah: I wouldn't go.

Dr Dryden: You wouldn't go. Now, which aspect of this particular problem would you like to work on first – going and speaking up, or guilt about not going?

Sarah: I'd prefer to go and speak up.

Dr Dryden: Okay. We can come back to the guilt later, if you want to – but let's see about going and speaking up.

In this portion of the transcript, Dr Dryden begins to explore Sarah's agenda item of being 'frightened to get on with people'. He encourages her to cite a specific instance of this problem, as this provides him with clarification as to the nature of the difficulty to which she refers. Also, discussion of problem areas on a more concrete, immediate level is likely to have greater relevance for the client, as it could assist her in dealing with problematic situations that she currently faces. This, in turn, may contribute to greater interest and involvement in the therapy.

Sarah describes the frustration and anger she experiences when her mother showers praise on her brother-in-law, and states that she would like to put a stop to this behaviour by assertively correcting her mother's misconceptions. As she also makes reference to the alternative of simply terminating contacts with her mother, Dr Dryden attempts to help her identify which goal she would most prefer to work on. In doing so he conveys the message that her guilt feelings are not inevitable, and that if Sarah chooses to work on them, therapy can help her to overcome them. Nevertheless, Sarah chooses to work on 'going and speaking up'. Dr Dryden accepts her preference in this regard, and makes a distinction between operating from a base of anger vs annoyance.

Dr Dryden: Now, when people speak their mind about something, they can do it out of displeasure and annoyance, or they can do it out of *anger*. Correct me if I'm wrong, but I'm picking up that you really feel quite *angry* toward your mum.

Sarah: Yeah, I do.

Dr Dryden: So if you spoke up at this point, would it be out of anger?

Sarah: Well, yes – it would be out of anger because . . . I suppose it's unfair to say, but I truly feel that it's her fault that I'm not very keen on life. Do you know what I mean?

Dr Dryden: Okay – we'll come back to that issue, because you seem to be blaming her.

Now, I make a distinction between annoyance and anger – let me tell you about it. I see annoyance resulting from really not *liking* what a person says – but anger is *blaming* the person, in addition to not liking what they say. See what I mean by that distinction?

Sarah: Yes.

Dr Dryden: Can you just recap for me what you've understood here?

Sarah: Well . . . you're saying that my anger at mum goes deeper than just annoyance at a thing she did – at one incident or something.

Dr Dryden: Or even a number of incidents – you could dislike a number of incidents that had occurred and still not *damn* her. So – do you want to speak up and share your annoyance, or do you really want to let her have your *anger*? What's your goal there?

Sarah: (pause) I just want to make her see that we go and see her as her children . . .

Dr Dryden: But you see, you're back to wanting to change her mind.

Sarah: Yeah.

Dr Dryden: And I'm saying that you may *never* be able to make her change her mind!

Sarah: Yes – I can see that.

Dr Dryden: Okay – let's start with your anger. When you go to see her and she's praising your brother-in-law up to high heaven and you're getting angry, what are you angry about?

Sarah: Well, it involves more than just my brother-in-law, you see. When we were all kids, I remember one incident where my dad was going to Pakistan on business – and he bought some gold watches to take along as a gift. He happened to drop one, and I picked it up – and even though I had no intention of keeping it, mum took it off me and said, 'You don't *really* think he'd buy *you* a gold watch, do you? That's for his friends in Pakistan!'

Dr Dryden: So I'm hearing you say it goes beyond one incident – there's a history of her putting you down. Right?

Sarah: Yeah! We're not good enough, you see, because we're not Pakistani.

Dr Dryden: And is that what you've come to believe about yourself? That you're not good enough?

Sarah: Yeah . . . I mean, I'm half-caste and I've spent half my life under a sun-ray lamp trying to get a tan – because I was raised to think that looks more beautiful.

Dr Dryden: So you did that in order to try and become more acceptable?

Sarah: Yeah.

Dr Dryden has offered 'operational definitions' of anger and annoyance, as per the RET concepts of inappropriate and appropriate negative emotions. In order to check on Sarah's understanding of the distinction he describes, he asks her to restate it in her own words.

In discussing her angry feelings toward her mother, Sarah makes reference to a long history of maternal comments and behaviours which, in her perception, communicated the message that she 'wasn't good enough'. Through inquiry, Dr Dryden identifies the fact that Sarah has to a large degree internalized this message. Her lack of self-acceptance and 'need' for her mother's approval have apparently led her to engage in certain extreme and unreasonable behaviours, such as spending inordinate amounts of time under a sun lamp.

Dr Dryden: Okay. Now, this is what I'm hearing: you become angry with her because she contributes to your not feeling very good about yourself, right? We could call that a *defensive* anger, which leads to your sort of blaming her. Now, what I'm saying is that you may have learned this negative attitude about yourself as a child, but you're now carrying it on yourself!

Your mum may never change – she may continue to sort of do you down – but how do you think you'd feel if *you* didn't do *yourself* down?

Dr Dryden has made a direct statement concerning the self-perpetuating aspects of Sarah's low self-worth. Here, it can be seen that the rational-emotive approach to addressing client problems differs radically from that recommended by a number of other approaches to psychotherapy. First, some therapies – such as psychoanalysis – do not tend actively to promote insights concerning the client's own role in producing and maintaining emotional disturbance. Rather, they are disposed to cite events in the client's history as being responsible for psychological problems. Second, a number of other forms of therapy would not introduce such a concept in as direct a fashion, believing that doing so represents an assault on the client's ego and may be likely to arouse resistance. It is apparent that the idea that she perpetuates a negative attitude toward herself is foreign to Sarah, as her initial response to Dr Dryden's statement evidences confusion.

Sarah: (pause) I don't really know what you mean, there.

Dr Dryden: Well, isn't she doing you down?

Sarah: Yes.

Dr Dryden: But in response to that, aren't you taking what she says and using it against yourself?

Sarah: Yeah – because she convinces you that she's right!

Dr Dryden: Okay – but who has *really* convinced you?

Sarah: She has.

Dr Dryden: I'm saying that *you* have! Can you see that? Because you could say, 'Isn't it fascinating, mum, that you think I'm no good – but you're wrong!' Right?

Sarah: (weakly) Yes . . .

Dr Dryden: You don't seem to be convinced about that!

Sarah: (chuckles) No . . .

Dr Dryden: But can you see that it's a possibility? You *could* have that attitude, right?

Sarah: Right . . .

Dr Dryden: We can look at it as an 'invitation'. When you go round to your mum's, it's like she's saying, 'Dear Sarah: *I* think you're no good, and I invite you to think of *yourself* as being no good.' Right? And in response to that, you seem to be saying, 'Dear Mum: Thank you for your invitation – you're right! I accept!' See what I mean?

Sarah: (chuckles) Yeah.

Dr Dryden: Now, wedding invitations usually have 'RSVP' on them. Do you know what RSVP means?

Sarah: No.

Dr Dryden: It means, 'Reply, if you please'. You turn the invitation over and you say, 'Thank you for you invitation – I accept, or I reject'. Now, could it be a goal of yours to be able to think, 'Thank you, mum, for your invitation to believe I'm no good – you're wrong!'

Sarah: Mm.

Dr Dryden: Do you see what I mean? The problem here is not so much what your mother is doing, but what *you* are doing inside your own head. You're saying, 'I'm no good!'

Sarah: Yeah – but you try having her visit your house . . . I mean, she makes you feel *so* miserable that you feel like it's a battle, like you're at war.

Dr Dryden: Only if your goal is to *convince* her that you're *not* inferior. You can certainly try and do that – but hadn't your primary goal be to convince *you* that you're not inferior?

Sarah: (pause) I know – but I could never imagine myself feeling any different.

Dr Dryden: Okay – but I'm hearing that on some level you say, 'I'm *not* living up to my mother's expectations – therefore, I'm-no-good!' Is that correct?

Sarah: Well . . . I suppose it must be.

Dr Dryden: Then prove to me that you're no good if you fail to live up to your mother's expectations. I want proof! You see, you've managed to convince yourself; now convince *me*.

Sarah: Well, I feel to blame that she feels as she does . . . not just about me, but – I think – about all of her children.

Dr Dryden: Okay – let's assume that you were to blame. You're really not, because that's *her* nutty idea. But assuming that you're correct – that you really are to blame – how does *that* make you no good?

Sarah: If I am to blame?

Dr Dryden: Yeah – how does that make you no good, worthless?

Sarah: It makes me feel terrible.

Dr Dryden: Because you're telling yourself *what* about being at fault?

Sarah: It makes me feel she's ashamed of us.

Dr Dryden: And if she is, that means what?

Sarah: That means I made her unhappy.

Dr Dryden: And if she's unhappy, that proves what about you?

Sarah: Well, I'd prefer to be a good daughter.

Dr Dryden: That's what you'd prefer to be, but let's assume you've been a *bad* daughter – again, probably not true – how would you feel about that?

Sarah: Ashamed!

Dr Dryden: Shame – do you know what shame means?

Sarah: That you can't look at people, you're ashamed . . .

Dr Dryden: . . . because you believe you're such a bad person! Isn't that what shame means?

Sarah: Yeah.

Dr Dryden: Right. Now, the attitude that underlies shame is the same sort of attitude that underlies *guilt*. Guilt is saying, 'I'm a bad person and I deserve to roast in hell', and shame is saying, 'I'm such a bad person that I'd better not show my face – because other people will see my badness!'

Sarah: Yeah.

Dr Dryden: But I'm still waiting for evidence that you are a bad, worthless person! I want evidence for that! All I've heard so far – and I'm only assuming that it's true – is that you haven't pleased your mother, right? Let's assume that's a bad thing, and that you may have done certain bad things. How does that mean that *you* are bad for having done those bad things?

Sarah: (sighs) Well, she never forgave me for marrying my first husband, because I was under age at the time.

Dr Dryden: Let's again assume that was a bad thing, although it may not have been. How are *you* bad for doing that bad thing?

Sarah: Well, I didn't stop and consider how she'd feel.

Dr Dryden: Again, let's assume that's bad. Can you see what I'm saying here? I'm making a distinction between *you* being bad, and *it* being bad. Do you see the distinction?

Sarah: Well, I suppose it is a bad thing to go off and get married without your parents' consent.

Dr Dryden: Let's assume that it is, just for the sake of argument. Now, aren't you saying that that makes you a bad person?

Sarah: Yeah.

Dr Dryden: I'm asking you to see the difference between *it's* bad and *I'm* bad. Do you see that at all?

Sarah: I don't really see the difference – because if you keep doing bad things, doesn't that mean you're bad?

Dr Dryden: Okay . . . (leaves seat) Hee haw! Hee haw! Hee haw! Hee haw! (returns to seat) I just got down on all fours and acted like a donkey – was that a stupid thing I did?

Sarah: Mm-hm.

Dr Dryden: Does that make me a stupid person?

Sarah: No.

Dr Dryden: Why not?

Sarah: Because I just know you're not a stupid person.

Dr Dryden: But I've done a stupid thing!

Sarah: You did it for a purpose.

Dr Dryden: (chuckles) But you married for a purpose as well, didn't you?

Sarah: (laughs) Yeah!

Dr Dryden: But what's the point I'm trying to make by going on the floor and acting like a donkey?

Sarah: You're proving that you can do something silly, but you're not necessarily a silly person.

Dr Dryden: And how can you *ever* be a bad person? In order for you to be a bad person, there's only one class of acts that you could ever, ever do – and what's that?

Sarah: To be a bad person?

Dr Dryden: Yeah – there's only one sort of thing you could ever, ever do – what's that?

Sarah: Only one thing?

Dr Dryden: Only one *class* of things you could ever do, if you really had a soul of badness.

Sarah: I don't know . . .

Dr Dryden: Think about it – you could only act in one sort of way – what would that be?

Sarah: I don't know.

Dr Dryden: Well, if a stupid person can only do stupid things, a bad person can only act in what way?

Sarah: A bad way.

Dr Dryden: So in order to be a bad person – not a human being that sometimes acts badly, sometimes acts well, and sometimes acts neutrally – you'd have to do only bad things. Do you agree with that?

Sarah: Oh, yeah.

Dr Dryden: You acknowledge it, but at the same time you believe you're a bad person. So – I want evidence that you only and ever act badly – and never act well!

Sarah: No – I mean, that's not true . . .

Dr Dryden: Now, I'm asking you this: what's more true – that acting badly makes you a bad person, or that it just means you're a fallible human being? Do you know what the word 'fallible' means?

Sarah: Yeah – like anyone else, you can do the wrong thing.

Dr Dryden: Right. So what's more true: that you're a bad person, or that you're a fallible human like everyone else who can sometimes act badly and sometimes act well?

Sarah: The second is more true.

Dr Dryden: Right. Now, I don't know if you really *believe* that, but you can acknowledge it – right? Our task is to help you really start believing it.

   Let's imagine that you could really accept yourself as fallible, that you could accept yourself even with the bad things you might have done. Do you think that you'd then continue to feel so ashamed and intimidated when you go around to see your mother? Imagine that you were really able to say to yourself,

'Okay, I'm going to *accept* myself – I don't like the fact that she's putting me down, but if she's implying that I'm a bad or worthless person, she's wrong.' How do you think you'd feel?

Sarah: Well, I'd feel a lot better.

Dr Dryden: Right. You've had unfortunate experiences in childhood, because you had some nutty parents who refused to accept you – but *you* have carried that attitude on. They're not *making* you feel that way, they're *inviting* you – and you're accepting the invitation. Now, can you see that?

Sarah: Yeah.

In his attempt to show Sarah the self-perpetuating nature of her low self-worth, Dr Dryden employs an analogy. He compares her mother's disapproving statements to 'invitations', which Sarah currently tends to 'accept'. He points out to her that when her mother puts her down, she can choose to reject the invitation. Thus, he indicates that one's worth is not contingent upon the approval of others.

Following this, Dr Dryden identifies one of Sarah's upset-producing beliefs ('I'm not living up to my mother's expectations – therefore, I'm-no-good!'), and asks her to cite proof to support it. Asking the client for proof of a particular dysfunctional proposition or belief is a frequently employed intervention within RET, and can sometimes help clients to see quickly that their self-defeating attitudes lack validity and cannot be factually supported.

Dr Dryden goes on to make a distinction between rating one's act (as good or bad) vs rating one's self (as a good or a bad person). In order vividly to convey the point that it is illogical to rate human beings globally on the basis of particular behaviours, he drops to all fours and mimics a donkey. Sarah is able to see that this silly act does not mean he's a silly person, and that in order for her truly to qualify for the label of 'bad person', she would have to commit *only* bad acts.

After Dr Dryden disputes Sarah's rating of herself as a bad person, he provides her with an alternative, more rational perspective: rather than judging herself in a global fashion on the basis of her behaviours, she can choose to view herself as a fallible human being who sometimes acts badly and sometimes acts well. The process of providing clients with a more rational personal philosophy is an important part of RET, as it helps to ensure that clients will begin thinking in less self-defeating, more adaptive ways after they have surrendered their irrational beliefs.

This section of the transcript concludes with Dr Dryden asking Sarah to imagine how she would feel and behave around her mother if she adopted a philosophy of self-acceptance. Sarah acknowledges that she would be less likely to experience upsets. Dr Dryden summarizes the message he has been trying to convey, and asks Sarah to restate it in her own words.

Dr Dryden: Right. Now, why don't you put into your own words what I've been saying.

Sarah: Well, just because mum and dad considered us inferior – more so mum – because of one thing or another – doesn't mean to say that we are!

Dr Dryden: That's exactly the point! Because she's your dear mother, you've taken her too seriously: 'Mum thinks I'm inferior, and she's right.' How about looking at your mother as a fallible human who might perhaps be wrong!

Sarah: Mm.

Dr Dryden: Now, what I'm saying is that you now acknowledge that, but I wouldn't expect you to *believe* it. That's one of the tasks of therapy: for you to go over that and think and think and think about it, and also to *act* as if you accepted yourself – right? We'll meet again next week, but in the mean time – if you agree – I'd like you to go over some of the things we've talked about, and write some of them down. Will you be going to see your mother this week?

Sarah: She's coming to me Sunday.

Dr Dryden: Right. You could prepare yourself for that meeting – before she arrives – by really showing yourself over and over that if she thinks you're inferior, she's wrong. You're a person with both good points and bad points, like everybody else. You're certainly not going to *like* the fact that she's going to harp on you this way, but *she's* a fallible human, too! She's got her own problems – and one of them is that she refuses to accept you as you are!

Do you think you can prepare yourself for that meeting?

Sarah: Yeah.

Dr Dryden: Okay – we'll meet again at the same time next week. But before you go, how have you found this session?

Sarah: (sighs) Like I did last week's – it tires me out!

Dr Dryden: (humorously) Yeah – I'm making you work, right?

Sarah: Yeah! You're making me think, you're making me see things differently . . . and yet it's so simple what you're saying. Just because *she* thinks I'm not good enough . . .

Dr Dryden: It's a simple idea – the challenge is getting yourself to really believe it and act on it.

Sarah: Yeah! I know . . . this I know!

Dr Dryden: Right, right . . . but again, is there anything I said that rubbed you the wrong way?

Sarah: Yes . . . Because I'm so angry with mum, it's hard for me to accept the fact that she's just another fallible human being. That's really going to be a challenge . . .

(End of recording)

The session draws to a close with Dr Dryden offering some suggestions regarding homework activities. He encourages Sarah to review and write down some of the ideas they have discussed, and suggests that she can prepare herself for her next meeting with her mother by doing so. He ends the session by asking her for feedback, and Sarah indicates that she finds the sessions tiring because 'you're making me think, you're making me see things differently'. She adds that she is finding it difficult to accept her mother as being simply another fallible human being; as will be seen, the content of the session that follows is germane to this type of issue.

The third session: teaching other-acceptance

The prior session dealt mainly with issues related to the self-perpetuating aspects of low self-worth and the possibility of adopting a philosophy of self-acceptance. Self-acceptance issues are frequently a focus during the initial sessions of RET, as many of the problems that clients present are related to negative self-rating. Clients may, for instance, rate themselves negatively for *having* emotional problems, believing that if they were stronger or more competent, such problems would not exist. When therapists explicitly deal with clients' self-rating problems early on in therapy, they are often able effectively to convey their concern for clients' well-being and to provide a significant degree of symptom relief. Clients are frequently quite receptive to RET's strong stance against person-rating, as it helps them to see that they don't have to blame themselves for being less than perfect.

The current session extends RET's anti-person-rating philosophy to other individuals within Sarah's interpersonal environment. It begins with the routines of agenda setting and obtaining feedback concerning previous interventions:

Dr Dryden: Okay – as usual, I'd like to start by setting our agenda and asking you if there's anything you might like to raise from last session. You were going to begin adopting a philosophy of self-acceptance, and *acting* as if you were accepting yourself – particularly with your mother. I'd like to find out how that went. What would you like to focus on this session?

Sarah: (softly) Being able to say 'no' to people, and not thinking I can never see them again because I've said 'no'. Once I've said 'no', I'm frightened to see them again!

Dr Dryden: Okay (writing) . . . Now, do you think that will take up the whole session, or are there other things you think we might get around to discussing?

Sarah: I don't think it'll take all of the session.

Dr Dryden: Right – in case we get through that, is there any other item you'd like to discuss?

Sarah: I think those were the three main problems, really. You know – sort of letting go of Peter and letting him get on with his life – which we discussed and I found helpful . . .

Dr Dryden: Okay – I'd like to check up on that, in fact.

Sarah: And, um – you sort of pointed out that I don't feel that . . . that I don't accept myself.

Dr Dryden: Mm-hm. Do you agree with that?

Sarah: Yes, I do! And you pointed out that one might be saying certain things to oneself, but it's up to me whether I believe them. I think that's very true.

Dr Dryden: Okay. So – are you saying that the three major issues you'd really like to focus on are with Peter, your mother, and saying 'no' to people?

Sarah: I'd like to be *myself* with other people, and have them accept me for what I am even if I've said 'no' and haven't done exactly what they've wanted. I'd still be able to go and visit and be friends – hopefully, what I imagine they're thinking isn't true – that she's a horrible person because she said 'no'.

Dr Dryden: What you're saying is that you imagine they're putting you down and thinking that you're horrible.

Sarah: From what you've discussed with me before, that's probably the conclusion I'd come to.

Dr Dryden: All right, I'd like to help you deal with that – in the event that people *do* think you're horrible when you *do* say 'no'. Right?

Sarah: Yeah.

Dr Dryden: Because it does happen from time to time, doesn't it?

Sarah: Yes, it does. Well, what actually happens to me . . . I get in a position where I say 'yes' to anything – and then I go about the task I've been asked to do with the wrong attitude.

Dr Dryden: Right. Okay, is there anything left over from our last session that you'd like to react to?

Sarah: I found what you told me very useful when mum came to visit me on Sunday. She said to me, 'Oh, your new carpet hasn't come yet!' I said, 'No, because if it was in the stockroom for months on end, it'd be a lot of rubbish by now.' I'm going to give her answers now – and if she doesn't like what I say, that's just hard luck because I haven't liked what she's said for about 38 years!

Dr Dryden: Right.

Sarah: I'm not setting out to be nasty to her – but where normally I'd have said, 'Oh no, mum – it hasn't come yet', and she'd say, 'Well, it's taking its time, isn't it?' I'm going to say, 'Well, I'm not bothered by it, so . . .'

Dr Dryden: What happened when you said that to her?

Sarah: She kept quiet.

Dr Dryden: Yeah – did that surprise you?

Sarah: Yes, it did a bit. She also asked about some curtains I'm having made, and sort of implied that I was spending too much of Art's money. I said, 'Well, I've worked also, so it's my money in the bank as well as his – and besides, you know very well that Art doesn't mind.'

Dr Dryden: Mm-hm. So again, you were speaking up to her.

Sarah: Oh, yeah – I let her know that it's not her business. It's actually my money that I've saved.

Dr Dryden: What I'm hearing from you is that you're determined to speak up, but not in a way that is sort of getting back at her. We spoke about 'revenge' last time . . .

Sarah: No – I feel sorry for her, because she wasn't able to show her kids the kind of love I've shown to my son. I've had a lot of pleasure from that, and I think she missed out.

Dr Dryden: Right. Now, have you found you've been worrying less about Peter, or worrying about the same?

Sarah: Well, there's no comparison between the way I've been lately and the way I used to be. Here's a good example of what you sort of discussed with me: he came home the other night, and he'd lost his bus pass. He said, 'Mum, will you give me £18 if I have to have another one?' I said 'If you can't look after your bus pass, Peter, it's not my problem.' He said, 'But I haven't got £18 – just my pocket money.' So I said to him, 'In that case I'll stop your pocket money until you've paid it back.'

It didn't even hurt me to say it! I thought, 'Bloody hell – he's 17 and he can't look after a bus pass!' I thought the only way to make him look after it would be to make him pay for it himself.

Dr Dryden: That's a good hypothesis – we'll have to see how it goes!

Sarah: But it didn't upset me! Normally, I'd do these sorts of things because I'd know they're right, but it would hurt me. I'd have thought, 'Well, I'm hurting *him*, really.' But this time I thought, 'I'm not hurting him, I'm doing him good – and I don't have to feel hurt if I know I'm doing him good.'

Dr Dryden: Right – but what if you had made an error and hurt him unintentionally? Would you then have to feel hurt?

Sarah: Well, I hope I could feel . . . I'm pretty sure I'll now feel . . . Well, it won't hurt him.

Dr Dryden: If it does?

Sarah: It won't hurt him to be hurt!

Dr Dryden: I see . . .

Sarah: You know, he's got this girlfriend now, and the other night she was telling him off because he'd been inconsiderate to her. I thought, 'Good for you – because he needs telling off.' It's about time somebody let him see that he can't have it all his own way – that's life, isn't it? He's got to have some things that hit him hard!

Dr Dryden: He's going to learn that the world doesn't revolve around him.

Sarah: Exactly – and this lovely young lady is helping him to see that.

Dr Dryden: Okay – so you're saying that even if you *do* make an error and he gets hurt, you're still going to be concerned . . .

Sarah: Well, yeah – I'd be concerned, but I'm not going to overdramatize it. I'll think, 'Tomorrow's another day and you'll get over it.'

Sarah has reported instances in which she was able to act more assertively with her mother, and less protectively toward her son. These incidents reveal that she is making connections between the content of her sessions and her life in the 'real world', and that she is deriving some benefit from prior interventions. The session continues.

Dr Dryden: Okay, good! Would you . . . Oh, never mind . . .

Sarah: What do you want me to do?

Dr Dryden: Um – I'm out of my favourite pipe tobacco. Any chance of your sort of nipping up to town and zooming right back?

Sarah: (laughing) No!

Dr Dryden: (mimicking confusion) Why not?

Sarah: Because we won't have our discussion, will we?

Dr Dryden: What? Yeah, we'll have it next week.

Sarah: (laughs) I don't believe you really want me to!

Dr Dryden: I do!

Sarah: Really!

Dr Dryden: Yeah! Will you do that?

Sarah: No!

Dr Dryden: Why not?

Sarah: Because I've got things to do and I've got to get back after this discussion!

Dr Dryden: (mimicking disappointment) Oh . . . all right.

   Okay – now how come you were able to say 'no' to me?

Sarah: (laughing) Because I trust you and I like you!

Dr Dryden: Right – and therefore, what? Because you trust and like me, what?

Sarah: You would still make me feel welcome when I came back.

Dr Dryden: So you're saying, 'The reason I'd be able to say "no" to you is because I'm pretty sure that you won't hold it against me.' Is that what you're saying?

Sarah: Yeah.

Dr Dryden: Okay – now in a sense, I occasionally do this sort of thing with people because it's one thing to *talk* about saying 'no', but quite another thing to actually get the experience of saying 'no'.

Sarah: The experience . . . I know, yeah.

Dr Dryden: Let's look at this particular issue of saying 'no' to people. Can you give me an instance where you wanted to say 'no', but were afraid to?

Sarah: Yes – my sister phoned me the other day, and asked me if I would have her little girl for a week because she's feeling tired and a bit down. In all honesty I wouldn't have minded, except for the fact that this week we've got carpet-fitters coming and decorating and so forth going on. Plus, I want to have time to think about our discussions – I've found them more useful after I've left and I think about them, and have some time to react to them. I thought that if I did this favour for my sister, it would just mess up what I'm finding useful to me – and for a change, I want to do what *I* want to do.

Obviously, I didn't want to go into all this detail on the phone with her, so I simply told her that it would be inconvenient because I've got a lot going on at the moment. She sort of pushed me about it, but I said, 'The best thing you can do if you're feeling that bad is to get some babysitters in and go off on holiday.' She didn't sound overly pleased to hear me say this, but she didn't react too badly – or, to put it differently, I didn't care if she reacted badly. But it's only because I've been . . .

Dr Dryden: You didn't care at all?

Sarah: I think I would've cared if she'd gotten mad and slammed the phone down. I'd have thought, 'My God, what've I done?' But she accepted that I said 'no', and didn't make too much of a fuss about it. But to be honest, I was only able to do that because I've been thinking about this issue coming up with us – and I was pretty sure that you'd say to me, 'You've *got to* say "no" if you don't want to do a thing!' And I've got to learn to do that!

Dr Dryden: Well actually, I wouldn't say that – do you know why?

Sarah: Why?

Dr Dryden: Because that would be giving you advice. In a sense, I would say to you, 'Well, let's look at the pluses and minuses of saying "no", and then you choose.'

Sarah: Yeah – that's really what I meant – that you would advise me to do what I felt was right for me at that particular time. That's what I've been thinking you'd say, anyway. I don't want to live my life for other people – and that's what I've been doing for years!

Dr Dryden: Right – but here was an incident where you said 'no'!

Sarah: I've got to be honest – I was able to do that because I've been coming to see you, and I feel as if you're behind me all the while. Also, that incident took place on the telephone – I didn't have to look at my sister. I don't see her that often anyway, because she lives some distance away.

Dr Dryden: But what if I said that I thought you were wrong – that you really ought to have said 'yes'.

Sarah: Well, I can honestly say to you that I really don't think I was wrong. I just haven't got the time, because I'm more concerned with getting myself right from the mental point of view.

I'm always bragging about how I want to be a good mum and a good wife – well, if I'm not right in myself, how am I going to achieve that?

Dr Dryden: Yeah – but what would you say to me if I said, 'No, look – the poor woman needs a rest – she's at the end of her tether!'

Sarah: I'd say it's just hard luck, because so do I. I don't need a rest in the way my sister says she does, but I need time. So I know that I was right – I'd have to disagree with you!

Dr Dryden: Okay – and how would you feel about *that*? Disagreeing with me . . .

Sarah: Not bad at all – but that might be just because it's you. I'm really not sure.

Dr Dryden: So again, perhaps you would feel free to disagree with me because you would predict that I wouldn't hold it against you.

Sarah: There's something in that.

Dr Dryden: So, do you have any fearfulness about meeting your sister again? You were saying, 'If I say "no" to people, I'm frightened to see them again.'

Sarah: Not with her, because my chances of seeing her before Christmas are nil. By then, she'll probably have had time to forget about it.

Dr Dryden: Okay – how about if . . .

Sarah: She came here today?

Dr Dryden: That's right – if you saw her today, how would you feel?

Sarah: Not too badly, I think. I'd probably feel that I had to bring the subject up again – even if she didn't – just to make sure I hadn't hurt her feelings.

Dr Dryden: And if you had?

Sarah: If I had . . . Well, I would probably feel a bit sad about it, but I would still stick to what I've got to do – what feels right for me and my family.

Dr Dryden: Okay. Now, is there any way of testing that out? Suppose I suggested that you deliberately go and see her, or phone her up and say, 'How are things?' Do you think you could do that?

Sarah: Yeah, I think I could – but she's not really the sister I tend to have problems with. I have another sister who's a lot like my mother!

Dr Dryden: So would you have a problem saying 'no' to that sister?

Sarah: Yes, yes.

At the beginning of this portion of the transcript, Dr Dryden employs a 'problem simulation' technique as a way into Sarah's difficulties with 'saying "no" to people'. As it turns out, she is easily able to refuse his request to run into town to get him some pipe tobacco; this is used to highlight the fact that she mainly has trouble with acting assertively when she believes it will be held against her.

As they start to discuss this issue, Sarah describes how she was able to refuse a sister's request to babysit by placing her own interests first. In reporting this interaction, she reveals the importance she places upon her therapy and 'getting myself right from the mental point of view'. Dr Dryden provides an additional problem simulation by 'disagreeing' with Sarah's stance with this sister, and establishes that she feels comfortable in taking issue with him. This incident in the therapy bears some significance, as it provides indications that first, Dr Dryden has managed effectively to convey his unconditional acceptance of Sarah, such that she trusts he won't act in a condemning manner toward her, and second, Sarah is not simply agreeing with his statements in order to maintain his approval.

Sarah reports that she experiences more difficulty in saying 'no' to one of her other sisters, and the transcript continues with Dr Dryden requesting a specific example of this problem.

Dr Dryden: All right, let's have a look at that – you'd *like* to be able to say 'no' to her?

Sarah: Yes.

Dr Dryden: Let's focus on an example where you'd have liked to have done that, but at that moment felt you just couldn't. Can you think of a recent instance?

Sarah: Well, my older sister – who's lovely in some ways – makes me feel a bit like mum does. She has a son just a bit older than mine who's recently married, and his young wife – who's pregnant – has been in and out of the hospital with all sorts of problems. I'd like to be of help because I love my nephew, but I feel that my sister has taken advantage of me and my husband. She'll phone me up and say, 'Oh, do you think you could run John up to the hospital because . . .' You know – she'll give me an excuse why *they* can't. But her excuse is usually something trivial, and my husband's been to work and he's tired . . .

Dr Dryden: And you're saying that when she does that – at times when it's inconvenient – you'd like to say 'no' but you can't.

Sarah: Yeah.

Dr Dryden: Okay. Now, what would stop you from saying 'no'?

Sarah: Well, two things: one is that my sister and her husband might think, 'Oh, she's everything mum said she is – nasty and selfish and spiteful – because she won't put herself out.' The other thing is that I would hate for my nephew to think I don't love him – because I really do!

Dr Dryden: Let's deal with those two issues one at a time, shall we? Let's assume that they *do* think you're nasty, and that mum was right. How would you feel about that?

Sarah: Well, it used to really upset me – I'd rather do the thing than have them think that about me.

Dr Dryden: Right.

Sarah: But now I think . . . I'd be able to say 'no' to them and just grin and bear it if they thought poorly of me. One day, I hope to be able to say 'no' and not give a damn what they think of me.

Dr Dryden: So you're saying your goal is to not care at all what they think of you?

Sarah: To a point, yes.

Dr Dryden: Not care at all? You see, I like to make a distinction between not caring at all about another person's opinion versus being *concerned* about it, but not deeming it crucial that they think well of you. Do you see that distinction? I'm not quite sure whether or not you're saying, 'My goal is not to be concerned *at all* with their opinion of me.'

Sarah: I'd prefer to have that goal than to continue as I've been.

Dr Dryden: Right. But can you see that there's a middle ground?

Sarah: Yeah – I do, like with everything that you tell me.

Dr Dryden: Now, which of those two do you want – do you want to be concerned, or do you want to not give a damn at all?

Sarah: I think I'd sort of like to be concerned. I wouldn't go out of my way *not* to help them, but I'd like to be able to say 'no' when the time's right – and if they don't like it, I'd hope to be able to accept that.

The next time I saw them, if they still didn't like it, I wouldn't allow us to continue on that subject – we'd talk about other things! They'd have to learn to live with something they didn't like . . .

Dr Dryden: But if they really continued to hassle you over this, week after week . . . then what?

Sarah: Well, I'd probably stop seeing them. But I don't think they'd . . . I realize that if I start to stand up for myself, people aren't going to go out of their way to cause me aggravation.

Dr Dryden: Okay. I think you're right, that perhaps in the past you over-exaggerated the degree to which people would hold it against you.

Sarah: Yeah.

Dr Dryden: But the reality is that some people *will* hold it against you – they *do* hold life-long grudges.

Sarah: Yeah, I know!

Dr Dryden: Now I'm asking, how would *you* cope if you said 'no' to your sister's family and they held a life-long grudge against you?

Sarah: I think, as I've said, I'd have to stop going to see them. I don't intend to go through life with a load of hassle and upset.

Dr Dryden: You're saying that from your perspective, you wouldn't want to expose yourself to that hassle – but you're also saying it's unlikely they'll do that.

Sarah: Yeah, yeah.

Dr Dryden: Okay – you could *cope* with it, 'though you wouldn't necessarily *like* it. You could tolerate the thought that they may think mum was right and you really are a nasty, selfish person. But let's look at the second issue – you would fear that your nephew would think you don't love him.

Sarah: Mm.

Dr Dryden: What would be upsetting for you if John felt that you didn't love him?

Sarah: Oh, I wouldn't like that at all!

Dr Dryden: You wouldn't like it, but would you continue to sacrifice yourself in order to ensure that he gets the feeling that you love him?

Sarah: To a point, yeah.

Dr Dryden: And that would be okay for you?

Sarah: Yeah. I mean, I've done it to the extreme before – now I'm saying I would do it only to a point.

Dr Dryden: Right. You see, one of the unknowns is that you can't *know* in advance whether John would think you don't love him if you refused to run him to the hospital.

Sarah: No, I don't know that – but I do like to show him that I love him.

Dr Dryden: Right – but does saying 'no' necessarily mean that you don't love him?

Sarah: Oh, no – it doesn't mean that.

Dr Dryden: And could you in fact talk with him about that?

Sarah: I could, yes! He's the sort of person that likes people with and without their faults – he sees people the way I wish everybody would.

Dr Dryden: So, even if John *did* think that you didn't love him, how long do you think that would last?

Sarah: Only like a tantrum, like with my son – for a few hours, I suppose.

Dr Dryden: Right – and in a sense, isn't there an advantage to showing your son and John that you're not prepared to do everything for them, but that you still love them?

Sarah: I think there's an advantage, certainly I do.

In discussing Sarah's difficulty with refusing her sister's requests to drive her nephew to the hospital, two issues become apparent: she is concerned that her sister and brother-in-law will think she is a nasty person, and she is afraid that her nephew will believe that she doesn't love him. Sarah is, however, able to recognize that it is unlikely her nephew's parents would condemn her forever, and expresses a position that suggests she would be able to cope with it even if they did.

With respect to her worry that her nephew will think that she doesn't love him, Dr Dryden makes several points. He emphasizes that she cannot know for certain that this is what John would come to believe, and highlights the fact that she can correct misunderstandings on this issue by directly speaking with him about it. Finally, he suggests that there are advantages to showing both her son and her nephew that although she cares for them, she will only extend herself so far.

It is noted that in discussing Sarah's issues with her sister's family, Dr Dryden employs an 'assume the worst' tactic ('. . . the reality is that some people *will* hold it against you – they *do* hold life-long grudges'). This strategy is intended to prompt the client to develop the means for coping with worst case scenarios.

Dr Dryden: So with respect to this particular issue – saying 'no' about running him to the hospital – are you saying that you could now say 'no'?

Sarah: On this particular issue I could, but with other issues I wouldn't. John went through some rough times with his parents, and he always used to come to me and say, 'I've left home'. I would take him in, and that would cause hassles with his mum. But there was no way – no matter what they said to me – that I was going to put him out on the street!

Dr Dryden: Yeah.

Sarah: I used to say to his mum, 'Look – you take him back and sort the problem out with him. I'm not saying who's right and who's wrong.'

Dr Dryden: Right – that's a situation where you wouldn't *want* to say 'no'.

Sarah: No! But I used to dread him coming because I knew what I'd be in for with his parents!

Dr Dryden: Ah – which would be what?

Sarah: Well . . . 'You've spoiled him, now he comes to you . . .'

Dr Dryden: And then how would you feel?

Sarah: I used to feel heartbroken, but no way would I . . .

Dr Dryden: But how would you feel *now* if they said that to you? Let's assume that once again John came over and you took him in, and they really gave you a hard time about it. How would you feel about that now?

Sarah: I'd feel sick, but I'd still hang on to John – I wouldn't put him out on the street.

Dr Dryden: What do you mean by 'sick'?

Sarah: I'd feel really bad about it, and I'd probably feel that some of what they were saying was true – that I've spoiled him, or shown him too much love.

Dr Dryden: Okay – but let me see if I can understand the 'sick' feeling – what would that sick feeling be?

Sarah: Well, it literally makes me feel sick. I think, 'Oh, God', and then I collapse in a chair and my stomach just sinks.

Dr Dryden: *They* would be criticizing you – but would you then criticize yourself?

Sarah: No – because I really can't see any wrong in loving somebody.

Dr Dryden: Okay – but when you say 'sick', do you mean that you'd feel depressed if they were to give you a hard time over John? I'm not quite sure what you mean by 'sick'.

Sarah: I'd really just feel sick – I mean, I actually am sick at times when people upset me.

Dr Dryden: Right . . .

Sarah: So I'd probably feel like that – I wouldn't eat, and I would smoke an awful lot.

Dr Dryden: Now, what would you be telling yourself about their criticism and feedback that would make you sick?

Sarah: I'd be thinking, 'Well, perhaps I have no right to love somebody else's son like that, or perhaps I *have* encouraged him a bit, or . . .'

Dr Dryden: And if I've encouraged him . . . ?

Sarah: If I've encouraged him, then perhaps I'm to blame for his behaviour.

Dr Dryden: And if I'm to blame . . .?

Sarah: If I'm to blame, so what? I'm still sticking by him – I can't help it!

Dr Dryden: Yeah, but then I don't understand how you'd feel sick. I can imagine you sort of calmly saying to yourself, 'Well, look – they're right – I am partially at fault, I have encouraged him. That may or may not be a weakness, but I'm going to accept myself with it.' Now, would you feel sick if you were saying that to yourself?

Sarah: I'm not feeling sick about saying that to myself – I'm feeling sick about what they're thinking.

Dr Dryden: Because . . .?

Sarah: Because it upsets me to think that they think I'm so horrible, when all I've done is love their son.

Dr Dryden: Because what about that is horrible?

Sarah: I just get hurt that they can't understand that I love their son – they should be pleased about it.

Dr Dryden: And I'm hearing, 'And they *should* understand!'

Sarah: Well, yeah.

Dr Dryden: Why should they? It might be desirable, but why *must* they?

Sarah: Well . . . They know how much I was with him when he was little. Our two boys were together all the time, and they were very, very close. I just love him like he's mine!

Dr Dryden: Yes – but can you see a distinction between saying to yourself, 'I would *like* them to acknowledge what I've done for him', and, 'They *must* acknowledge what I've done for him!'

Sarah: They don't have to – I just wish they wouldn't give me such a cut-and-dried response like, 'When he comes to you, chuck him out.' They might as well say to me, 'Go tear your heart out!'

Dr Dryden: Are you also angry with them?

Sarah: I am to a point, because I fail to see how they can treat their son like that. I mean, I just can't – and nobody's going to be able to make me . . .

Dr Dryden: But I'm hearing two things: 'How can they treat their son like that', and, 'How can they treat *me* like that?'

Sarah: (laughs)

Dr Dryden: Am I wrong?

Sarah: How can they say, 'Go and cut your heart out, Sarah' – because that's what they're really saying when they tell me to throw him out.

Dr Dryden: Yeah, but do you know what the real answer to, 'How can they do that to me?' is?

Sarah: No . . .

Dr Dryden: The real answer is, 'Easily!' They don't seem to have any trouble doing it! But I think at the time you really *are* thinking, 'They *should not* do this to me.'

Sarah: Well, they shouldn't – they shouldn't say . . .

Dr Dryden: Why *shouldn't* they?

Sarah: Well, I just don't know how people can be so hard, so unfeeling.

Dr Dryden: But you're really saying again that they *shouldn't* be so hard, and they *shouldn't* be so unfeeling. What's the reality?

Sarah: Well, they are.

Dr Dryden: Now, do you believe that reality exists? That what exists exists?

Sarah: (pause) Yeah, I suppose it does.

Dr Dryden: But you see, when you say that they *shouldn't* do that, you're really saying that what exists . . . *should not exist.*

Sarah: Mm.

Dr Dryden: Does that make sense?

Sarah: I know . . . I'm not going to change it, am I? I'm not going to change what exists. But I'm still not going to throw John out!

Dr Dryden: No, no, no – you see, that's not your problem – whether or not you throw John out is really not your problem. Your problem is that feeling of being sick – which, as far as I can see, stems from, 'They shouldn't ask me not to take him in. They should realize what a sensitive soul I am, and treat me accordingly!'

Sarah: Well, yeah – I suppose that really is what I'm saying.

Dr Dryden: But why *should* they realize that you're a sensitive soul? I would agree with you that it's desirable, but I'm asking you why *must* what is desirable exist?

Sarah: Well, it doesn't always, does it now?

During this portion of the session, Sarah makes reference to the 'sick' feeling she experiences when her nephew's parents make a fuss about her willingness to take him in. Dr Dryden attempts to gain clarification as to the nature of this feeling, as identification of an inappropriate negative emotion will frequently provide hints as to the client's operative irrational beliefs. As Sarah is unable to provide a more specific label for the affective state to which she refers, Dr Dryden takes a different tack and directly asks her to describe the thinking that accompanies it. This approach enables him to identify the irrational beliefs she subscribes to with respect to her sister and brother-in-law. It appears that she believes, 'They *should* understand and appreciate that I love their son and go out of my way to care for him!' Dr Dryden works to dispute this belief ('why *should* they realize that you're a sensitive soul?'), and attempts to show Sarah that she is refusing to accept the reality of the situation as it currently exists.

Dr Dryden: Okay, you're starting to acknowledge that now. Let's imagine that you took that and really worked on it – went over and over it with yourself – and showed yourself that, 'I don't *like* them treating me this way, but (a) I can take it, and (b) there's no reason why they *shouldn't* do it, as it's their value system.' Do you think that you would feel *sick* when they next did that?

Sarah: No, not the way you've put it now – I mean, in terms of saying that's what they value.

Dr Dryden: That's right.

Sarah: Because it's not so bad or wicked to them – it's just the way they are.

Dr Dryden: Right – they've got their own particular value system. And incidentally, you're also saying that they *should* share *your* value system. Why should they?

Sarah: No, they shouldn't have to.

Dr Dryden: Right . . .

Sarah: Because I wouldn't want to share theirs!

Dr Dryden: That's right! So can you see that your problem isn't really about whether to take John in or throw him out – it's about your attitude toward the behaviour they direct at you!

Sarah: Yeah.

Dr Dryden: And it's not, I think, that you're putting yourself down – which you rightly pointed out to me. It's really that you're saying – like many people do – that, 'Because I think that my approach is a caring and humane one, other people *should* share it.'

Sarah: Yes, I see what you're saying.

Dr Dryden: You've been demanding that since you love John and are somewhat sensitive over that issue, his parents should take that into account and not say certain things to you.

Sarah: That's what it's amounted to.

Dr Dryden: But can you see that by showing yourself that there's no damn reason why they *have to* act as you would like – although it might be highly desirable . . .

Sarah: But they don't have to – that's not their value system.

Dr Dryden: Now, can you imagine yourself really working on that attitude for yourself?

Sarah: Yeah, I can.

Dr Dryden: Right – and can you see that you won't feel sick? You still won't *like* it . . .

Sarah: No, I won't like it – but that's just the way they are.

Dr Dryden: That's exactly it!

Sarah: And I'm the way *I* am, and I'm prepared to keep John if it makes me feel happier. I'll just put up with the way his parents are – I don't have to like it!

Dr Dryden: Right – and you don't have to feel sick!

Sarah: I won't feel sick, right.

Dr Dryden: That's right – because in a sense, my goal here is to help you do what you think is the right thing without needlessly sickening yourself.

Sarah: Mm. Just as I want other people to accept *me*, I must accept other people.

Dr Dryden: You don't *have* to, but it would be desirable.

Sarah: Yeah – it would be a lot easier for me, wouldn't it? It would make life a lot simpler.

Dr Dryden: That's right – if you really accepted that they have the right to act as they do. By the way, who hands out rights these days? Who determines what's right and wrong?

Sarah: Who determines it? You have to determine it yourself, I suppose.

Dr Dryden: That's true to a large extent, although we do also have the laws of the land. But who's the only person who could strip you of your right to take John in?

Sarah: Well, nobody could, could they?

Dr Dryden: You could, by telling yourself, 'I have no right'. See that?

Sarah: Mm. Yeah, but I'm prepared to do wrong when emotions come into it.

Dr Dryden: But would you be doing wrong by your value system?

Sarah: No, no.

Dr Dryden: But by *their* value system, you would.

Sarah: Well, it'd be hard luck, you know.

Dr Dryden: Right. Now, one of the things that you did last week was to put into practice what we talked about. That's a very important part of therapy. Can you think of any way of putting into practice what we've talked about here? More specifically, is there anything you could do between now and next week about saying 'no' to people?

Sarah: Yeah, lots. John's wife started labour today, so no doubt his folks will be on the phone asking me to do a bit of the dirty work. I should do what pleases me – so, if it doesn't please me, I won't do it. If they think that I'm horrible and nasty, they have the right to think that – I'm not going to change what they think.

Dr Dryden: Right.

Sarah: I can just take each incident as it comes, and if I *can* and *want* to do it, I *will* do it – because it suits me. And it doesn't matter if they criticize me occasionally, because that's life . . .

Dr Dryden: Yeah, right. You're not going to adopt a philosophy of 'The only person I'm going to please is me, and I don't give a damn about anyone else' – but you're starting to learn that you *can* please you, and that you *can* say 'no' – particularly when you feel that a given thing is really inconvenient, and that others are trying to use you.

Sarah: Mm.

Dr Dryden: See that?

Sarah: I *do* believe that they know I'm afraid of saying 'no' . . .

Dr Dryden: And play on it?

Sarah: Oh, definitely!

Dr Dryden: Okay – you can work on what you've described, because it sounds like it's probably going to come up. We'll continue next week.

Was there anything about this session, again, that you didn't like? Anything I said that rubbed you up the wrong way or wasn't particularly helpful to you?

Sarah: No! I can't believe it when you actually put it in terms that . . . it's so simple, and you're so right when you say, 'John's folks have the right to be what they are!' I mustn't expect them to be like I am!

Dr Dryden: You can hope!

Sarah: (laughs)

Dr Dryden: But you'd best not *demand*!

Sarah: No, no.

Dr Dryden: Anything that was particularly helpful, apart from that?

Sarah: That was very helpful, yes – and I should just go out now and practise!

Dr Dryden: That's it! I'll see you next week.

(End of recording)

Sarah has recognized that her sister's family has its own particular value system, and that she has been upsetting herself by internally demanding that they share her perspective. Dr Dryden helps her to see the relationship between her irrational beliefs and her negative emotional consequences, and emphasizes that she can do away with her 'sick' feeling by giving up her demands. She insists, however, that she will not change her characteristic response to her nephew's conflicts with his parents, and that she will continue to care for him as she sees fit. Dr Dryden supports her in this position, as it appears merely to reflect her own desires and preferences. Rational-emotive therapists typically do not attempt to modify a client's value system; rather, they try to help the individual to see the consequences of subscribing to particular values, and the pernicious effects of escalating these values into absolutistic shoulds and musts.

As the session concludes, Dr Dryden asks Sarah to think in terms of how she might apply the material they have discussed. Here, he is encouraging her to design her own homework assignment; this approach can often result in a homework activity that has special relevance for the client and is thus more likely to be enacted. Sarah anticipates that her nephew's parents will be in contact with her to request favours connected with the impending birth of their grandchild, and states her intention only to assent to those she wants to perform.

The fourth session: learning how to cope with adverse circumstances

As session four begins, Dr Dryden states his agenda items and asks Sarah to add her own. She indicates that she is unsure about what to focus on, so Dryden uses review of her problem list to prompt her recall of specific issues and problem areas.

Dr Dryden: Okay – once again, let's set up our agenda. Also, I'd like to find out how your general mood is these days, and how you did with saying 'no' to your family. What would you like to focus on today?

Sarah: Well, I think my mood has improved, generally. I'm not sure what else to focus on.

Dr Dryden: Let's go back to your problem list, and we'll see if anything occurs to you as we run down that. The first item was having to say 'no' to people, the second item was having to change plans – is that a problem for you?

Sarah: Mm.

Dr Dryden: Okay – we really haven't looked at that yet, have we? The third item was 'rowing' – you say that you don't know how to make up or give in. Fourth item was, 'I hate going to see mum, although I do every week.' We worked a little bit on that. Finally, you wrote, 'Art's family makes me feel like an outcast – even if I *am* half-caste, they don't have to show it.' Well, we've worked a little on that, also.

Sarah: Mm.

Dr Dryden: So, would you like to choose any of those to focus on today?

Sarah: Yeah – when I *do* row, I don't know how to give in.

Dr Dryden: Okay, rowing and giving in – we'll see where that takes us. But first, let's start off with your general mood – you were saying that you feel rather better?

Sarah: Yeah, I do. I saw a friend the other day that I haven't seen for about four years, and usually I'd cross the street and dodge into a shop. This time I made an effort to stop her, which is not like me, normally – and I felt quite confident talking to her. I even took her telephone number and said I'd keep in touch with her.

Dr Dryden: To what do you attribute the difference?

Sarah: Well, as I said, normally I would've tried to avoid her – and hope that she hadn't seen me.

Dr Dryden: Because if she saw me . . . what?

Sarah: She'd know how I felt – about being frightened to meet people, and not wanting to talk to them.

Dr Dryden: And if she knew . . .?

Sarah: I'd be embarrassed or ashamed, I suppose.

Dr Dryden: You'd feel ashamed. Now, this time she still might have remembered that you're rather frightened to meet people, but you actually stopped her and spoke to her. What was different this time?

Sarah: I think she seemed a bit shocked that I'd made an approach to her. She looked a bit like I'd imagine I used to feel when somebody stopped me, you know. But then we started chatting and laughing . . .

Dr Dryden: Right – but how did you *get* yourself to make the approach?

Sarah: Well actually, I heard her voice and I thought, 'That sounds like Louise' – and I didn't hesitate, I didn't even have to think about it.

Dr Dryden: Okay – but can you see that implicitly your thinking had changed? Before, you were focused on, 'Oh, she's going to see me and see how frightened I am, and I'm going to feel ashamed.' In the present case, you obviously weren't thinking that . . .

Sarah: No!

Dr Dryden: But what *were* you thinking implicitly that assisted you in going up to meet her?

Sarah: I simply thought, 'Oh, that's Louise', and I just thought that I wanted to make her see me. I thought, 'Well, I'll stop and talk to her', and I didn't feel frightened or anything.

Dr Dryden: You didn't feel frightened, whereas before you would have?

Sarah: Yes, yes.

Dr Dryden: Frightened of what, before?

Sarah: Well, for one thing, frightened that she might have asked me about the divorce – and that's something I wouldn't have wanted to talk about. I'd have felt ashamed, and all of the other things I used to feel. I just didn't stop to think about any of that – in fact, I found myself telling her about my ex-husband, and how he's married again and happy . . .

Dr Dryden: Does that mean you no longer feel as ashamed about that?

Sarah: Well, I don't feel so guilty. I definitely don't feel as guilty as I used to.

Dr Dryden: Is it possible that you were *implicitly* more accepting of yourself, in case she did ask you about those things?

Sarah: Yeah – I must've been, yeah.

Sarah has chosen to focus on the issue of 'rowing' with her husband. Prior to launching discussion of this issue, however, Dr Dryden makes an inquiry regarding her general mood. This leads to her report of being able easily to approach and start a conversation with an old friend that she hadn't seen for some time. As Sarah indicates that this behavioural episode represented a positive deviation from her usual fashion of handling such situations, Dr Dryden asks questions intended to elicit the helpful self-talk that might have accompanied it. His goal here is to identify and underscore attitude changes that are allowing Sarah to act in a more self-confident manner.

Sarah, however, does not appear to recognize that Dr Dryden is asking her to review the underlying attitudes that might have come into play in the situation she has described. As such, he directly suggests to her that this reported change in her behaviour may have been related to increased self-acceptance. The session continues with additional inquiry concerning mood and homework activities.

Dr Dryden: Okay, good. How about your depressed moods?

Sarah: Um, sometimes I'm a bit depressed in the mornings, and I'll take my time getting the day started. But then I decide I'll get myself active, and go take a shower and make myself look a bit better.

Dr Dryden: Right – so that doesn't last.

Sarah: No – I make an effort to try and stop that – because I think that hundreds of people must be going through the same situation.

Dr Dryden: Are you pursuing the idea of voluntary work?

Sarah: Yes. I went to the probation office yesterday, and they sent me a letter saying they'd like me to go down and help out the social workers with some of the less urgent cases. They'd just like people who will sort of befriend somebody – and I thought that's really what I need for myself – so it's helping both ways, you know.

Dr Dryden: Right. When do you start that?

Sarah: Well, they're sending letters out to five different clients – I'll be calling just to befriend them, and to offer any bit of help they might want.

Dr Dryden: Good. Now, have you had any reactions from last week's session that you want to bring up?

Sarah: Um, yeah – John's wife had a baby a few hours after I left here – we'd been talking about John . . .

Dr Dryden: That's right, yeah.

Sarah: . . . and naturally I was excited for him, and wanted to phone him up right away. But they haven't rung *me* up and asked me to do anything out of the ordinary.

I'll still be a bit soft with my family – I know that. It wouldn't be me otherwise. But I want to be able to draw the line when they try to *use* me, and be able to face the fact that if they don't like it, they don't like it.

Dr Dryden: Right – but you haven't had an opportunity to test that out yet.

Sarah: Well, I did a little bit. Mum asked me to wash her quilt covers for her, and I said I would. But I told her not to come on a certain day demanding them back, because I didn't know how soon I'd be able to get them dry in this weather. Normally, I would have just used my tumble drier if I couldn't get them dry outside, even though I won't use it for myself unless I have to.

Dr Dryden: So you decided you would wash them for her – and that was okay by you?

Sarah: Yeah, that was fine.

Dr Dryden: So what you really said to her was, 'Don't hassle me about it'. What if she *does* hassle you about it?

Sarah: Well, it's just hard luck because I'm not going out of my way – I haven't even washed them yet.

Dr Dryden: So if she were to hassle you about it, are you going to tell her, 'Well, mum, I'll do it in my own time?'

Sarah: Yeah, I will. I feel confident about telling her that she just might have to wait. I don't need to say it nastily, or try to rub her up the wrong way – I can simply state the facts to her.

Dr Dryden: What if she gets upset?

Sarah: Well, I won't really be bothered if she gets upset, because I know she's lucky I'm saying I'll do it.

Dr Dryden: Okay. Will you get angry with her? 'How dare she get upset with me . . .?

Sarah: No, no.

Dr Dryden: How come?

Sarah: I don't know how come. I just know that . . .

Dr Dryden: Well, before you were saying, 'Because I'm doing these nice things they should recognize it and they should be . . .'

Sarah: Well, I've started to recognize that they are what they are! If they get upset, that's probably a shame for them – but I'm not going to let myself become upset because they are the way they are.

Dr Dryden: Right!

Sarah: I still know that I'm being pretty good to them, even though I might be blowing my own trumpet . . .

Dr Dryden: Yeah – is it going to help change them at all by privately demanding that they not be the way they are? If in your own head you're saying, 'They mustn't do this' – is that going to have any effect on them?

Sarah: No, it's not. They're not going to change.

Dr Dryden: They *might* change, although we can't know for certain. Your mother, for example, might realize that you're now putting your foot down, and she might then stop hassling you – or she may not, because she might have a problem there. But you seem to be saying, 'I'm certainly not going to *like* her hassling me about doing these things, but I'm going to show myself *that's* the way *they* are – I don't like it, but that's reality!'

Sarah: Yeah, it is.

During the review of prior homework activities, Sarah reports an incident in which, according to her perception, she was able to act somewhat assertively with her mother. Anticipating the possibility that her new attempts at assertiveness might sometimes elicit negative responses from others, Dr Dryden asks how she might respond if her mother gets upset with her. Sarah's answer indicates that she would be unlikely to engage in negative self-rating if faced with such an event.

Dr Dryden then goes on to inquire whether Sarah might become angry if hassled by her mother. In the ensuing dialogue, he links the content of the last session (concerning the issue of accepting others as they are) with the situation currently under discussion. Thus, he manages to expand the sphere to which a philosophy of other-acceptance can be applied. He reinforces the point that Sarah's internal demands concerning family members' behaviour are quite unlikely to modify the way these individuals act, and summarizes the more rational attitude that she seems to be in the process of adopting. He next turns to consideration of the problem area that Sarah has chosen to focus on.

Dr Dryden: Okay. So you're working on saying 'no'. We'll keep that on simmer and come back to it – okay? But let's go to the main item, which is 'rowing and not being able to give in'. Could you say a little more about that?

Sarah: Well, people would hassle me and get me upset. And then my poor husband would walk in, and I couldn't even look at him! I think I probably felt ashamed that I'd got so hassled, and that I let people get me upset. But he'd walk in nice and pleasant and say something like, 'Hello, love – have you had a nice day?' – and I'd snap back at him, 'Well, do I *look* like I've had a nice day?'

He hadn't done anything to deserve that! He's the one person in my life that *doesn't* hassle me. He's absolutely great! And yet he seems to get the blame for everything – including things that I thought Peter had done.

Dr Dryden: Because you weren't able to confront these other people?

Sarah: Yeah, that's what I think.

Dr Dryden: So you weren't able to confront them – that's what we call 'kicking the cat'. Because you couldn't kick back at them, you let good old Art have it – right?

Sarah: Yeah – it's really horrible.

Dr Dryden: You still do that – is that what you're saying?

Sarah: Well, since I've been coming here, I've thought about these things. I've thought, 'Well, you're using Art as a whipping boy, and it's just not right. You either get the guts to speak up to the people that are hurting you, or you just stay away from those people.' I've got to do *something*, and not blame Art for what other people are doing!

Dr Dryden: Well, you don't *have* to – but it might be very wise!

Sarah: It *is* wise – it's just absolutely unfair to treat such a good human being that way.

Dr Dryden: Okay – you said that since you've been coming here, you've been thinking about this issue. What's been happening on that?

Sarah: Well, I don't think Art knows what's happened to him, because I've been so nice to him and not so bad tempered.

Dr Dryden: Has he remarked on that?

Sarah: Yes, a couple of times – but this is an example of how he's *so* good. He doesn't badger me, he lets *me* talk about these sessions if I feel I want to. And to be quite honest, I haven't discussed very much of it with him. I've been too busy sorting it out myself. But I've joked a little bit by saying, 'Don't you think I'm better tempered since I've been going there?' And he'll remark, 'I don't know what he's doing to you, but he's doing you good.' I know he's happier – in the past, he must've been on edge all the time – and maybe even wondered why he'd married me.

It appears that Sarah has developed a pattern of displacing her angry feelings on to her husband when unable to confront other individuals with whom she experiences difficulties. She indicates, however, that she has been thinking about this issue, and makes reference to positive changes in her manner of relating to Art. Dr Dryden picks up on this, and asks Sarah if her husband has commented on it. Here, he is attempting to utilize the observations of a significant other to check on his client's progress in therapy. Although the report he receives is 'second hand', it does seem to indicate that Sarah is trying to think and act differently outside of her therapy sessions.

Dr Dryden: Okay – so, what I'm hearing is that in a sense, you're talking about something you *used* to do, and don't do so much now.

Sarah: Yeah – but I think that sometimes Art will still aggravate me simply because of his placidness. He would be so placid when I spoke nastily to him, and I'd think, 'You bloody fool – if this was the other way around, if I was some man – I'd turn around and slap your face and say, "Don't complain to me if you've had a bad day! I'm a hard-working bloke and I do everything I can for you." ' Actually, it used to rub me up a bit that he didn't retaliate!

Dr Dryden: Well, let's look at that. At point 'A' we have Art's placidness. Then, at point 'C', we've got your feelings. How would you *feel* about his placidness?

Sarah: Well, it can sometimes annoy me, you know.

Dr Dryden: Right. But you see, I make a distinction between annoyance and anger. Let me share it with you, and we'll see which feeling you mainly have.
  Annoyance is, 'I don't like this trait of placidness in Art – and although I might tell him that I don't like it, I'm going to remind myself that that's the way he is!' But anger is, 'He's placid, and he damn well *shouldn't* be – he *should* come back at me, he *should* stand up for himself!' Do you see the difference between the two?

Sarah: Yeah.

Dr Dryden: What's the difference?

Sarah: I'm not accepting it – I'm not accepting him for what he is.

Dr Dryden: Yeah – and you're demanding that . . .

Sarah: He be something different.

Dr Dryden: But even if you didn't demand and you accepted him the way he was, that wouldn't necessarily mean that you'd *like* his placidness. You might strongly *wish* that he would stand up for himself. You might even tell him that, and he might say, 'That's just not my way'.

Sarah: Yes, he has – because I have said that to him.

Dr Dryden: So you can see the difference between annoyance and anger? And I don't see that you have to change your feeling annoyed about it, because that just reflects your own particular preference.

Sarah: Mm.

Dr Dryden: But anger means that you're escalating that preference into a real strict demand.

Sarah: Yeah – sort of saying, 'You've *got to* change to suit me'.

Dr Dryden: So if you made a prediction for the future, which do you think you'd be more likely to feel according to the definitions we've used: annoyed or angry?

Sarah: Just annoyed.

Dr Dryden: Right – that's not a problem, you see. You're not going to like this placidness, because you've got your own set of preferences.

In this portion of the transcript Dr Dryden again describes the distinction between anger and annoyance, and establishes further linkage between irrational other-directed demands and significant emotional upsets. He asks Sarah to predict whether she will be more likely to experience anger or annoyance toward Art in the future, and indicates to her that annoyance is less likely to result in serious problems, as it merely reflects her own preferences.

Sarah: Right. In the past I knew how badly I was behaving, and I would think, 'You'd better change, Art, and stop me'. I wanted somebody to stop me from being like that!

Dr Dryden: Because you felt powerless to do anything about it yourself.

Sarah: Exactly, yeah. I knew *I* couldn't stop me . . . now I realize that I was saying, 'Art, *you've* got to stop me'.

Dr Dryden: Yeah – but as you realize that you *can* do something about your emotions, you may no longer demand that he has to stop being placid.

Sarah: Exactly . . . Hopefully, if I can control my own emotions, I'll probably be very glad I've got a placid man! I probably won't even say that I don't like it – do you know what I mean?

Dr Dryden: Yeah – that's a good point! You may have been demanding that he be sort of aggressive toward you because you believed that was the only way you'd get out of it – like you'd be shocked or threatened out of it.

Sarah: Yes, even threatened – because I hated myself for what I was doing.

This excerpt suggests that Sarah now acknowledges that it is possible for her to exert some control over her emotional responses to various people and situations. She sees that as her capacity in this regard increases, she may rely less on external factors (e.g. her husband) to assist her.

Dr Dryden: That's right – but let's look at that. Let's assume that in the future you *do* take it out on Art, okay? Now, how would you feel about *you* for doing that bad thing?

Sarah: Well, absolutely ashamed – more so now because I'm so aware that I can, if I want to . . .

Dr Dryden: Ah! If you were to lapse, what would your conclusion be about you?

Sarah: Well, I think I'm still entitled to make some mistakes, because I'm a human being.

Dr Dryden: Yeah, but would you feel ashamed if you reminded yourself of that?

Sarah: No, no.

Dr Dryden: Because shame is, 'Since I now know what to do, I have to do it 100 per cent of the time! I *mustn't* lapse, and if I do that proves that I'm . . .'

Sarah: I might have thought like that before, but now I won't.

Dr Dryden: All right – it really does sound like you're in the process of changing some of your fundamental philosophies. You *might* lapse, you see, but then you can show yourself that you're a human being who's going to lapse, as humans do.

Here, Dr Dryden has broached the issue of backsliding in therapy. His implication is that 'lapses' are to be expected, as Sarah is a human being who will occasionally make errors. He indicates that when she does lapse, she can still accept herself as a fallible person and choose to refrain from negative self-rating.

Sarah: Well, I did lapse the other morning. We had a carpet-fitter coming to do Peter's bedroom, and I woke up a bit late. I got panicked thinking about all the things that had to be done as preparation, and started bawling at Peter because *I* was running late.

Dr Dryden: But what were you upsetting yourself about?

Sarah: Well, 'plans' not coming off smoothly.

Dr Dryden: Ah – should we go to that item?

Sarah: If you like, yeah.

Dr Dryden: (chuckles) Well, no – if *you* like!

Sarah: Well, I planned to get up and do Peter's room – with his help, obviously – so that the carpetman could just walk in, fit the carpet, and leave. Then I'd be able to go through my usual routine of cleaning the rest of the house – and it just seemed that everything was going to go to pot. I thought, 'Oh, I'm late – so everything's going to have to go wrong, isn't it?'

Dr Dryden: It sounds like you've got two attitudes in there. The first has to do with the fact that you *like* things to go smoothly and according to plan. But it seems like you're not *just* saying that you'd *like* things to go according to plan – you're saying they've *got to*. If they don't, what?

Sarah: Oh, well – somebody near me – usually Art – would get it!

Dr Dryden: I'm hearing this: 'Things have *got to* go according to plan, and I *can't stand* the frustration of their going wrong! And because I'm frustrated with the world for not working according to plan, and because Art is the nearest available part of that world, he's going to get it!'

Sarah: (laughs) Yes!

Dr Dryden: It's usually good and desirable that things go to plan, but let me ask you – why do they *have to*?

Sarah: Well, they don't really *have* to! It's just that I feel so much calmer in myself when they do.

Dr Dryden: Yeah – because if they do, you don't then insert your absolute demand that they go right. But if they go wrong, then you bring your demanding philosophy to the plan – can you see that?

Sarah: Mm, yeah.

Dr Dryden: But I'm saying that even if they don't go according to plan, again, you're not going to like it – so you probably won't feel absolutely calm about it – but if you really showed yourself, 'Well, I don't like it, but I can *stand* it', do you think you'd then tend to let Art have it?

Sarah: No, because I was going to let Peter have it the other morning, but halfway through I thought, 'It's not *his* fault I got up late – and I don't like what's happening, but it's no good blaming him. It's just best to get on with it as best you can, and maybe it'll fall into place. And if it doesn't you still can't blame Peter.'

Dr Dryden: Right – and if it didn't fall into place, what?

Sarah: If it didn't, I wouldn't be happy – but at least I wouldn't be getting at somebody about it. I was coping with it within myself.

Dr Dryden: So the next time you find yourself upsetting yourself – not just getting sort of annoyed, but really upsetting yourself because you're demanding that your plans *have to* go right – what could you tell yourself?

Dr Dryden and Sarah have begun discussing the upsets she experiences when her plans fail to unfold as she would like them to. Dr Dryden quickly points out to her that she is turning a preference into a demand, and starts to dispute her irrational belief that 'things have *got to* go according to plan'. Although he indicates that surrendering this belief will not necessarily lead her to feel calm when her plans don't work out, he suggests that it could result in less self-defeating emotional and behavioural responses to such unfortunate situations. Finally, he poses a question intended to prompt her into formulating self-talk which she can use to deal with upsets when they occur. Sarah responds:

Sarah: Well, if they don't go right, I'll just have to cope with the situation as best I can – and definitely not blame other people around me, because it's not their fault. Even if it is their fault it's *still* gone wrong. Other people sometimes *will* be to blame, I suppose, and I've got to accept that.

Dr Dryden: There's a difference between saying they're *responsible* and they're to *blame*. Saying they're to blame is really saying they are *rotten* – how dare they interfere with my plans!

Sarah: Yeah, well – I really believe now that I'll be able to cope with it, because it's not the end of the world.

Dr Dryden: (mock surprise) It's *not* the end of the world?

Sarah: (laughs) No, it's not – because I can catch up the next day. And if I can't, there's going to be another day.

Dr Dryden: And what if you *never* catch up?

Sarah: Exactly . . . it doesn't really matter if everything isn't done. I'd *prefer* that it was, but it's not going to be the end of the world – and I'm definitely not going to hurt Art and Peter over it. Not as far as I can help it, anyway – do you know what I mean?

Dr Dryden: Again, you may lapse – but then you can spot what you're doing and show yourself, 'Oh, I'm probably *demanding* – not just preferring – that things go well'. And then you can ask yourself, 'Well, why *must* things go well?' And as you just answered it: 'They don't *have to*, although that would be nice.'

In this last remark, Dr Dryden has provided an abbreviated description of the process by which Sarah can dispute the irrational belief that 'Things *must* go well'. As stated here, this process involves identifying the operative irrational belief, asking oneself a disputing question ('Well, why *must* things go well?'), and providing a rational response.

Sarah: No, they don't have to. And I know that I'm very, very lucky to have such an understanding husband as Art. I'm extremely lucky!

Dr Dryden: But watch out that you don't set yourself up to put yourself down – because it sounds like you're saying, 'Since I'm so lucky, I must really be *stupid* for spoiling what I've got by kicking Art. I darn well *shouldn't* do that – what a worm I am for taking it out on my poor old husband.' Can you see how you might set yourself up like that?

Sarah: Yeah.

Dr Dryden: But now if you lapse and go back to blaming Art, what could you show yourself about *you* for lapsing?

Sarah: Well, I don't know . . . let's say, for instance, that Art came home tonight and I got a bit snappy with him. I'm not going to be frightened to turn around and be nice to him again, because I'm pretty sure he hasn't condemned me. I used to worry that he'd think, 'Oh, I don't want to be close to her.' I didn't like myself for what I was doing, so I thought, 'How can *he* like what I am?'

Dr Dryden: So therefore, 'Because he might not like me, I'm not going to turn around and be nice to him, because he might condemn me more.' Is that what you're saying?

Sarah: Yeah, well . . . he'll come over to me and be so nice, and I'll sort of push away – prolonging the process of making up, I guess.

Dr Dryden: Because what would you be telling yourself?

Sarah: Because I'd be telling myself, 'He can't *really* mean it, he can't *really* want to be living with me . . .'

Dr Dryden: Yeah – 'Because *I* think I'm a no good turd, he must!'

Sarah: Yeah, yeah – but he doesn't because he knows that one minute a person can be like a little angel and the next minute like the devil. That's okay – he must love the angel part of me enough to put up with the devil part.

Dr Dryden: He accepts you with your good and your bad.

Sarah: Exactly!

Dr Dryden: Right – but what I'm hearing is that *you* are now starting to be more self-accepting about your good and bad parts, too.

Sarah: Yeah – because I know I may always tend to be a bit quick-tempered and sharp-mouthed.

Dr Dryden: But you can actually recognize that that's your *tendency*, and really get after yourself when you do flare up. You can ask yourself questions like, 'What am I telling myself, what am I demanding?' You see, I can also be pretty quick to temper, particularly when driving in a car and somebody else gets in my way. I might get angry, but then I'll quickly show myself what I'm doing. I'll ask myself, 'Why the fuck do I *have to* get my way? Why is it *more than bad* that they drive poorly?'

I'll still be annoyed because I don't *like* it, and I still have the tendency – like you – to be quick-tempered, but then I work on that and accept myself *with* my tendencies.

Sarah: Well, this is what I hope I can do, you know.

Dr Dryden: You will, if you keep working at it.

Dr Dryden has again made reference to the issue of lapsing back into dysfunctional emotional and behavioural habits, and reiterates his message that Sarah does not have to put herself down when this occurs. He states his observation that she seems to be approaching greater self-acceptance.

He encourages Sarah to recognize that she may have a tendency to anger herself quickly, and discloses that he can be somewhat similar to her in this regard. He describes circumstances in which he is 'quick to temper', and how he works to deal with his anger and to accept himself with his self-acknowledged tendencies. Selective therapist self-disclosure can represent a powerful intervention within RET, as it provides a vehicle by which real-life applications of rational-emotive philosophy can be illustrated. In addition, it allows the client to view his or her therapist as another fallible individual who continues to work at countering the human tendency toward irrational thinking. This, in turn, can function to enhance rapport and convey the message that it is indeed possible to modify one's upset-producing attitudes and asumptions.

Sarah: Yeah . . . I do see things looking much better – I feel a lot more confident about the future than I did.

Dr Dryden: Let me make a suggestion. I originally said that we've got ten sessions at our disposal – but we can spread them out more. How would you feel about seeing me again in two weeks?

Sarah: Yeah – because by then I probably would have had a few more experiences to cope with, and I'd be able to come back and tell you how I reacted to them. Hopefully, it would be for the better – but you know, they might *not* be for the better.

Dr Dryden: Right – because you might lapse. But if you do, you can work on accepting yourself and perhaps on *understanding* why you lapsed – because if you're not accepting yourself, you'll have a hard time going back and understanding the lapse.

Sarah: Mm.

Dr Dryden: You might say to yourself, 'Oh, I shouldn't have done it, I shouldn't have lapsed – what a bad person I am' – and that will block you from understanding it.

Sarah and Dr Dryden have agreed to let two weeks go by before they meet again. Dr Dryden suggests this course of action because he perceives that Sarah is making progress with respect to her problem areas, and because he suspects that the longer period between sessions will likely provide her with more opportunities to apply the tools she is acquiring. He makes the point that a self-accepting approach can set the stage for continued insights into the means by which she creates upsets for herself, and turns attention to the task of identifying a homework activity.

Dr Dryden: Okay, is there anything related to this problem list that you think you could work on? You could deliberately *force* yourself into particular types of situations, to actually make quicker progress.

Sarah: Um . . . how can I force myself?

Dr Dryden: Well, for example, are there people you're avoiding that you'd like to see?

Sarah: Well, I don't want to meet any of the people I used to work with, because I just didn't like them. But I'm glad to say that's because I don't *want* to, and not because I'm frightened to.

Dr Dryden: Right.

Sarah: That's really the truth! As far as the family is concerned, I'm going to see them anyway – we're pretty close, you know.

Dr Dryden: What about meeting new people?

Sarah: Well, I will be meeting new people. I'm looking forward to doing this work with Social Services, and . . . I'm not frightened now if Art asks me to go out – because I used to worry that I didn't look good enough. But I know by the things he says that *he* thinks I look good enough – and he's the one that really matters.

Dr Dryden: But what if he suddenly changed his mind and said, 'Oh, God – you've suddenly turned ugly, dear!'

Sarah: (laughs) Well, it's just hard luck because I can't do anything about it! He'll never be like that – he's such a nice person! But I'm not so worried about how I look, anyway. I mean normally, I never would have come to see somebody like yourself without first showering and blow-drying my hair!

Dr Dryden: (humorously) You mean you haven't showered yet!

Sarah: (laughs) No, and I haven't blow-dried my hair! But in the past I would've been stupid enough to go through all that to come here, just to go back home and do housework. Then, I'd have to do it all over again to look right for when Art came home.

Yesterday I had to go to Social Services, so obviously I had to do myself up a bit to look respectable. But when I came home, I didn't do it all over again for when Art came in – and his reaction was nil! It's as if a few weeks ago I would have expected Art to say, 'Oh, you haven't just showered and changed – you don't look all nice for me!'

Dr Dryden: That's interesting. Because you're becoming more accepting of yourself, I think you're now able to see Art more as he is – without inventing all of these things he might be thinking about you.

Sarah: Yeah – I thought I had to be glamorous all the while.

Dr Dryden: Because, 'How else could he accept me if I wasn't?'

Sarah: Exactly, yeah. But I don't believe that now.

Dr Dryden: Okay – so what you're saying is that you *are* going to meet new people, and see how you react to them. There will also probably be an opportunity to go and say 'no' to people.

We've looked at your own family's attitude toward you – we haven't yet really looked at Art's family. You've said his family makes you feel like an outcast.

Sarah: Yeah, they do –and I haven't had a chance to . . .

Dr Dryden: Where do they live?

Sarah: They don't live too far away.

Dr Dryden: Well, is there any opportunity for you to go 'round and see them? You could create an opportunity to practise accepting *yourself*, even if they make derogatory remarks about you. How about that? Do you think that would be a good thing to do between now and a fortnight?

Sarah: Yeah – I know what you're saying. I might try going down to see his mum, because I think that's important as far as Art's concerned. I want him to keep in touch with his mum.

But to be quite honest, I now feel that if they don't particularly like or want me, for whatever reason, I *really* don't care anymore. So, I don't find it that important whether I see them or not. Before, I didn't want to see them – but I thought, 'Well, that makes it even worse – I've *got to* see them.' But I don't *have to* see them – I don't have to go down and please Art's mum!

Dr Dryden: That's right! But you could develop the flexibility – because as you say, perhaps the only motivation for seeing them is that it's important to Art.

Sarah: Yeah – I feel it's fair that Art sees his family as much as *he* wants to. I can't say exactly how much that is, but I do know that he'd like to see his mum.

Dr Dryden: From what I'm seeing, we're really getting to grips and you're making an improvement on all of these problems – can you see that?

Sarah: Yeah – I really think that I'm feeling better about a lot of things.
Dr Dryden: Okay – well, we'll stop . . .
(End of recording)

Dr Dryden has suggested to Sarah that she can 'force' herself to encounter problematic situations, such that she will actually be *creating* opportunities to practise applying a more rational philosophy. This represents a change from the approach utilized in prior sessions, where homework activities tended to be directed toward events that were already in the making. This past strategy can be described as a *reactive* approach to homework, whereas the current approach which Dr Dryden promotes can be considered *proactive*. When clients actively place themselves in the situations with which they experience emotional and behavioural difficulties, they are stepping out of their usual role of being a passive responder. This can allow therapeutic progress to occur more quickly and efficiently.

Sarah at first appears confused by the concept of 'forcing oneself', but then catches on to this idea and considers the possibility of visiting her husband's family with the object of working on self-acceptance issues. As the session ends, therapist and client agree that Sarah is making strides in dealing with her problem areas.

5 The middle sessions

The fifth session: review of progress on original presenting problems

Given their initial agreement to meet for a total of ten sessions, the fifth session represents the halfway mark for Dr Dryden's therapy with Sarah. As such, he begins the session by requesting a review of her original presenting problems. Sarah, in turn, raises an issue concerning her 'right' to be upset or annoyed. This item is added to the agenda for the session.

Dr Dryden: Well, this is our fifth session if we include the first one . . .
Sarah: Yeah.
Dr Dryden: . . . and since we're halfway through the course of treatment, I'd like to review how things are going.
    What would you like to focus on today?
Sarah: Well, really, I feel a lot better about everything.
Dr Dryden: Yeah.
Sarah: So – I don't really know. I think I've still got to learn to control my feelings, and . . .
Dr Dryden: Which feelings?
Sarah: Like when something upsets me or annoys me – because there is a difference between being upset and annoyed.
Dr Dryden: Right.
Sarah: I *am* learning to sort of calm down – but sometimes I have a right to be annoyed, and sometimes I have a right to be upset. So – I'm not really sure where I have to let people get away with something, and where I have to stop and say, 'Well, you *are* wrong – don't do that!'
Dr Dryden: Okay, we'll talk about that: the right to be upset and annoyed. But first, let's review the items on your problem list and see how we get on.
    Your first item was having to say 'no' to people . . .
Sarah: I don't think I listed them in terms of priority.

Dr Dryden: Right. How are you doing on saying 'no' to people?

Sarah: A lot better. I *do* feel that I have the right to say 'no', and I no longer feel that people are going to condemn me as badly as I thought they would.

Dr Dryden: Yeah – but if they do . . .?

Sarah: If they do, I really don't care that much – that's really true! But – I want to point out that I'm not going to go out of my way to say 'no' just to prove this point.

Dr Dryden: Right, right.

Sarah: Do you know what I mean? I'll say 'no' if I feel I've got to because of the circumstances. But I don't want to try and make out that I'm suddenly becoming a hard person who's going to say 'no' just for the sake of doing it. I don't want to be like that; that wouldn't be me.

But there's nothing wrong in saying 'no'. When I can justify it for myself, that's all that really matters. For instance, I told you that I got a job – and I made it quite clear at the interview that within reason, I would be flexible with my hours. But I take a lot of pride in looking after my home and my family, so I'll only be flexible with the job if it doesn't interfere with those things.

Dr Dryden: Would you have been able to do that before you came to see me?

Sarah: No – in fact, I wouldn't have gone to the Jobcentre with the attitude that I had. I used to sort of go, and crawl in and look on the board, and come away.

Dr Dryden: (chuckles)

Sarah: And I only used to go if I was absolutely bored out of my mind – I don't know why, but I used to think it was so degrading. But after coming to see you I thought, 'How stupid to think it's degrading'.

Dr Dryden: Right. You mean you would crawl in because you'd be ashamed?

Sarah: I'd be ashamed because I was depressed and fed up and thought that I looked horrible, and all of those silly things that I used to think.

Dr Dryden: Right, yeah.

Sarah: But after seeing you, I thought I should pursue what I like most – and that's a routine. I like a routine – it keeps me happy, and I think it benefits the family as well. So, I decided I would handle each day like I was already working. I would get up in the morning, do the housework, get myself tidied up, and go to the Jobcentre – as if that was my job every day. And that's how I got this job!

In conducting their problem review, Dr Dryden first asks Sarah for an update on the issue of saying 'no' to people. In responding to his inquiry, she makes reference to two important cognitive changes she has experienced: she now believes she can accord herself the privilege of refusing a request ('I *do* feel that I have the right to say "no" . . .'), and also no longer expects that others will totally condemn her if she does so. In addition, she reports that even if she *is* condemned, she will not tend to magnify the importance of such an event.

It is interesting to note that some of Sarah's remarks indicate that she is attempting to integrate the behaviour of assertively refusing requests with other aspects of her personality. She states that she doesn't want to give the appearance of becoming a 'hard person' who will 'say "no" just for the sake of doing it', because 'that wouldn't be me'. These comments can serve to underscore the observation that it may be unwise for therapists to push too hard for sweeping changes in a client's behavioural repertoire. Just as a used-car salesman is likely to lose a sale when he pushes a Rolls-Royce on a customer interested only in basic transportation, the therapist may jeopardize rapport and arouse resistance when a 'hard sell' approach is used to advocate radical modifications in well-entrenched behaviour patterns. Each client is likely to possess a particular view of self which influences the degree and types of changes they will be willing to make.

Sarah goes on to relate how her new attitudes about saying 'no' will affect the way she deals with her work schedule, and describes her use of a disciplined routine to assist in the process of finding employment. The session continues with Dr Dryden's inquiry concerning another issue from Sarah's original problem list.

Dr Dryden: Right – good! Okay, let's move on to problem number two: having to change plans.

Sarah: Well, I still sort of have butterflies at the thought of having to change plans. But funnily enough, the hours for my job are different every day.

   Now, some people might say, 'Well, what's the matter with that?' But if somebody had offered me a job like that before I came to see you, I would have been upset by the lack of a routine – do you know what I mean?

Dr Dryden: Right.

Sarah: With an attitude like that, I probably would have spoiled the interview.

Dr Dryden: But what if you made some plans now, and something *really* went wrong to disrupt them – how would you feel about that?

Sarah: I probably would get upset – but . . .

Dr Dryden: And *then* what would you do after you got upset?

Sarah: (chuckles) Well, they may have me locked up for this – but I have little chats with you even though you're not there!

Dr Dryden: Okay – and what do you say?

Sarah: (laughing) Well, I say to myself . . . Like when I went for the interview, the woman said to me, 'You'll start at nine o'clock on Monday, ten o'clock on Tuesday, twelve o'clock on Wednesday, and we're not quite sure about Thursday'. I thought to myself, 'Not quite sure about Thursday! How can you say that to me?'

   But then I thought, 'Now, if you were telling your therapist about this, he'd say, "What's so bad about it? *Why* can't you do it?" ' And I said to myself, 'Well, there *is* no real reason – I'm just making up reasons.'

   Really, I think that over the years of my married life I've set myself into such a routine, that it's become habit – and I'm frightened to break it. I think things aren't going to go right if I break routine – but that's not true!

Dr Dryden: So you're saying that you might become upset initially, but then you'd say, 'Okay, so I'm upset – what am I telling myself?' Or, you might imagine *me* asking you that same question, and then you'd answer it!

Sarah: Yeah, that's what I've been doing, actually.

Sarah reports that she copes with her upsets about disruptions to her routines by having imaginary 'little chats' with Dr Dryden. He responds by asking her to describe these chats in order to assess whether her coping self-talk is indeed rational, and also to reinforce her use of this self-initiated cognitive intervention.

   It is not unusual for clients to report that they have imaginary conversations with the therapist between sessions. Ellis (1983), in fact, has described such a phenomenon in his work with clients:

Often, my clients tell me that when they are trying to do something that they are afraid of, and are having great difficulty doing it, they literally hear my voice saying, forcibly repeating: 'Now what are you afraid of? What the fuck difference does it really make if you get rejected? What's really going to happen to you that's so terrible?' and so on. And they then go and do the things they've been terribly frightened of doing.

A client's fantasied conversation with a therapist may sometimes take the form of an involved dialogue; alternatively, it may simply consist of a single question which prompts the client to engage in rational thinking: 'What would Dr X say to me about this situation?' These 'conversations' can be viewed as an intermediate step in the client's endeavour to acquire and exercise a more rational philosophy of life. They may indicate that the client recognizes the adaptive and self-enhancing value of such a philosophy, but does not yet quite trust him or herself to utilize it competently. As such, the 'presence' of the therapist is used as a source of confirmation and encouragement. Ideally, as the client continues to progress in therapy, independent utilization is accomplished and the therapist's 'presence' fades.

Dr Dryden next makes an inquiry concerning Sarah's conflicts at home.

Dr Dryden: That's good! Okay, the next problem is rowing: 'I don't know how to make up or give in.'

Sarah: Mm. Well, I've been very good there. Because things are so much better, I haven't been so touchy. So, obviously there haven't been many rows lately. But I really do suffer with premenstrual tension [PMT] – that is true.

Dr Dryden: Right, okay.

Sarah: It's not a made-up thing – I really do have it. The other day I happened to be on the phone when Art came in, and I usually sort of wait on him and give him his tea. But this time he got the tea out of the oven himself – I was keeping it warm, you see.

Dr Dryden: Mm-hm.

Sarah: I had a tea towel in my hand while I was talking on the phone – and when he came back in, I noticed he'd taken a clean towel out. Well, this sounds very silly, but I said to Art, 'Why did you take another clean towel out?'

Dr Dryden: This was when you were under the influence of PMT?*

Sarah: It was the very beginning – I get worse day by day.

Dr Dryden: Okay – so at the beginning you . . .

Sarah: At the beginning, I told him off for taking the tea towel out. He didn't say anything, but then Peter piped up and said, 'Well, does it matter?'

It *did* matter to me, because I'm the one that has to handle all the washing, and I'm the one that has to get it dry! So I said to myself, 'I *do* have the right to be annoyed! I *do* have the right to get upset!'

It's okay for Peter to sit there and think, 'Oh, what a trivial thing – just

---

* On reflection I (WD) would have been wise to suggest to Sarah directly that she consult a Well Woman clinic for her PMT symptoms. She had seen her GP about this but considered that he had neither the time nor the understanding to help her (see p. 108). A Well Woman clinic would have offered her both and it was an error of omission that I did not suggest such a referral.

because he's taken another tea towel!' Perhaps in his eyes, it was trivial – but it *wasn't* to me!

Dr Dryden: Right.

Sarah: So, I let him have it nicely!

Dr Dryden: What's he interested in? What sort of things is Peter interested in?

Sarah: Peter's interested in everything, you know . . .

Dr Dryden: What is he *mainly* interested in?

Sarah: Well, I'd say the things he's interested in at college – he's training to be a social worker.

Dr Dryden: Yeah – but does he have any hobbies?

Sarah: Hobbies? Well, he likes to collect records – and he's got a girlfriend . . .

Dr Dryden: The point I'm trying to make is that something *he's* passionately interested in, *you* might find trivial for yourself. Right?

Sarah: Oh, yeah.

Dr Dryden: But as you say, even though *he* finds your concern trivial, you have a right to consider it important.

Sarah: Yeah. If we were talking about a different time of year when you could hang half a dozen towels out, and know they would be dry in a couple of hours . . .

Dr Dryden: Is that one of the things you wanted to bring up under the right to be upset and annoyed?

Sarah: Yeah!

Dr Dryden: Right. We can come back to that at the end – okay?

Sarah: But if that happened today and Peter said that to me – well, I probably would've hit him with a tea towel!

Dr Dryden: Because . . .?

Sarah: Because now I've *really* got premenstrual tension – and anybody's likely to get it!

I *am* controlling it, perhaps better than I would have a couple of months ago. But I'd be kidding myself to say it's not there, so all I'm really doing is bottling up the tension that I feel.

Something stupid will make me cry – and I mean *really* cry. Then I start feeling so upset, and I'll think about all of the silly things that used to upset me . . .

Dr Dryden: Right – well, what would you do if that happened now?

Sarah: Well, even talking to you on my own wasn't working so well today – because . . . I don't know, I really feel . . .

Dr Dryden: But you attribute that to the premenstrual tension?

Sarah: I do. I know that's what it is, because I've had this so often, for so long, that I *know* the difference in myself.

Dr Dryden: Right.

Sarah: But hopefully, like every month, it will go away and I'll be what I consider to be normal again.

Dr Dryden: But how does your family react? Do you tell them that you're having this problem? And do they accept it, or what?

Sarah: Yeah – I've told them, and they accept it. But obviously, it's not pleasant for them – I can't predict what's going to upset me at a given time.

I can't say to Art or Peter, 'Well, don't do a certain thing, because *that* will upset me'. So, they really can't avoid it, because I don't know it until it happens. You know – it's just something that will flare up.

Dr Dryden: But do you regard that to be a problem for you?

Sarah: Yeah, I do . . .

Dr Dryden: In what way is it a problem for you?

Sarah: Well, I feel I'm causing unpleasantness, unnecessary unpleasantness for people.

Dr Dryden: And if I am . . .?

Sarah: Well, I don't like that!

Dr Dryden: No – you don't like it, but how do you feel about it?

Sarah: I feel that I want to be able to *stop* it!

Dr Dryden: And if you can't, because it's premenstrual tension . . .?

Sarah: If I can't, I just have to live with it!

Dr Dryden: By telling yourself what?

Sarah: That they'll have to put up with me the way I am.

Dr Dryden: Or not!

Sarah: Or not put up with me.

Dr Dryden: And if they don't?

Sarah: If they don't, they can do the same as I feel sometimes – there's a door, and they can walk out of it!

Dr Dryden: But I was thinking that you might make yourself feel rather guilty.

Sarah: No, I don't actually feel guilty. I feel more sorry than guilty. There's a difference, of course.

Dr Dryden: Yeah, it *is* sad if they're upset.

Sarah: But I hadn't looked at it like that until you said it. I mean, normally I would feel *so* upset at making them upset, that I would get angry . . .

Dr Dryden: Yeah, but what would the upset be about?

Sarah: The fact that I'd be feeling so guilty – and the more guilty I felt, the more angry I'd become. Do you know what I mean? So actually, it *has* been better, really.

Dr Dryden: You became angry because you would somehow blame them for making you feel guilty? Is that what you're saying? Or, is it because you felt bad about yourself . . .

Sarah: Because I felt bad about myself – I thought, 'Why, of all people, do I have to get that disgusting thing: premenstrual tension?'

Dr Dryden: Yeah. 'Why can't my neighbour get it, and I be spared?'

Sarah: Yeah – I think, 'Why can't I be spared that . . .'

Dr Dryden: And do you still believe that?

Sarah: Well, I do wish that I didn't have it, but I wouldn't wish it on somebody else!

Dr Dryden: Yeah – and when you say, 'Why should I have it?' you're really saying 'I *shouldn't* have it!'

Sarah: Mm

Dr Dryden: Now, why *shouldn't* you have it?

Sarah: There's no reason I shouldn't have it – I'm a woman, and if I happen to get it, I get it.

Dr Dryden: Yeah . . .

Sarah: But . . . talking about it now, I don't feel so guilty as I would've felt. Last month I probably would've been feeling a lot more upset, because on top of everything else, I'd be feeling guilty.

Dr Dryden: Right – but now you recognize that you don't have to feel guilty.

In reporting on her difficulties with 'rowing', Sarah makes reference to the impact that premenstrual tension has on her moods, and consequently, her behaviour. Although she is concerned that her behaviour may sometimes contribute to unpleasantness for her husband and son, she makes statements that suggest she is refraining from global negative self-rating. This issue receives additional treatment further on in the session. At this point, however, Dr Dryden continues with an inquiry concerning Sarah's relationship with her mother.

Dr Dryden: Okay, let's go on: 'I hate having to go and see mum, although I do it every week.'

Sarah: Well, this is very strange, it's all coincidence, but – mum's had a falling out with her only son. One of my sisters has become a Jehovah's Witness, so mum's not visiting her too much, because she's afraid of anything like that. Another sister has just become a grandmother, so all of her time is taken up with her granddaughter. And my other two sisters live some distance away, so mum rarely sees much of them.

So, suddenly . . . it seems that I'm the only one left for mum to come running to – do you know what I mean?

Dr Dryden: Right.

Sarah: I've always felt pity for her – but I think now it's a little bit more. But I wouldn't *dream* of showing that I pity her.

Dr Dryden: Yeah . . .

Sarah: And I feel that more than ever now, I'm a sort of support for her. I won't always make the effort to go and see her, but I'll ring her up and say, 'If you're fed up and you haven't got anything to do, pop up.'

Dr Dryden: Yeah – but do you dread it when she does?

Sarah: No – I don't, because . . . I suppose it's not a very nice thing to say, but her troubles have made me feel that I can be kinder to her. Genuinely kinder – not put on, if you know what I mean. I feel as if she needs *me* for a change.

Dr Dryden: Because . . .

Sarah: She's suddenly been cut off – I don't know why it is.

Dr Dryden: But how would you feel if she suddenly made peace with her son, and . . .

Sarah: They all sort of had time for her again?

Dr Dryden: Yeah – how would you feel about that?

Sarah: Well . . . I hope I can feel like I do now! In a way, it would be a relief – it's a bit frightening to think that I'm suddenly sort of babysitting her, if you know what I mean. I've got to look after her. But . . .

Dr Dryden: But do you feel you can put limits on that?

Sarah: Yeah – I feel I *can* put limits on it. To be quite honest, she's expecting me over tonight, or tomorrow night. Well, I'm definitely not going tonight, and tomorrow night I want to go and see my sister's new granddaughter. So, I'm not going either night.

What I should do is just ring up and say, 'I'm sorry, I can't make it – but you know that you're coming on Sunday for dinner.' She's getting so that, within reason, she realizes she ought to be grateful – she knows I'll be fair with her.

Dr Dryden: But you *could* say that.

Sarah: I could.

Dr Dryden: And if she still regarded you as being inferior because you're not fully Asian – how would you feel about that?

Sarah: She does still think that way.

Dr Dryden: Yeah – and how do you feel about that?

Sarah: I don't care – I think she's silly! You know, you want to feel sorry for her more than anything.

Dr Dryden: Okay – let's move on: 'Art's family make me feel like an outcast – even if I *am* half-caste, they don't have to show it.'

Sarah: Well, I told you before that I don't see a lot of them – and the more I think about it, the less important I find them. But I still toy with the idea that it's not a very nice relationship from Art's point of view.

I usually need an excuse to go, and Christmas is coming up. We'll definitely be going down to see his mum, to talk about Christmas presents and anything special that she might want.

I think I might draw the line at that: simply making sure that I keep things on a friendly basis with Art's mum. But that will really be for *his* sake – even if you actually have to lie sometimes, I don't think it matters that much – as long as you're doing it for the right purposes. And the right purpose will be to please Art.

His mother's not going to *hurt* me – I don't know whether I thought she was before – but let's put it like this: whatever she says or doesn't say now won't hurt me, because she's very immaterial to me. As for his sisters – if they happen to be there, I'll just say 'hello'. If they want to continue a conversation with me, that's fine – if they don't, that's fine, too.

Dr Dryden: Right.

Sarah: I know that they think I'm snobbish. Well, that no longer bothers me so much. If I'm honest with myself, I can see that I've probably been a little bit jealous of them – jealous of their confidence and their appearance. It's best to just treat it as it is, and not be frightened of it – you know.

Sarah describes circumstances with her siblings which have led her mother to become more dependent on her. Dr Dryden ascertains that she feels comfortable in placing limits on the amount of time and attention she gives to her mother's demands, and obtains evidence that Sarah no longer gives so much weight to her mother's opinions concerning her 'inferiority'. In asking about her relationship with Art's family, he is also able to learn that she is coping better with their rejecting attitudes toward her. Attention is then shifted to the problem area which received treatment in the initial session.

Dr Dryden: Okay, let's look at the first problem you brought up: 'Peter is my life'.

Sarah: (laughs) Oh, no! Well really, he is – I mean, I absolutely love every hair on his head, and it's right down here (gestures to heart) so you know how much I love him! But . . .

Dr Dryden: 'But he's the *only* thing in the world for me!'

Sarah: God, no – he's not!

Dr Dryden: (mock surprise) He's not?

Sarah: (laughs) No, he's not. I mean, I want everything that he wants for himself – but *he* must go out and get it, *I* can't do it for him.

I used to feel guilty if he tried for something and he couldn't get it. One of his lectures ran very late the other day, and he didn't get home until ten o'clock. Normally, until I started seeing you, I would've been almost in tears for him thinking, 'Oh, isn't it terrible – what can I do? Perhaps I *pushed* him to college', and all. Well, I've encouraged him, but I *haven't* pushed him.

It's like you've told me: each person has his own choice. He doesn't *have* to go to college – and if he does, the rewards are his, not mine.

Dr Dryden: And if he doesn't?

Sarah: And if he doesn't, well, he doesn't. He'll do what other people have to do, and go and work in a shop like I do. And I consider myself lucky that I've got a job!

Dr Dryden: Okay, good. I was going to ask you – have people commented on the changes in you?

Sarah: Well, funny enough, my sister did! But she put it down to my not working . . .

Dr Dryden: (humorously) Right – the rest has done you a world of good!

Sarah: Yeah! I thought, 'Oh God, if only you knew – I've got a miracle worker – but I'm not sharing him with you!' I didn't tell her – I haven't told anybody, only Art. Peter has a sense that I'm seeing someone, because the other night when I rang you up he said, 'Who's this therapist?' I'm afraid I lied to him a bit – I said, 'Oh, the doctor has asked a number of women who've been on different drugs over the years . . .'

Dr Dryden: To volunteer for a project.

Sarah: Yeah! And he believes it, and I think it's enough for him to know – I should hate him to think I'm having a lot of problems. I don't want him to think that I can't cope.

Dr Dryden: Because . . . if he thinks you can't cope?

Sarah: Well, I believe he's so much like me, that it could rub off on him . . .

Dr Dryden: But what would stop you from teaching him what we've worked on here?

Sarah: Well, funny enough . . . because he wants to be in the type of work that you're in, he's wanted to know all the ins and outs. He's said, 'Well, what do you talk about?' I told him, 'He's just asking questions to find out why so many women have turned to drugs.'

Dr Dryden: So your goal is not to tell him about . . .

Sarah: No, I'm not ready to talk properly with Peter about it yet – but I have been discussing it more with Art. Before, I wasn't even prepared to let Art know too much. He knew I was seeing you, but I talk with him more about it now.

Dr Dryden's inquiry concerning Sarah's relationship with her son reveals that she is maintaining her stance of not being overprotective with him. Although she obviously loves Peter, she seems to be keeping an appropriate emotional distance and is allowing him to be responsible for his own life decisions.

Sarah appears, however, to have some reservations about disclosing the true nature of her therapy contacts to Peter. She expresses her concern that he might think that she is unable to cope, and that this might 'rub off on him'. Dr Dryden suggests that Sarah might actually be able to facilitate Peter's own coping capacity, by teaching him the principles of a rational philosophy of life. Nevertheless,

Sarah indicates that she is not yet willing to be that open with him about her therapy. Dr Dryden continues the session by moving on to Sarah's agenda item concerning her 'right' to be upset or annoyed.

Dr Dryden: Okay. Well, let's sort of briefly look at 'Do I have the right to be upset or the right to be annoyed?' What do you want to raise about that?
Sarah: Well, when I am upset or annoyed . . . I mean, what do I do? Do I let off steam? And what do I do after?
   The way it stands now, I say what I'm going to say, and then I just clam up. I become unapproachable – at least, that's what Art says I am.
Dr Dryden: Can you give me an example of what you mean?
Sarah: Well, take that example about the tea towel. Before I started coming here, I wouldn't have spoken to Art or Peter because I thought I was wronged. I would've just walked out of the room.
   The reason I tell myself that I'm not going to speak to them is because, really, I don't know what to say to them. It's as if I can't immediately be nice after I've been nasty.
Dr Dryden: Why couldn't you be nice?
Sarah: I don't know what to say! So I walk out of the room . . .
Dr Dryden: But if you *did* know what to say, would you say it?

Sarah has indicated that she finds it difficult to reconcile with family members after she has become upset with them. In responding to this, Dr Dryden asks questions intended to assess whether this problem stems mainly from an emotional obstacle (i.e. an inappropriate negative emotion – such as anger or guilt – that makes it difficult for an individual to approach others in a friendly, forgiving manner) or a skills deficit (i.e. a lack of knowledge and experience regarding the behaviours involved in reconciliation). As noted in Chapter 2, this is an important distinction to make, as it allows the therapist to formulate hypotheses as to the types of intervention strategies that may prove most helpful.

Sarah: Well, I walked out of the room, but then I thought, 'This is stupid – I'm going right back to square one. I'm not speaking to them because I don't know what to say, and because I'm afraid they're going to think I'm horrible. Well, they're *not* going to think I'm horrible, so I *can* go back in and speak to them!'
   So I went in, really trying to act as if nothing had happened – but I have to admit, it was an act. I brought myself to say something to Peter – I asked him if he had a pen I could borrow. But I felt like I was giving in – which is what I've said I find hard to do.
Dr Dryden: When you say 'giving in', it sounds as if you see it as a sort of battle.
Sarah: Not that it's a battle – I see it as if I'm cornered. I've got no escape, so I might as well give in.
Dr Dryden: Escape from what, though?
Sarah: From being allowed to shout my mouth off – and I don't want the unpleasantness that causes.
Dr Dryden: Yeah – but do you feel that if you've shouted, you've done something that you can't apologize for?
Sarah: I've never been able to apologize 'til recently!

Dr Dryden: Could you say, 'Well, look – I'm sorry I shouted at you. I'm having some premenstrual tension and that might explain it'. I mean . . .

Sarah: No, I didn't say that to them, but . . .

Dr Dryden: But would that be something that you could say?

Sarah: I might be able to work on it now, but before, I would have said 'no'.

Dr Dryden: Well, what would've stopped you from saying that, before?

Sarah: It sounds stupid, but they'd probably fuss over me – and I'm not quite sure if I like that. I *do* like it, but I find it embarrassing as well.

Dr Dryden: But then, how could you handle it if that happened?

Sarah: Well, I have trouble with it.

Dr Dryden: But how *could* you handle it, if it happened?

Sarah: Now?

Dr Dryden: Let's say that in that particular incident you went back and said, 'Look, I'm sorry that I snapped at you – I'm having premenstrual tension', and they started fussing. Now, what could you do – if you don't like being fussed over?

Sarah: Oh, I'd probably get embarrassed and start crying or something – and I don't want that to happen!

Dr Dryden: Would your crying be due to the premenstrual tension, or would it be because of your embarrassment?

Sarah: Well, probably both. Normally, I would just get embarrassed and . . .

Dr Dryden: Because, 'If they . . .'

Sarah: I would shove them away – I'm sure I would!

Dr Dryden: And what's your goal?

Sarah: I don't know, but I'd have to say, 'Get off!' I do that.

Dr Dryden: Because, 'If they fuss over me, that means . . .' what?

Sarah: I should hate them to feel sorry for me, I think.

Dr Dryden: Because, 'If they feel sorry for me, that means . . .' what?

Sarah: (laughs) That means . . . I don't want to be felt sorry for. That means there's something wrong with me!

Dr Dryden: Ah! So if they feel sorry for me, I'm *pitiful*!

Sarah: Yeah!

Dr Dryden: Well, *are* you pitiful if they feel sorry for you?

Sarah: I dunno.

Dr Dryden: Well, think about it.

Sarah: (long pause) I just can't stand the thought of them . . . I mean, I like normal, friendly relationships – and I don't object to Peter fussing over me. Considering how rarely he does it, it's laughable.

Dr Dryden: You mean it's mainly Art.

Sarah: Yeah – I should hate . . . because Art will do it, he'll say, 'Oh, c'mon love', and put his arm around me. And I can't help it – I say, 'Get off!' because I don't want him to feel sort of – I don't know – sorry for me.

Dr Dryden: Because again, aren't you saying that you're a pitiful creature if he feels sorry?

Sarah: I don't know . . .

Dr Dryden: Well, if you just thought, 'Look, I don't like it, but it doesn't mean that I'm a pitiful person', would you still tend to feel embarrassed?

Sarah: I can't say that I don't *like* it. I can stand Art's fussing – if everything's fine.

But I don't want him to fuss if something's wrong – which is ridiculous, and I almost sound barmy as I go on.

Dr Dryden: Yeah . . .

Sarah: I think I can't stand facing the fact that something's wrong – and I think if they make a fuss, they're proving that something's wrong.

Dr Dryden: And if there's something wrong . . .?

Sarah: (half laughs) I don't like it!

Dr Dryden: But there's more to it than that, isn't there? You're saying, 'If there's something wrong . . .' what?

Sarah: Well, I want Art to pretend it's *not* wrong.

Dr Dryden: Because if there *is* something wrong, what would that mean?

Sarah: That I've caused some sort of scene or something.

Dr Dryden: 'And if I've caused some sort of scene . . .'?

Sarah: Well, I don't like myself!

Dr Dryden: Right!

Sarah: (chuckles) Ohh!

Dr Dryden: You seem to be saying, 'If Art fusses, I would have to acknowledge that there's something wrong – and if there's something wrong, I would have caused it. And if I caused it, then I'm to blame – and that makes me a . . .' – what?

Sarah: Horrible person.

Dr Dryden: That's right. But how are you a horrible person if you – for example – shout at somebody for a tea towel?

Sarah: Well, I'm not really.

Dr Dryden: (humorously) Of *course* you are! It's pretty obvious – you're thoroughly despicable for doing that act, aren't you?

At the start of this portion of the transcript, Dr Dryden makes a suggestion to Sarah concerning a behavioural response she might utilize as a means of 'making up' with Art and Peter ('Could you say, "Well, look – I'm sorry I shouted at you. I'm having some premenstrual tension and that might explain it".'). This, in turn, leads to Sarah's statement that she becomes embarrassed when family members fuss over her. In order to determine the content of the cognitions that contribute to the onset of this feeling, Dr Dryden makes use of a series of open-ended questions (e.g. 'Because, "If they fuss over me, that means . . ." what?'). The use of such questions is part of the process of *inference chaining* (Dryden 1987b; Moore 1983), which is a technique applied by rational-emotive therapists to identify a client's underlying irrational beliefs. By utilizing inference chaining, the therapist can often identify problems which are not immediately apparent from the client's initial description of events.

In this case, the inference chaining process leads to identification of the following sequence of cognitions: 'If I'm fussed over by family members, it proves that there's something wrong – I've caused a scene. If I've caused a scene, that proves I am a *horrible person*.' Thus, Sarah engages in negative self-rating when her upsets prompt Art and Peter to act in a conciliatory manner toward her. Dr Dryden goes on to dispute her conclusion that she is a horrible person, which serves to initiate discussion concerning the issue of 'rights':

Sarah: (laughs) No! I mean, I *do* have the right to moan, don't I?

Dr Dryden: Well, we'd better look at exactly what you mean by, 'Do I have the right?' Saying, 'I have the right' does not necessarily mean that I *am* right, that I am correct – because I might be in the wrong.

If you're in the wrong, you have the choice of either accepting yourself or condemning yourself.

Sarah: You're saying I have the right to have these feelings, to get annoyed – but that I have to sort of cope with it after. I have to cope with the outcome . . .

Dr Dryden: Well, I've been helping you to distinguish between a feeling like annoyance, which is based on your *desires* – and anger, which is based on your demands. Remember that? We talked about the difference between desires and demands.

I think you have the right to *both* of those, but I think that the feelings based on the demands are going to get you into trouble with *you* – you'll be likely to feel depressed and angry.

Sarah: Mm.

Dr Dryden: They'll probably also get you into trouble with other people. If you shout and scream at them, they're not going to like that. If, however, you say to them, 'Look, I don't *like* that', or, 'Stop that!' and you're just feeling annoyed – they still may take offence, but it's less likely.

Sarah: Mm.

Dr Dryden: So, saying that you have the *right* to do something doesn't necessarily mean that it's a good thing to do. You could say you have the right to *murder* – but that's most likely going to be a bad thing!

Sarah: (chuckles) Yes!

Dr Dryden: Does that help to clarify it a bit?

Sarah: Yeah.

Dr Dryden: Perhaps you could tell me in your own words what it clarifies.

Sarah: Well, it makes me see that I'm allowed to express myself – nobody's going to get too uptight about that – providing I don't let it get out of hand and *demand* that people do and see things my way.

Dr Dryden: I think you brought up the question of rights once before: 'Do I have the right to take John in?' Remember? I asked who could deprive you of your rights, and you said only *you*.

We could say that you can give yourself the right to feel and act as you wish, but the important thing is to consider whether your feelings are based on *desires* or *demands*. You have the right to have either, but you're more likely to do yourself in if you're internally *demanding* something.

Sarah: Mm, yeah.

Dr Dryden: Let's examine this in the context of the tea towel incident. Did you have the right to be furious about that?

Sarah: Yes, I still think so because . . .

Dr Dryden: Right – but where's your fury going to get you?

Sarah: Nowhere. I'll just have two people looking at me as if to say, 'Oh, God – she's got premenstrual tension again' – and I'll think, 'How dare you be annoyed with me!'

Dr Dryden: But that's anger.

Sarah: Yeah, I know.

Dr Dryden: You're saying, 'You damn well *shouldn't* feel annoyed with me – you should understand!'

Sarah: Yeah.

Dr Dryden: Well – why *should* they?

Sarah: Yeah – but they always expect *me* to understand how *they're* feeling!

Dr Dryden: And therefore . . .?

Sarah: So . . . I still occasionally think I should expect them to understand how I'm feeling.

Dr Dryden: But 'expect' is a little vague – it seems to be somewhere between hoping and demanding.

The point is, being human you *are* going to demand things – but you can identify that when it occurs, and ask yourself, 'What am I telling myself? Am I saying that they *must* do this, or they *must* do that? If I *am* saying that, how can I challenge it?' See what I mean?

Sarah: Yeah – actually, I've been doing a lot of that with Peter.

Dr Dryden: Right.

Sarah: You know, I've never told Peter, 'You've *got* to', because I know you can't get away with that with a teenaged boy . . .

Dr Dryden: Right.

Sarah: . . . but there have probably been times when I've implied it. He'll often work with his father on a Saturday – that's one of the main times that they see each other. If he didn't work, it meant he didn't see his dad.

So – many times I would say to him, 'You *are* going to work tomorrow, aren't you?' I'd more or less be demanding that he go – so that he would see his father.

Funny enough, there hasn't been that much work for the past three weeks – and obviously, they can't have kids doing the work when that's the case. He's said to me, 'I suppose I've got to go down anyway, haven't I?' And I've said, 'Well, that's up to you, Peter.'

Dr Dryden: In other words, 'You don't *have* to.'

Sarah: Don't have to . . . I said, 'I'll be pleased if you go, but if you choose not to, that's between you and your dad.'

Dr Dryden: But have I clarified for you in any way this notion of rights?

Sarah: I don't have the right to demand that Peter go and see his dad – that I don't, no.

Dr Dryden: But I'm saying you *do* have the right to do that! You may, however, choose not to exercise that right . . .

Sarah: I might have the right to *feel* that way, but I don't have the right to demand that someone live their life the way I want them to – do I?

Dr Dryden: I'm saying you do! You *do* have the right to internally demand that, but you may choose not to exercise that right. When you say that you don't have the right – it's really saying, 'I *must* not do it!'

Sarah: Well, I do feel now that I mustn't make commands on people!

Dr Dryden: Right. But you see, you may be giving yourself a problem about that. You start off by saying, 'Well, yes – I *have* been demanding that they must do it my way' – but now you're saying, '*I* must not demand such things.' Do you see that?

Sarah: Oh, yeah – I go to the other extreme!

Dr Dryden: That's right! People in this type of therapy can wind up doing that if we're not careful – they conclude, 'I *must* not demand!'

Sarah: Mm, yeah. You're demanding that you not demand!

Dr Dryden: Exactly! You have the right to do it . . .

Sarah: I have the right to do what the hell I'd like, but I'll suffer the consequences!

Dr Dryden: That's it! Okay – let's finish up now. When would you like to meet again?

Sarah: Well, last time you suggested a fortnight.

Dr Dryden: What do you feel?

Sarah: I think a fortnight sounds good.

Dr Dryden: Okay, then – a fortnight.

(End of recording)

Dr Dryden has attempted to help Sarah see that she has the 'right' to feel angry toward others and to internally demand that they act as she would like, but emphasizes that she can choose not to exercise this right. The choice of not exercising this right is presented as the more rational alternative, as an individual's other-directed demands are likely to contribute to significant emotional upsets and lead to interpersonal conflicts.

As the session nears its end, Dr Dryden points out to Sarah that she may be harbouring the belief that 'I *must* not demand'. Since RET attempts to teach individuals that the absolutistic demands they apply to themselves, others, and the world can result in self-defeating emotional and behavioural consequences, it is perhaps not surprising that some clients begin to subscribe to this particular irrational belief. Rational-emotive therapists attempt to remain sensitive to this possible development within therapy, as this self-directed demand has the potential to lead to negative self-rating. Here, the sequence of cognitions may take the following form: 'I can see that I'm very upset; that's an indication that I'm engaging in irrational demanding. The fact that I'm demanding – as I *must* not – means that I'm a weak, hopeless person who will never get better.' Sarah seems quickly able to grasp Dr Dryden's statements concerning this additional type of irrational belief, and the session ends with agreement to meet again in two weeks' time.

The sixth session: troubleshooting and identification of additional problem areas

The problem review accomplished during the fifth session clears the board for consideration of other issues. Thus, the current session provides an opportunity for troubleshooting (with respect to previously raised issues) and identification of additional problem areas.

Dr Dryden: Okay – let's get our agenda together. I'd like to go over what we talked about last time: coping with Art's fussing when there's something wrong. Also, we touched on the possibility that you could subscribe to the belief, 'I *must* not demand'. Perhaps we can look at that some more, as well.

What would you like to put on the agenda today?

Sarah: Um . . . being able to cope when Art makes a fuss – or when I've started something . . .

Dr Dryden: Has that cropped up in the past two weeks?

Sarah: Yeah, yeah. But I think I handled it better than I normally do.

Dr Dryden: Okay – so you want to discuss 'How to Deal with Fussy Art' – right?

Sarah: (laughs) Yeah.

Dr Dryden: Right. How about your mood? How's your mood been lately?

Sarah: Pretty good. When I do get a bit down, I find that I cope with it a lot better. It doesn't seem so important now if I wake up and I don't feel on top of the world. It doesn't matter that much . . .

Dr Dryden: Right.

Sarah: I used to think that it mattered *so* much – that you have to wake up in the morning feeling great.

And – I do definitely realize that I'm not out to please anybody – not even you, anymore! I have to watch that I don't say . . .

Dr Dryden: (humorously) Aha!

Sarah: . . . what I think is the *right* thing to say to you. I've had to be careful that I wasn't saying what I thought perhaps you wanted to hear. I've thought about that . . .

Dr Dryden: Uh-huh, yeah . . .

Sarah: It would be all too easy for me to say what I thought you might want me to say, rather than what I really felt. I think that I may have been doing that, perhaps the last few times.

I've thought about it after I've left, and I've told you about how I'll have a conversation with you when you're not there . . .

Dr Dryden: Uh-huh.

Sarah: And I've thought, 'Be careful you don't say what you *want* him to hear'.

Dr Dryden: And what do you think I want to hear?

Sarah: Well, I was really happy when you said that you were going to use our tapes because you were pleased with me– but then afterward I thought, 'Don't get excited and start trying to please him . . .'

Dr Dryden: Right!

Sarah: '. . . You've got to keep being realistic – you're going for therapy, you're not trying out for a part in a play!' (laughs)

Dr Dryden: That's right, yeah! Do you think, for example, that last time you might have exaggerated how much improvement you've made?

Sarah: No, I don't think I exaggerated – but I've got to be careful that I don't. Do you understand what I mean?

Dr Dryden: Right.

Sarah: I have to be careful that I don't exaggerate how much better I'm doing. Everything I tell you is absolutely true, but you might notice that from now on I'm going to tell you when I *do* have moods.

Before, knowing that you'd be pleased, I might have told you, 'Well, I'm feeling a lot better!' But – I would have neglected to add that I still have moods. I'm really still the way I was when I first came, except that I feel I'm more in control of myself.

Dr Dryden: (humorously) Right – we haven't brought about a complete personality change, then.

Sarah: (laughs) No, I'm still moody Sarah!

Dr Dryden: Moody Sarah, okay.

Sarah: Well, I like myself a lot better – that is true. And I don't really care so much about what other people think. I even went to see Art's brother – remember I mentioned that I don't bother much with his family.

Dr Dryden: Right.

Sarah: Well, I must admit that they did ring me up first, and asked us to go to a party over Christmas. But I felt myself being perfectly natural on the phone – I didn't get too excited, and I didn't say, 'Oh, thank you for asking me – I humbly accept!' I just said, 'Well, I'll speak to Art, and if he says it's okay, sure we'll make it.' I didn't act as if they were doing me a big favour, like I normally do.

Dr Dryden: 'What a privilege – inviting a shit like me!'

Sarah: (laughs) Yeah! I didn't feel like that. I just thought, 'Well, it's nice of them to ask'.

I don't make efforts to fuss with them anymore – but it was nice to think that somebody had made a move that I hadn't made. I thought, 'You've got more guts than I have.' I appreciated that.

At the start of this session, Sarah has made statements which indicate she is becoming less needy with respect to maintaining the approval of significant others. Significantly, she relates her awareness that she may have been trying to please Dr Dryden through her behaviour during their sessions, and states that this may have caused her to be overly positive in her reports concerning her progress. She goes on to say that she will try to provide more accurate reports in the future.

Rational-emotive therapists attempt to provide their clients with unconditional acceptance, meaning that they choose to act in a non-condemning fashion even when clients behave in very negative ways. By conveying unconditional accept-ance, therapists hope first to teach clients indirectly that they never have to rate *themselves* negatively on the basis of their traits and behaviours, and second, to show clients that they don't have to worry about maintaining the therapist's ap-proval. Even with the therapist's unconditional acceptance, however, some clients will still act in an approval needy fashion. Thus, it is important for therapists to remain alert to this issue, such that the client's 'need' for the therapist's approval can be directly addressed (and remedied) within the therapy.

The session continues with additional consideration of an issue discussed dur-ing the prior session.

Dr Dryden: Okay. Well, 'What do I say after I've gotten annoyed?' It sounds like the title of a book!

Sarah: (chuckles) Yeah.

Dr Dryden: You stated last time that you don't know what to say after you've snapped at Art or Peter. Have you had any experiences with that recently?

Sarah: Yeah – I did snap at Art the other day. I don't know if I mentioned it to you before, but sometimes I feel that he's hanging around and watching me. He'll sit in the kitchen and wait for tea to be finished up, but I'd prefer it if he just went into the other room and put his feet up.

If I'm in a mood, as we might call it, I tend to snap at him and say, 'Oh, for God's sake – get out of here!' Then I feel horrible that I've said it, because I know he doesn't mean any harm. In fact, I suppose it's nice that he wants to be in the same room with me – but it does tend to get on my nerves. So, I told him off and ordered him into the other room – and then I felt miserable about it.

Dr Dryden: What did you feel miserable about?

Sarah: I felt miserable that I'm unable to cope with something like that. There's women who would be so glad . . .

Dr Dryden: Cope with what?

Sarah: I don't know – I feel as if I'm under pressure if he's sitting there. I feel as if I've got to make conversation with him, or somehow please him. I work in a little shop, you know, and I haven't got anything exciting to talk about!

Dr Dryden: Okay – you infer that he expects you to talk to him, and then you feel under pressure.

Sarah: Yeah.

Dr Dryden: Then you sort of get angry with him for . . . what?

Sarah: I feel he's expecting me to do something I can't always do – so I think, 'If you go into the other room, then you won't be expecting me to do anything. You'll be watching telly, or discussing something with Peter.'

Dr Dryden: And when you snap at him – then how do you feel?

Sarah: I feel miserable. I wish I *could* talk to him every single night he comes in – but even better, I wish that I could just nicely say to him, 'Go put your feet up in the living room, instead of being under my feet.' But it seems I don't stop to think like that – I let myself get all worked up . . .

Dr Dryden: So there's three issues here. First, you get angry with him because you think he's expecting you to do something you find difficult. Then, you get angry with yourself for not being able to do it. Finally, you don't know what to say after you've snapped at him and he's gone in the other room with his tail between his legs.

Sarah: (laughs) Yeah.

Dr Dryden: What *do* you say, then?

Sarah: Well, this is where I'll clam up. I don't know what to say, and I'll think, 'Now I've just spoiled a perfectly decent evening.'

I wouldn't mind sending Art to you, because I don't think he knows what to say, either! I think he sits there and thinks, 'Oh God, I've really done it now!' It's just such a shame for him.

Dr Dryden: Okay – well, what are the sorts of things that you *could* say to him at that point?

Sarah: Well, I suppose I could do what *he* does eventually – he'll sort of say, 'Oh c'mon, forget it.'

Dr Dryden: And you'd like to say that?

Sarah: Yeah. I prefer him to say that than to pretend absolutely nothing happened – I can't stand that. Sweeping it under the carpet just annoys me.

Dr Dryden: So what would *you* like to be able to say?

Sarah: I'd prefer to do what Art does most of the time . . .

Dr Dryden: Which is what?

Sarah: 'Oh c'mon – let's forget it!'

Dr Dryden: So you'd like to say that to him – what stops you?

Sarah: I suppose some of it's pride . . .

Dr Dryden: Because, 'If I make the first move and acknowledge that perhaps I was in the wrong, that would mean . . .' what?

Sarah: That would mean I was wrong . . .

Dr Dryden: And if I was wrong . . .?

Sarah: That would again prove that I'm not a very pleasant person.

Dr Dryden: Now, can you see the jump there?

Sarah: Mm.

Dr Dryden: You went from 'I've done something unpleasant' to 'I'm not a very pleasant person'. Can you see the sort of jump that you're making?

Sarah: (in a small voice) No, not really.

Dr Dryden: Well – have I ever spoken with you about the difference between the 'Big I' and the 'Little i'?

Sarah: No.

Dr Dryden: Okay – let me just write this out for you. I'm writing a big block 'I' here, and I'm making lots and lots of little 'i's' inside of it. Now, I'm going to circle one of the little 'i's'.

Take a look at this: the big 'I' represents you in your wholeness, your totality – right? But as you can see, you're made up of lots and lots of little 'i's'. You have lots of behaviours, lots of thoughts, lots of feelings. Now, how many little 'i's' do you think you're made up of?

Figure 1   The Big I/Little i diagram

Sarah: I suppose thousands, if you put it like that.

Dr Dryden: That's right! Now, the one I've circled is what you've just said to Art, which wasn't very pleasant – right? How does that one unpleasant . . .

Sarah: It doesn't make me a *whole* nasty person!

Dr Dryden: That's right!

Sarah: Mm.

Dr Dryden: Now, if you were to regard what you said as unpleasant and undesirable, but didn't jump to '*I* am an unpleasant person', what sort of difference do you think that would make?

Sarah: There's a big difference between saying there's a *little* part of me that can be nasty and snappy, and saying that all of me is! The way you've put it now – and thinking about what you've said in the past – I'm not *always* like that. Far from it!

Dr Dryden: Right.

Sarah: In fact, I *do* go out of my way *not* to be like that – because I know I *can* be snappy.

Dr Dryden: So, if you could accept the 'Big I' as having lots of 'Little i's' – some good, some bad, and some neutral – do you think that would help you to speak to Art?

Sarah: Yeah – probably.

Sarah has described a particular scenario in which she tends to act angrily toward her husband, and has indicated that she would like to be better able to act in a friendly, conciliatory manner after such an incident has occurred. Dr Dryden attempts to show her that she is basing a global negative rating of herself upon a discrete behavioural episode, but Sarah indicates that she is unable to see the 'jump' in reasoning that such thinking requires.

Dr Dryden chooses to illustrate this point graphically by providing Sarah with a 'Big I/Little i' diagram (see Lazarus 1977). With this visual model she is able to grasp easily the illogical aspects of rating one's total self on the basis of particular actions or characteristics, and acknowledges that refraining from such negative self-rating could help her to accomplish her goal of 'making up' with Art.

RET is a psychoeducational approach to therapy; as such, rational-emotive therapists are concerned with developing and utilizing strategies for effectively teaching the tenets of sound mental health. As noted in Chapter 2, the use of visual models represents one such strategy, as some clients may acquire new concepts more efficiently through the visual channel. In fact, the authors' personal experiences indicate that the well-timed presentation of a visual model during a particular therapy session may for some individuals be the best recalled (and arguably most significant) feature of an entire course of therapy.

Dr Dryden: Well, why don't you try it and see. Also, I don't know how you feel about saying you're sorry – do you find it hard to apologize?

Sarah: Um – I find it hard to apologize to Art. But I *have* taught myself to do it with Peter.

Dr Dryden: Yeah.

Sarah: On the whole now, I can say I find it *reasonably* easy to say 'sorry'.

Dr Dryden: Normally, people find it hard to say 'sorry' because then they would have to admit to themselves or to others that they made a mistake – and of course, they *shouldn't* make mistakes!

Sarah: Mm. Thinking about it now, it seems that each time I say 'sorry', I'm thinking to myself, 'Oh, there's *another* part of me that's not very nice'.

Dr Dryden: Yeah – and therefore, what?

Sarah: Therefore I start thinking that the 'Big I' is all horrible. But it's not true when you put it like this, you see.

Dr Dryden: That's right – because there's lots and lots of 'Little i's'. And also, can't the 'Little i's' change, as well?

Sarah: Mm – yeah.

Dr Dryden: For example – some of the things you *were* doing at the start of therapy, you're no longer doing.

Sarah: Yeah that's true. I'm being a bit more honest about the therapy with Peter now, because he told me that he told his lecturer at college that I'd volunteered to see some therapist! You know the story I gave him . . . (laughs)

Dr Dryden: (humorously) Right – it will soon be all over town – you realize that!

Sarah: Well, Peter's started to look at you as some sort of god, because I'm improving. He's said, 'This experiment's doing you a world of good, mum – you're not even so house-proud as you used to be!' So it's obviously doing *some* good . . .

Dr Dryden: Right.

Sarah: And Art said there's definitely an improvement – he's *really* pleased.

Dr Dryden: Okay – but let's go back to the beginning of this. Let's assume that Art comes in from work, sits down at the table, and he *is* expecting a conversation!

Sarah: (laughing) I know!

Dr Dryden: Let's assume that! Now, how would you like to feel – how would you like to deal with that? And let's say you're not particularly in the mood to make conversation, right?

Sarah: Yeah – but I must emphasize it's not so much my mood . . .

Dr Dryden: Yeah . . .

Sarah: It's not knowing what to say. As I've said, I haven't got anything very exciting to talk about!

Dr Dryden: Okay – I'm hearing that you really have three choices. One is to snap at Art and say, 'Get in the other room!' The next is to say, 'Would you please mind going into the other room?' And finally, you could choose to talk about trivialities.

Sarah: Yeah – that's what I find myself doing, most of the time. Art will tell you that I'm a chatterbox! That makes me laugh – I wish he wouldn't say it, because it puts me under pressure! He *thinks* I'm a chatterbox, when really, I'm quiet.

Dr Dryden: And therefore, what? 'Because he thinks I'm a chatterbox . . .' what?

Sarah: I hate to think . . . It upsets me when I *haven't* got a lot to chat about, or when I don't want to talk about trivialities.

Dr Dryden: Yeah – and what's upsetting about that?

Sarah: Well, then I feel he might think I'm sulking. I mean, he's even asked me, 'Is something wrong?' And I'll think, 'God, no – there's nothing wrong. Just because I can't chat all night . . .'
 I can't do that seven nights a week!

Dr Dryden: And do you tell him that?

Sarah: Yes, but I don't tell him in a very nice tone of voice.

Dr Dryden: Right, okay – you're feeling angry – because, 'If he thinks I'm sulking and I'm really not . . .' what?

Sarah: Well, that annoys me!

Dr Dryden: Wait a minute – do you find it annoying, or are you angry about it? Remember we were talking about the distinction . . .

Sarah: Yes – it used to kill me! It used to make me want to burst!

Dr Dryden: Right – but how do you feel now?

Sarah: I don't feel so bad now – I really mean that! But I do think . . .

Dr Dryden: (humorously) You're not just saying that because we're going to put you on the telly soon?

Sarah: (laughing) No, no – no. (Pauses) I'm handling everything better – but I do get annoyed. I still think . . .

Dr Dryden: And of course you have no right to be annoyed!

Sarah: (pauses, then chuckles) Oh, I'd forgot that – I've a right to be annoyed! I do have a right to be annoyed, but I don't see why he should expect me . . . or why he should assume I'm in a mood because I'm quiet. I mean, I *have* told him these things . . .

Dr Dryden: Again, I'm not sure whether you're feeling annoyed or angry. Normally, when people say, 'Why should he think this way?' they really mean, 'He *shouldn't* think I'm in a mood!'

Sarah: Yeah – well, I go as far as saying he should know me well enough now to know . . .

Dr Dryden: But why *should* he?

Sarah: Well, you know – I do have . . . I suppose it's like two personalities. If he doesn't recognize that by now . . .

Dr Dryden: Yeah . . .

Sarah: Well, he's a bit slow – it's as simple as that.

Dr Dryden: 'And he shouldn't be slow!'

Sarah: (laughing) Well, he annoys me if he's slow! Surely he should know that by now.

Dr Dryden: But can you accept the fact that perhaps he really doesn't? Or, as is often the case when a person worries over their partner's mood – perhaps *he* needs your approval . . .

Sarah: Mm.

Dr Dryden: And he can't stand thinking that you're really *dis*-approving of him. Therefore, he has to check and check and check.

Sarah: That is true – he *is* like that!

Dr Dryden: Right – and therefore, since he's *like* that . . .

Sarah: (musing) Mm – I should be rational about him, more understanding . . .

Dr Dryden: That could be wise – because after all, does it make sense to say, 'Okay, he is like that – and he *shouldn't* be that way!'

Sarah: Well, now you've really made sense. He *does* need my assurance – do you know what I mean? He likes to make sure that he hasn't upset me, that *he's* not the reason for my being quiet.

I think what's really happening is that I get upset that he needs my assurance. I think, 'Surely he should know that my being quiet doesn't mean he's done anything – he couldn't *be* any better than he is!' I'd be asking for God, you know, if I asked for anything better.

Dr Dryden: Right . . .

Sarah: I think, 'Can't he see how nice he is? Why does he need to keep having my approval?' That's *really* what I think is happening.

Dr Dryden: Yeah – because he, like you, has got his own set of problems.

Sarah: (chuckling) Ohh, yeah.

Dr Dryden: (chuckling) Right? He's a human being with a problem – an *approval* problem.

Sarah: Yeah.

Dr Dryden: People who seek approval may see that the other person's not being so bubbly, and they attribute that to themselves!

Sarah: Yes, he's blaming himself.

Dr Dryden: If you were to really acknowledge that, and when he did that said to yourself, 'Well, there's Art with his approval problem' – would you then snap at him so much?

Sarah: No, no. What you say now is *so* true. You know, I realize he's a little bit like myself – and I've just been demanding that he should *know* me.

Dr Dryden: Yeah – and you're also demanding that he shouldn't have a problem – when he's got a problem!

Sarah: Yes, yes . . .

Dr Dryden: When we use the word 'problem' here, you know what we mean – he has a *tendency* to . . .

Sarah: Yeah – he needs me to say everything's fine. I'm sure I can find the right words, without sort of being dramatic about it.

Dr Dryden: So – let's go over this. He comes in, and you're not particularly in a chatty mood. He's sitting there – almost like a little puppy who wants a bit of approval – and you snap at him. He goes away, and then you blame yourself. You don't want to publicly acknowledge that you made a mistake, because you might blame yourself even further – right?

Now, can you *imagine* a whole different ballgame . . .?

Sarah: Yeah.

Dr Dryden: Now, why don't you take us through your new way of handling that. He comes in . . .

Sarah: Yeah – he comes in, and he usually gives me a kiss on the cheek, and he says, 'Have you had a nice day, love?' And normally I'll just say, 'Yeah, all right', and we'll chat.

But in a mood, I'd snap at him and tell him to get out of my way and stop asking stupid questions. What sort of day does he think I've had, working in a little shop?

But now – listening to you – I'd probably say, 'Yeah, it's been all right – but go inside and put your feet up', or something like that.

Dr Dryden: Because you'd be telling yourself what about him?

Sarah: All he wants is my approval. He wants to know that I'm still happy, even though I'm quiet. He's got a bit of insecurity too, like I perhaps do about other things . . .

Dr Dryden: Yeah. Incidentally, I also wonder if you're getting annoyed because you think he *expects* you to chat, and you really sort of feel that you *should*, even when you don't feel like it.

Sarah: Yes, that is true, yeah.

Dr Dryden: Why *should* you when you don't feel like it?

Sarah: Well, this is it – I shouldn't if I don't really want to. But it would be nicer if I were able to say to him, 'Oh, go put your feet up a bit, love, while I finish off the table . . .'

Dr Dryden: 'Because I'm not in the mood to chat', or whatever.

Sarah: Yeah, yeah. It all sounds so simple now – but it didn't seem simple when it was happening.

Dr Dryden: Right – because it all sort of happens very quickly . . .

Sarah: Yeah – you don't stop and think.

Dr Dryden: Right – but let's even assume that you *do* snap at him. Now, how can you handle that?

Sarah: Well, recognizing Art for what he is, it will be much easier to just go in and say, 'Oh, c'mon', and give him a nudge. I mean, I'm not the lovey dovey type – it's no good saying I'll fling my arms around him and all that. But I probably *could* give him a nudge and say, 'Oh, c'mon – let's turn the telly on', or something like that.

Dr Dryden: Right – but how about if you start to blame yourself? How could you handle that?

Sarah: Well, usually once I blame myself I try to pass the blame on to Art. But to be truthful, I don't think I'll react like that now.

When you've really hit home on a subject with me, I haven't reverted right back to where I was. I might go halfway back, but then I've been able to stop myself and think my way through – do you know what I mean? I'll be so aware of this now, I can't really ever see me being *so* bad again.

Dr Dryden: Yeah, okay . . .

Sarah: With Peter, you know, I've *never* reverted back. (Humorously) I'm after an Oscar, that is true – I've gotten nearly there . . .

Dr Dryden: We'll give you the Client of the Year award at the end of treatment!

In this portion of the transcript, Dr Dryden identifies certain 'shoulds' that Sarah is placing on Art and his behaviour. In the course of discussing these other-directed demands, he advances the hypothesis that Art's actions may reflect his need for her approval. Sarah seems to regard this as a very useful 'insight', and states her belief that it will help her to deal with his apparent approval-seeking behaviours in a calmer, more understanding manner.

Rational-emotive therapists will occasionally offer hypotheses as to the self-created needs and irrational beliefs held by significant others within the client's interpersonal environment. This can sometimes assist clients in developing a greater understanding of the factors which influence these others to act in certain ways, and can function to increase their *general* awareness of the manner in which attitudes and beliefs impact upon affect and behaviour. Such a device is best used with caution, however, as some clients will be only too willing to focus on other individual's problems, rather than their own.

Sarah: (laughs) With certain things, like I said, you've *really* gotten to me – and I'm able to control them. I'm not saying that I haven't had any of the old feelings, but I'm definitely in better control.

Dr Dryden: Right – that's usually what occurs. You realize what's happening, and then you sort of challenge it.

But let's move on to what you wanted to talk about – Art fusses, and you want to push him away. It's similar to what we've just been discussing, isn't it?

Sarah: Well, it's *really* the same sort of thing that we've been talking about. I realize now that he sort of wants to make a fuss and make up quick because he can't stand my disapproval.

Dr Dryden: Right.

Sarah: Hopefully, I'll be in better control of myself when those situations come about.

Dr Dryden: Okay, right. Now, what about the issue of, 'Do I have the right?'

Sarah: Yeah – I do have the right to do anything, as long as I'm prepared to suffer the consequences. (Chuckles) Or the pleasures, as the case may be!

Dr Dryden: Actually, I was listening to our last tape the other day, and I was thinking about this issue. The word 'right' has a lot of peculiar meanings in the English language, and I was wondering whether it might be better to look at it as, 'Do I have the choice?'

Sarah: Mm, yeah. I was thinking about that conversation we'd had as well, because I wasn't sure whether you'd got my real meaning. But I came up with my own conclusion: I do have the right to do what I want to do, but I must take the consequences, whether they're good or bad. That's a decision I have to make.

When I decide to be pleasant or unpleasant, I've got to suffer the consequences or the pleasures, haven't I?

Dr Dryden: Right. Okay – let's move on to, 'I *must* not make demands. Now that I see what I'm doing, I'm demanding that I must not do it anymore!'

Sarah: (laughs) That's it, yeah! I mustn't demand that I mustn't demand!

Dr Dryden: That's right! You could really have very interesting conversations with yourself!

Sarah: Mm, yeah.

Dr Dryden: Have you worked on that during the past two weeks?

Sarah: Yeah. Well actually, that came up last night – I demanded something of Peter. He's artistically inclined, and I asked him if he'd draw me some pictures for Art's little nephews. He said, 'Oh, I'll do them later.' I just said, 'I want them now – do them NOW!'

Peter said, 'There you go – demanding again!' I mean, it was all rather light and pleasant, but I *was* demanding – I wanted them done then. I thought, 'Get him now while he's not doing anything.'

Dr Dryden: Yeah – and when you noticed that, how did you react?

Sarah: When I noticed that I felt, 'Well, he has the right not to be in the mood, just as I have the right to demand if I'm willing to suffer the consequences.' So, I just laughed and let it go – and I still haven't got the pictures! (Laughs) But I'm not upset about it!

Dr Dryden: (laughs) Right, okay!

Sarah: I can demand, by all means. Sometimes I'll get what I demand, but sometimes I won't. Hopefully, I won't be upset – just as I wasn't last night.

Dr Dryden: Yeah, okay – well, we've run out of issues here.

Sarah: (laughs) Yeah. Well, I should get my Oscar now!

Dr Dryden: You want it now? I haven't had it made yet!

Sarah: Honestly, I *do* feel much better. I really do, and I really appreciate every session that we've had. Each one has done something for me – I really believe that.

Dr Dryden: Okay, but let me ask you – since the time that you made the problem list, have you thought of any additional issues that you'd like to bring up?

Sarah: Not really, no – I don't think so. I *would* love you to see how I handle my mother now . . .

Dr Dryden: Yeah, right!

Sarah: She came knocking on the back door Monday evening, and I can't say I was really in the mood to see her. That was the evening I said to Art, 'Will you get out from under my feet!'

When she came in she said, 'Are you rowing?' I said, 'Yes I am – and if you don't like it, go lump it!'

Dr Dryden: (laughs) Right!

Sarah: So she went into the living room, and I just made tea and forgot about it. And she shut up – she didn't ask any more questions!

Dr Dryden: Right.

Sarah: So – that's got to be good. She's still generally welcome, but I put her in her place when she needs it.

Dr Dryden: Right – okay.

Sarah: When it happened, I thought, 'Well, I've just told her to shut up. Now what do I do? I know – I'll just act perfectly natural, go in the living room, and put my feet up.' And I started talking about my oldest sister, because it happened to be her birthday.

Dr Dryden: Right.

Sarah: So that was great – things just carried on sort of naturally after that. But I felt pleased to tell her to mind her own business – if I want to row, I will. That was *my* business, wasn't it?

Dr Dryden: Right – or rather, wrong! I think you made a terrible mistake there!

Sarah: (laughs) No, I don't think I did!

Dr Dryden: (humorously) Yeah, you did – you'll never get your Oscar now! I'll have to give it to somebody else!

Sarah: (laughs) I really feel so happy now – I've gained an inner happiness, if you know what I mean. I'm like a child, I get excited about things – but would you believe, my ulcer plays me up more, now.

Dr Dryden: Oh, that's right. You did tell me about your ulcer. What are you taking for it?

Sarah: Um, I don't know what they call it – it's some little white tablet I have to take fifteen minutes before my food. (Hushed tone) And of course, the doctor's told me to stop smoking!

Dr Dryden: Have you?

Sarah: I've cut them down, but I haven't stopped. And the more excited I get, the more I want to go for a cigarette – but I'm frightened to tell him that. I mean, he'll say, 'You imbecile! I've sent you to a therapist, it's done you good – and now you smoke more!' Well, I'm not smoking *more*, but the fact remains I haven't quit.

Dr Dryden: So you get excited, and then you get a pain? Is that what you're saying?

Sarah: Not so much pain – it's like butterflies, or like when you're waiting to see the dentist.

Dr Dryden: That sounds like excitement – and then you go for a cigarette?

Sarah: Well, I *tend* to.

Dr Dryden: Why do you go for the cigarette?

Sarah: When I used to be depressed, I'd tend to go for a cigarette – and smoke in a depressed state.

Now, I'm going straight to my sister's from here – the one that's got the little granddaughter – and I bet you the first thing I'll do is prop myself in an armchair and light up. I'll think, 'I'm so happy – and it's so nice to be relaxed'.

Dr Dryden: It's so nice to be relaxed . . . and therefore, what?

Sarah: You know – enjoy life, have a cigarette! (Laughs)

Dr Dryden: How would you feel if you said 'no' to yourself?

Sarah: I'd be really pleased! I mean, I know I'm doing more harm than good inside. And – I know the doctor's going to murder me.

Dr Dryden: Well, why don't you try an experiment? When you go to your sister's tonight, and also at other times when you're feeling excited and happy, see how you *feel* after saying 'no' to yourself. Some people start to feel uncomfortable after they've said 'no' to themselves – if that happens to you, it might be a good opportunity for you to *tolerate* feeling frustrated. You see what I mean?

Sarah: Tolerate being frustrated! (Laughs) That sounds terrible!

Dr Dryden: What's terrible about it?

Sarah: (laughs again) I mean, I'm so happy . . . I don't want to be frustrated in any sense of the word!

Dr Dryden: Oh, right! But you see, you're really saying, 'I don't want to be frustrated in the *short term*', but then you're ignoring the *long-term* consequences of smoking.

Sarah: A lot of it is definitely habit, you know.

Dr Dryden: Yeah – but do you really *want* to cut down?

Sarah: Oh, yeah – for one thing, I'd love to put on some weight. I mean, I'm like a rake. I just want a nicer figure – and I think it's perfectly normal for a woman to want a nice figure.

Dr Dryden: (humorously) So *eat* the cigarette!

Sarah: (loud laughter) Oh, that's true – that would be eating more!

Dr Dryden: Okay – you think that, 'Because I'm happy, I might as well go whole hog and have the cigarette'.

Sarah: That's probably what I'm saying to myself. I'm thinking, 'Oh, I'll be happy to have a cigarette – there's no end to this happiness!' But there *will* be if I carry on smoking!

Dr Dryden: Exactly! Now, why don't you remind yourself of that?

Sarah: That's right. I mean, I *have* cut down . . .

Dr Dryden: How much do you smoke now?

Sarah: Oh, between twenty and thirty.

Dr Dryden: One of the things that might be helpful to you initially is for you to become more *aware* of when you smoke. Are you aware of what you're doing?

Sarah: I am – I know, for instance, that I tend to smoke more in the mornings, and then it tends to die down after that. Then, my real anxiety hour is around five or six o'clock, when I'm dolling up and trying to do the tea at the same time.

Dr Dryden: When you're what?

Sarah: (laughs) What I call dolling up – making sure I look decent for Art when he comes in.

Dr Dryden: (humorously) That's called the glamour-puss syndrome!

Sarah: That's it, that's it! I'm trying to get ready for Art and I'm cooking the tea – and I tend to smoke a bit more.

Dr Dryden: Right . . .

Sarah: And then it doesn't really bother me too much in the evening – except for times like this, when I'm going visiting.

Dr Dryden: Okay – but what is your goal?

Sarah: Well, I'd like to be able to say I want to get off cigarettes completely, but to be honest, I like to smoke. So – if I knew I could stick to only five or six a day, or smoke only after meals, I'd be absolutely delighted.

Dr Dryden: So your goal is to limit yourself to six. Okay, then – what would stop you from doing that?

Sarah: (humorously) When I sit in here with you, nothing! But . . .

Dr Dryden: But when you're out in the 'real world'?

Sarah: Well, we haven't discussed cigarettes before . . .

Dr Dryden: Okay, let's assume that you can only smoke after meals – of course, you could have twenty-six meals!

Sarah: (laughs) I'd come back here looking so fat!

Dr Dryden: That's right! But let's assume you're going to have four meals a day, so that means you're only going to have four cigarettes, right?

Sarah: Right.

Dr Dryden: Now, when would you be most vulnerable to exceeding that limit?

Sarah: In the morning.

Dr Dryden: After breakfast, or before?

Sarah: After breakfast – I sit and look at all the housework, and I'll think 'Oh, I'll have a cigarette before I tackle that'. Then, I'll have another before I go off to my job.

Dr Dryden: Okay – so at those times you have the thought, 'Well, I'll have a cigarette'. Now, how would you feel if you responded to that thought by telling yourself, 'No, I won't'.

Sarah: On some occasions I *can* say 'no' to myself. But while I'm doing the housework, I'll do a job, and have a cigarette – and do a job, and have a cigarette. It's like a reward, if you know what I mean.

Dr Dryden: So you're saying, 'Because I've done such a tedious task, I deserve the cigarette'.

Sarah: That's what I must be saying, yeah.

Dr Dryden: How would you feel if instead you said to yourself, 'No, I'll have something else as a reward'.

Sarah: Well, nothing else interests me. I'm not the type to eat sweets or snacks. If I never saw another sweet, it wouldn't bother me.

Dr Dryden: (exaggerated, incredulous tone) The only thing that would reward you would be the cigarette?

Sarah: Yeah – I mean, if you gave me a bottle of whisky I wouldn't know what to do with it. I'd probably just throw it away!

Dr Dryden: (laughs) Okay – but how about if you cut out the cigarettes and didn't replace them with anything else? How would you feel?

Sarah: Well, I *have* done that at times – and I just feel lost and a bit bored, I suppose.

Dr Dryden: You'd feel lost and bored – now, what would stop you from tolerating those feelings until you got involved in some activity other than smoking?

Sarah: Well, I definitely will try it.

Dr Dryden: Yeah – that's what I call tolerating frustration. See what I mean?

Sarah: Oh, yeah – I know what you mean. I've been doing that with Peter's bedroom – he keeps it like a pigsty. But he's nearly 18, and it's *his* pigsty!

Dr Dryden: Right – although you don't like it, you can tolerate it.

Sarah: I *have* been learning to tolerate that. I walk past his bedroom door with my eyes shut, and just make sure that *mine* looks like Buckingham Palace.

Dr Dryden: And I think you could also learn to tolerate the frustration of not having a cigarette when you want it!

Normally, when people want to cut down, they really have two goals: they want to reduce the number of cigarettes they smoke, *and* they want to rid themselves of the frustration. Now, these two goals are usually incompatible, so they have a choice – they can choose to tolerate the frustration in order to reach their long-term goal, or they can sabotage their long-term goal by having a cigarette in order to relieve the frustration.

Sarah: Mm.

Dr Dryden: Now, which do you want?

Sarah: I'd prefer to be able to cut down and put up with the frustration – because I know that eventually, I'll get rid of that frustration.

Dr Dryden: And you can – if you tell yourself, 'Yes, it's unpleasant, but I can *stand* it', and then focused on something else.

Sarah: Yeah, I can see that that could work. I *am* learning to stand frustration, because I've already done that with Peter's bedroom. As trivial as that might sound to you, it was really annoying to me. It used to make me really angry! (Laughs) I wanted to punch him!

Dr Dryden: (humorous tone) Yeah – because after all, Sarah *deserves* order!

Sarah: (laughs) Yeah! Well, I don't get it with Peter's bedroom, and I've learned to live with that. I'm not even that aware of it anymore, unless I go in to change his sheets. Then I think, 'Oh, what a pigsty'. So I hurry up and change the sheets, and I come out.

But it wasn't like that in the beginning – and I suppose this cigarette business won't be, either. I used to sulk at Peter, and sit there quite frustrated and annoyed. I don't do that any more, and I find it's one less room to keep clean.

Dr Dryden: Right, exactly. So do you think you could actually practise thinking that you *are* going to stand not having what you want in the short term, in order to get the long-term helpful benefits?

Sarah: Yeah – I think I can definitely have a good try at it. During the four hours I'm at work, the thought of a cigarette doesn't even bother me!

Dr Dryden: Because you're involved?

Sarah: I think it's because I'm involved, and because it would look most unlady-like to be smoking behind a counter.

Dr Dryden: What sort of shop do you work in?

Sarah: Well, would you believe . . . it's a tobacconist! So, if I can go without a cigarette at work for four hours, I can do it at home for four hours, can't I?

Dr Dryden: That's right – and sort of limit yourself to a certain number.

Okay – it's been two weeks since we last met. Would you like to extend that a bit?

Sarah: Um, yes. Let's say three weeks. That will give me three weeks to let you know how I'm getting on with my smoking habits. (Laughs) And I'll be able to look my doctor in the face, and say I'm *really* trying!

Dr Dryden: Right! So, three weeks then . . .

(End of recording)

After a brief review of several other issues and areas, Dr Dryden and Sarah turn their attention to her cigarette smoking. According to her report, Sarah now tends to smoke when she's feeling happy or excited, and also uses cigarettes to reward herself for completing household tasks. Dr Dryden suggests that she give herself an exercise in frustration tolerance by saying 'no' to herself when she has the urge to reach for a cigarette; Sarah, however, initially balks at the idea of courting frustration. Dr Dryden responds to this by indicating that she is over-focusing on the short-term discomforts of refusing to smoke, and tending to disregard the long-term health hazards of continued tobacco consumption.

After describing the times of day when she is most apt to smoke, Sarah sets herself the goal of reducing her smoking to five or six cigarettes per day. Dr Dryden elicits from her that she might tend to 'feel lost and a bit bored' if she refrained from using cigarettes as rewards, and suggests that she could attempt to tolerate these feelings until she distracts herself from the urge to smoke by engaging in some other activity. At this point Sarah is able to grasp the concept of tolerating frustration, and relates that she has learned better to tolerate the frustration of her son's disorderly bedroom. The session ends with agreement to let three weeks pass before meeting again.

It can, of course, be frustrating to deny oneself certain pleasures in the short term in the service of attaining a long-range goal. Thus, low frustration tolerance (LFT) can represent a major obstacle to modifying self-defeating habits such as tobacco smoking and overeating. In order to assist clients in overcoming this obstacle, rational-emotive therapists will teach individuals to identify the irrational beliefs which contribute to LFT (e.g. 'I *must* have what I want when I want it; I *can't stand* being deprived'), and will frequently encourage them to take on goal-oriented homework activities which are likely to provoke significant degrees of discomfort and frustration. When these feelings are experienced through enactment of the homework activity, the client is presented with an opportunity to dispute his or her operative irrational beliefs. This can lead to the development of greater frustration tolerance, and ideally will carry the client closer to desired goals.

The seventh session: anticipating termination

In terms of establishing an agenda for the current session, Dr Dryden indicates that he would like to conduct a follow-up with respect to Sarah's upsets with her husband and her attempts to reduce her cigarette consumption. In addition, he states that he would like to discuss her reactions to the approaching end of treatment. Sarah adds her own agenda item by making reference to her continued difficulties with premenstrual tension.

Dr Dryden: Okay – as usual, let's get our agenda together.
Sarah: Mm-hm.
Dr Dryden: It's been three weeks since we last met, right? I'd like to find out how things have been going.
   Last time we spoke about Art's fussiness, and your reaction when he sort of wants to chat. Also, cigarette smoking – I'd like to get an update on that. Finally, I'd like to get your reaction to the fact that we're approaching the end of treatment, and how you feel about that.

Have you got anything you'd like to put on the agenda?

Sarah: No – only that I've been keeping track of dates, and I find that I can't cope as much as I'd like to around the time of my periods. I did mention that once before . . .

Dr Dryden: Mm-hm.

Sarah: Everything just gets out of hand, then.

Dr Dryden: You've noticed that, have you? How long does it last for?

Sarah: It starts about a week before, and it's all right a couple of days after. I suppose in all, its about ten days.

Dr Dryden: Right – so it's about a third of the month, isn't it? Okay, we'll discuss that. But first, how's your mood been since our last session?

Sarah: Everything's been absolutely great, except for that eight to ten days. I just can't control myself then, and I don't want to talk to anybody. I don't even like the phone to ring, or the thought of answering the door. It's just like looking at another person – and the more I try to stop it, the more I get upset.

Dr Dryden: Mm-hm.

Sarah: But it's just as if a cloud's lifted from me when it's over – and I can look back at it and think, 'How stupid'. But I know it's going to happen again, and I know there isn't anything I can do.

Dr Dryden: Right – as you said, you've been keeping dates. Had you noticed this before you started to come here?

Sarah: Yes, and I had complained to the doctor about it. It seems such a shame that . . . everything seems so nice, and then this happens and spoils everything! But I must say that once it's over, I'm back to being able to cope.

But on those days I *can't* cope, and it used to cause so much damage. I could never put things right afterward – do you know what I mean?

Dr Dryden: Right. And now you're saying you *can* put them right?

Sarah: I'm saying that I *can* be normal afterward – but it seems so miserable to know that I've got it coming again.

Last year, I remember trying to sort of plan my holiday around it. We were going to Italy, and you have to book up a good five or six months in advance. I tried to work it out so that I wouldn't be going during those weeks. As it turned out, it all went crazy and I did go those weeks – and I had a horrible holiday!

Dr Dryden: Mm-hm.

Sarah: I know that that time is definitely at the root of the trouble – I'm sure of that now, more so than ever.

Dr Dryden: I think it's important, perhaps, to distinguish between emotional experience which is mainly determined by psychological factors, and emotional experience which is mainly determined by changes in the chemistry of your body.

Sarah: Mm.

Dr Dryden: They may interrelate, but I think we have to explore further to what extent . . .

Sarah: Yeah – perhaps I was exaggerating when I said it was the root of the trouble. It probably isn't the root of it.

Now that I'm better able to cope with life, I know that things can be a lot better. I feel much stronger and more confident in myself. But I still dread that week, because it's as if I have no control whatsoever over what happens.

Dr Dryden: Right – and for how long do you dread the event?

Sarah: I might think, 'Well, I've got two weeks to go, and then it's going to start coming on.' And each day gets worse as it gets closer.

Dr Dryden: So, if we break that down a bit further, you've got the upset you experience during that ten-day period, and you've also got some prior time when you feel anxious about it. Is that correct?

Sarah: Mm-hm.

Dr Dryden: Okay – why don't we look at that some more a little bit later? Right now, I'd like to hear how you feel about some of the issues we've already worked on.

Sarah: I feel great about most things. Even the smoking – I mean, it's not what the doctor would advise, but I'm smoking less and I feel better.

Dr Dryden: What are you down to?

Sarah: I'm still having six or seven a day – but when you consider it used to be at least twenty on an average day, I feel I'm doing much better. I already feel the benefits of it, and I'm eating better.

Dr Dryden: So it used to be between twenty and thirty, but now it's about six.

Sarah: (laughs) Well, I buy ten every day, and then I make sure I give Art some! That might sound unfair, but he smokes anyway – so I sort of insist that he have a couple or three of mine.

Dr Dryden: Right. And how do you feel about the target you've set for yourself?

Sarah: I feel great – I feel that I'm really achieving something.

Dr Dryden: Mm-hm, good. What sort of strategy have you been using to keep the smoking under control?

Sarah: (chuckles) Well, I've been telling myself that I'll put on weight and I'll look better – and you know how I feel about looking better! Also, the money's nice, because I put the extra money in a box to go toward things Peter wants for college.

Dr Dryden: So you're really stressing the positive consequences of *not* smoking.

Sarah: Mm-hm.

Dr Dryden: And that seems to help, does it?

Sarah: Yeah, it does. And I like being able to say 'no' when people offer me one, you know.

Dr Dryden has learned that Sarah is doing relatively well with her goal to reduce the amount of cigarettes she smokes, and makes an inquiry as to the strategies she has utilized to carry this off. This is therapeutically useful information to possess, as it could provide clues as to the types of interventions which Sarah finds helpful. She indicates that she has been reminding herself of the benefits to be accrued by smoking less, including weight gain and extra cash. The session continues with attention turned to other issues.

Dr Dryden: Right! I think that's important.

Now, what about your reaction to Art when he sort of sits down and stares at you – as if he wants either your approval or chats.

Sarah: That's been working great, because you told me all about the 'Little i's'. That was working out fine until this week, when I really couldn't cope.

Dr Dryden: Oh, you're in this period now, are you?

Sarah: No, I've *just* got over it – that's why I'm feeling so great. But this time last week, I was having difficulties. All the things you said to me were going through my mind, but it was as if you had told them to somebody else. It just wasn't making any sense to me; it didn't give me any feelings.

Dr Dryden: Okay – we'll come back to that.

How do you feel about the fact that this is our seventh session? We were going to have ten in all, so we're sort of working toward the end. How do you feel about that?

Sarah: I've got mixed feelings, really. Today I'd say, 'Well, I feel quite confident, so it really doesn't matter'. But at other times I'll think, 'What's going to happen when I'm not going any more?' You know – who's going to advise me, and am I going to feel as confident as I do now?

Dr Dryden: Mm-hm. Well, who's been advising you in the last three weeks?

Sarah: Well, you – because as I've told you, I sort of have talks with you between sessions. I go over in my mind what you say to me.

Dr Dryden: Right – but is it true that *I've* really been reminding you, or is it more true that you've conjured up my image and . . .

Sarah: Yeah, I suppose that's true – but it's nice knowing that I can come to you. I mean, when I was feeling really down last week I kept thinking, 'Oh, I'll be glad to go and tell the therapist about this, because I'm sure he can work a miracle!' At those times, I feel like there'd be nothing if not for you.

Dr Dryden: Mm-hm.

Sarah: I don't feel quite that strongly about it today – but in a fortnight's time I probably *will* feel like that again.

Dr Dryden: So again, is it when you're in that premenstrual time? Would it be correct to call it that?

Sarah: Yes, that's what I usually call it.

Dr Dryden: You feel as if you don't have any control, and therefore you would look to me to . . .

Sarah: Mm, definitely.

Dr Dryden: What could I do for you during that time?

Sarah: Well, to put it in my terms, you'd be the only one to convince me that I wasn't insane. No one else could convince me – I'd say to myself . . .

Dr Dryden: Could you convince *yourself* that you weren't insane?

Sarah: No, I couldn't. No, I think not.

Dr Dryden: Well, how could *I* convince you?

Sarah: (laughs) Well, you convince me about everything else!

Dr Dryden: Okay – but what arguments do you think I would use to convince you during that period?

Sarah: I don't know – you'd probably just tell me that I'm under stress, or that I'm letting things get out of hand, and that I'm capable of controlling it.

Dr Dryden: Would you believe me?

Sarah: Yeah – I believe everything you say, don't I?

Dr Dryden: Okay – now, why would you believe *me* and not *you*?

Sarah: (pause) Because you're even more honest with me than I am with myself. I think we *do* tend to kid ourselves sometimes – which might not be such a bad thing, now and again. But . . .

Dr Dryden: So if I said to you, 'Okay, look – the reason you're like this is that you're under stress, and to quite a large extent it has to do with the changes in your body chemistry' – you would find those arguments convincing because they came from me?

Sarah: I think so, yeah. But I'd probably think, 'I know you're right, but can I just go and sleep until it's all over?' That's just how I feel – I think that I'd like to go to sleep, wake up, and have it all be over.

Dr Dryden: So even if I stated those arguments to you, they wouldn't be convincing at that time – because you'd say, 'Okay, that all sounds very true – but I really want to go and sleep'.

Sarah: Probably – I would just like to close my eyes and have that part of the month go away.

Dr Dryden: Okay – but in a sense, you seem to look at me as having some sort of magic that you don't have.

Sarah: Well, I don't know if I simply want someone to tell me I'm sane, or if I want someone to tell me off and say, 'C'mon, now – don't be so stupid!' I think you're the only person I wouldn't get upset with if you *were* to really shout at me – because I'm convinced that whatever you say to me is for my well-being.

Dr Dryden: Yeah.

Sarah: And none of it's for you. I know it's your *job*, but nevertheless . . .

Dr Dryden: Is it possible that you're tending to idealize me?

Sarah: Well, I don't know – but as far as I'm concerned, you're the most understanding and sensible person I've ever been able to talk to. You're not *emotionally* involved with me – and you're not going to lie to me, or cheat me, or anything.

Dr Dryden: So you're saying that when we finish, you won't have that relationship any more.

Sarah: No – I won't, will I?

Dr Dryden: Okay – does that suggest anything to you about the sorts of relationships you have at the moment?

Sarah: You mean with other people?

Dr Dryden: Yeah.

Sarah: Well, yeah. I mean, to some extent, people are going to say certain things to me just to be kind – or just to be the opposite. I don't know – some people can just be nasty . . .

Dr Dryden: Right.

Sarah: As much as Art cares about me, he's going to say *some* things for his own welfare. But I know whatever you say to me is . . . well, I just take it to be true, and I believe you.

Dr Dryden: *Anything* that I might say to you?

Sarah: Well, no – because I know when you're twisting something to sort of make me see a point.

Dr Dryden: I guess it's sort of a natural reaction to feel sad when a relationship has ended – and I see our relationship as a special sort of relationship, wherein I'm trying to help you. But it sounds a bit like you're saying, 'Oh my God, I'm never going to see Dr Dryden again – I *need* his help, I'm *lost* without him!'

Sarah: I suppose it's a little bit like that, 'though perhaps not quite as strong as you're putting it. Whenever I'm feeling a bit rough, it's nice to think, 'Well,

I'm sure that when I've discussed this with Dr Dryden I'll find there's some simple way of handling it'. I always feel better after I've spoken to you about things.

Dr Dryden: Right – but you've mentioned that you're kind of having these conversations with me in your mind. Do you feel that in any way you're learning to be your own therapist?

Sarah: Yeah – I think sometimes I've helped myself with things that you've said, and I've put them into practice. Even with this premenstrual tension – I might not be *feeling* better, but I think I'm handling it slightly better.

Dr Dryden: Right. But how would you feel – if right now – this was our last session?

Sarah: I wouldn't be very happy about it – I'll be honest, no.

Dr Dryden: Yeah – how would you feel?

Sarah: I'd feel a bit like I'd done an exam, and I'd be thinking, 'Oh God, I can't wait for the results'. I don't know if that makes any sense.

Dr Dryden: Mm-hm – can you elaborate on that a little bit?

Sarah: Yeah – I'd sort of be waiting to see how I'd react without you in the future. I'd be watching myself every day, thinking, 'There's another day you didn't have to go to him'. I mean, I know it's been three weeks, but nevertheless I knew I was coming back to you.

Dr Dryden: What difference did that make to you?

Sarah: Well, it made a hell of a lot of difference when I was going through the premenstrual tension. I mean, I've been to the doctor and I've told *him* – and he's very kind and nice – but he doesn't seem to have the time or the understanding that you have. I know he's got another thirty patients waiting for him, and I guess I don't tend to tell him properly.

Dr Dryden: Okay – but what if you didn't have me to tell in that way – what would that mean to you? You're saying, 'Okay, I know I can tell Dr Dryden about this'. But what would it mean to you if you couldn't because I wasn't there?

Sarah: Well, that's when I start to think that something is absolutely wrong with me up here (gestures to head). I think that you're the only one who's going to convince me that isn't so.

Dr Dryden: Okay – and why am I the only one? What's so special about me?

Sarah: To begin with, you helped me to feel that I wasn't insane – because I was quite convinced that I was when I first came here!

Dr Dryden: Right – but let's have a look at that. Is it true that I somehow magically said something and that you magically felt that you weren't insane – or was it more the case that I asked you to question certain things, and you came to your own conclusions?

Sarah: Yeah, I suppose that *is* true – but only by discussing things with you was I able to do that. So if next week I felt I was insane, and I wasn't coming to see you . . .

Dr Dryden: Let's assume you do – let's assume you weren't coming to me, and you started to think that you're insane, right? What do you think I would say to you, if I was there? I really wouldn't be there, but let's pretend that I was – what do you think I would say to you?

Sarah: You'd probably ask me to go through the different incidents that I'd found upsetting – we'd look at each incident, and you'd probably make me see them in a different light.

Discussion of Sarah's thoughts and feelings concerning treatment termination leads her to communicate her belief that she needs Dr Dryden to help her deal with premenstrual difficulties. Here, she indicates that she thinks he is the only individual who would be able to convince her that she is not insane when she experiences herself as being out of control. Dr Dryden recognizes that Sarah's beliefs in this regard could interfere with her ability to function independently after treatment has ended, and thus pursues a strategy intended to facilitate her confidence in her own coping skills.

Dr Dryden: Okay – I'd like to help you to realize that you *don't* need me. I suppose I have been helpful, but it appears you're under the impression that you some-how *need* me to help you work things out. Let's see if that's true.

Just imagine that this was our last session, right? Next week, you start to feel that you're insane. Now, can you speak aloud the sort of dialogue you'd have with yourself?

Sarah: I'd start to think that this was a waste of your time and mine, and that . . .

Dr Dryden: No – I mean the sort of dialogue you'd have with yourself to combat the notion that you're insane.

Sarah: What I'd be saying to myself?

Dr Dryden: Yeah! What would you be saying to yourself?

Sarah: I'd probably be convinced that it was premenstrual tension coming on, and I'd think, 'I can't wait for this to be over – and if it's not over soon, I'll probably do something stupid – like walking out of the house!'

Dr Dryden: But what would you say to specifically combat this notion that you're insane? You'd think, 'Yes, this is really premenstrual tension . . .'

Sarah: But then I get myself convinced that it's not, and I think, 'Oh, I'm going to put myself under a bus because I can't stand this!' I mean, I really have said such things to myself.

Dr Dryden: Okay, but how could you challenge that notion?

Sarah: I think that I can't do that because of Peter – what's Peter going to do? Poor Art never comes into it – I always think that he's big enough to look after himself. But if I keep sane, it's because of Peter. I can't have Peter coming out and finding his mother dead – these are the sorts of things I say to myself!

Dr Dryden: So you're saying, 'I'm insane because I want to throw myself under a bus' – right?

Sarah: Well, I know that I can't just go to sleep 'till it's all over – so I'll think, 'If I just had an accident and broke both my legs, they'll let me go in hospital and put me to sleep. Then I'll be asleep until it's passed.' But I know I'll just have to face it again the next month – even if I slept it off *this* month, I can't sleep it off every month!

Dr Dryden: But let me come back to this: how could you, on your own, question this notion that you were insane?

Sarah: Oh, well – I say to myself, 'Am I going mad, or is it premenstrual tension?' I look at my dates, and I convince myself that it is premenstrual tension.

Dr Dryden: Right. And do you believe yourself?

Sarah: I have to! I mean, I only *half* believe it, but . . . I *have* to believe it, otherwise I can't carry on the day! That's why I can't even wait for darkness to come, so I can go to bed.

Dr Dryden: Now, what would I be able to say that would be more convincing to you?

Sarah: I don't know – I don't know what you'd actually say, but I'm sure that you could convince me that . . .

Dr Dryden: Well, try to imagine. Imagine that I suddenly appeared at your shoulder – right? What would I say that you'd find convincing?

Sarah: Well, you always manage to stop me feeling depressed, and that's really the root of what I'm feeling at those times.

Dr Dryden: Okay, what would I say? Imagine it.

Sarah: (pause) Well, I could probably imagine it a lot more if it was actually happening than if . . .

Dr Dryden: But just really try – what would I say to you if I magically appeared and you started to feel undepressed? What would I say to you?

Sarah: You'd probably tell me that it all has something to do with the chemicals in my body, and that it will eventually all be over, and . . . I'd probably say to you, 'Yes, but what do I do until it's over?'

Dr Dryden: And what would I say to you at that point?

Sarah: 'You've just got to carry on; you've just got to learn to cope.'

Dr Dryden: Yeah – and would I tell you *how* you could learn to cope?

Sarah: You would probably tell me how, but I don't know what you'd say. I don't know how to cope at those times.

Dr Dryden: Okay – well, have we dealt with this yet in therapy?

Sarah: No . . .

Dr Dryden: We've dealt with coping in other situations, haven't we?

Sarah: Yeah – but I don't feel like the same person, then.

Dr Dryden: Okay – but again, imagine what I would say to you. As you said, I might tell you that you can live through this; that it's only premenstrual tension. What else would I say to you about learning how to cope – based on what we've talked about already?

Sarah evinces helplessness with respect to her ability to convince herself that she is not insane and can cope with her premenstrual tension. Dr Dryden responds to this by asking her to try and imagine what he might say to her that would help her to deal with her problems in this area. Here, he is capitalizing (in a therapeutic sense) on Sarah's earlier reports that she has imaginary 'little chats' with him between sessions.

Sarah: Well, I do remember thinking that I'm sort of allowed to . . . I mean, I look terrible at the time – and that doesn't bother me any more. That used to bother me, but I figured the hell with that . . .

Dr Dryden: I'm allowed to what?

Sarah: With respect to what I look like – it makes me look terrible. I always look tired and drawn.

Dr Dryden: So I would say that you can live through it – right?

Sarah: And you would probably say, 'Well, so what if you look a mess?' And I would have to agree with you there.

Dr Dryden: (writing) Okay . . . 'You can live through it; so what if you look a mess; it's only premenstrual tension.' What else would I say to you that would help you to cope with it?

Sarah: I've just thought of this, and it's a good point to remember when it happens . . .

Dr Dryden: What's that?

Sarah: Let's say my sister pops up and she says, 'Oh God, you look terrible'. Well, I don't have to feel ashamed to say to her that I *feel* terrible, and that I can't stand this premenstrual tension.

Dr Dryden: So you're saying that you can admit it to people.

Sarah: Thinking about it now, yes.

Dr Dryden: 'I do look terrible' – and that would help you?

Sarah: Yeah – not so much saying that I look terrible, but that I *feel* terrible. I needn't be ashamed to say that I feel terrible.

Dr Dryden: And what would you say to yourself implicitly to not feel ashamed?

Sarah: That it's premenstrual tension, and that it will all be over in a few days.

Dr Dryden: Okay – let's have a look at this. I'd come down and I'd say, 'You can live through it; so what if you look a mess; it's okay to admit that you feel terrible; it's only premenstrual tension, you're not going mad.' Right?

Sarah: Mm.

Dr Dryden: So it's like a magic lamp, isn't it? It's almost as if you're saying, 'Oh, I need Dr Dryden – let me rub the lamp'. Then I'd appear and I'd say these things to you.

  Would they be convincing for you? Or would I need to say a few other things before I went back into my lamp?

Sarah: No, you're probably right. Just the fact that I could sort of refer to you in my mind would probably help me to cope better. I mean, I said some of the things you've just written down.

  But there is one problem – if people sort of . . . say my sister said, 'You look down; you look rough'. Well, I'd start crying! I can't stand that, you know!

Dr Dryden: What would I say to you about crying?

Sarah: (laughs) I don't know!

Dr Dryden: Based on what we've been talking about, do you feel *ashamed* about crying?

Sarah: Yeah, a bit of that.

Dr Dryden: Okay – what would I say to you about feeling ashamed about crying?

Sarah: (laughs) Crying is nothing to be ashamed of! I suppose it's a normal . . .

Dr Dryden: (writing) 'Crying is nothing to be ashamed of.'

Sarah: Yeah.

Dr Dryden: Okay – can I now go back into my lamp?

Sarah: (laughs) Yeah – I think so.

Dr Dryden: Okay – I disappear into my lamp, right? How do you now feel after I've appeared, whispered these things into your ear, and have disappeared again?

Sarah: Well, I feel confident again, I suppose.

Dr Dryden: Yeah. Have you noticed anything special about what we've been doing?

Sarah: (pause) What do you mean?

Dr Dryden: Well, we developed a number of things to help you cope, right? Who developed them?

Sarah: Well, I'm saying what I think *you* would say to me!

Dr Dryden: Mm-hm, okay . . .

Sarah: I suppose I said them, so I suppose *I* developed them. But I need you to say, 'Well yes, that's right!'

Dr Dryden: Why do you need me to say that?

Sarah: Because I trust you more!

Dr Dryden: You trust me more than who?

Sarah: (laughs) Me!

Dr Dryden: What is it about *you* that's not very trustworthy?

Let's imagine that you were in the type of situation we've been talking about, right? There's Sarah, feeling pretty uptight about having premenstrual tension. Just sort of close your eyes and try to picture that.

Picture yourself, on your own, really acknowledging that you *are* feeling poorly. Imagine that you're saying to yourself, 'Okay – I *can* live through this. So what if I look a mess? It's okay to feel terrible and admit that, and there's nothing to be ashamed of if I cry. It's due to premenstrual tension.' Can you imagine *you* saying those things to yourself?

Sarah: Yeah, I can . . .

Dr Dryden: Now, how do you think you'd feel as a result of that?

Sarah: Well, if it's worked like it has for other things, I suppose it would be all right.

Dr Dryden: Now, why then do you need me to come and rubber stamp it: 'Well, Sarah, you're doing a great job here!'

Sarah: (laughs) Well, I might not – but until tonight I was pretty sure that I would. I should probably go away thinking I *don't* need you as much as I thought – do you know what I mean?

By asking her to imagine what he would say to help her, Dr Dryden has elicited from Sarah a list of coping statements that she might use when she experiences premenstrual tension. Sarah is able to see that *she* has formulated these statements, and acknowledges that Dr Dryden's 'rubber stamp' is not required to confirm their validity.

Dr Dryden: Well, let's test that out. Do you want to make a note of the arguments that you've used, or do you think you can remember them?

Sarah: No, I'd rather make a note of them.

Dr Dryden: Okay – let me give you pen and paper. I'm just going to tell it to you as it came out of your mouth.

(Hands Sarah writing materials) You were saying, 'I can live through it; I'm not insane for having these feelings, it's just due to premenstrual tension; so what if I look a mess; it's not shameful to feel terrible and to admit it; and there's nothing to be ashamed of if I cry.'

Now, there's one other belief that I'd like you to challenge: 'I *need* Dr Dryden's help with this!' How would you challenge that?

Sarah: The best I can do at the moment would be to say, 'I'll try and do it on my own'.

Dr Dryden: Mm-hm. Sort of a 'Let's see' attitude, you mean.

Sarah: (still writing) Yeah.

Dr Dryden: Now, can you think of any way to practise these things in advance of the event?

Sarah: Well, yeah – because as I've said . . .

Dr Dryden: How could you practise in advance?

Sarah: Well, I've just sort of put into practice some of the things that you've said to me, and talked to me about – and I *do* see things in a different light.

Dr Dryden: But I'm asking if there's any way you can *practise* going over some of these arguments *before* you get into that mood.

Sarah: Yeah – because the last time I came here I think I left a little bit early, and I started to walk down. Then Art went driving past, and I had to walk all the way back. Where normally I would have hit the roof and thought, 'How dare you not see me!' I sort of laughed about it.

I've learned to laugh at things a little bit more now. Unfortunate things are going to happen, and I *try* to react differently, I try to look at things differently . . .

Dr Dryden: (humorously) Yeah, but I wasn't there to rubber stamp it! I mean, how could you possibly help yourself? I wasn't there! You *need* me to be there and rubber stamp it for you!

Sarah: (laughs) No, I don't! But it *is* true – you did teach me to look at things in a different light.

Dr Dryden: Well, okay – but suppose I had tried to teach you the opposite. Would you have believed me? Suppose I had told you, 'It really *is* shameful to feel certain ways; you really *shouldn't* do that!'

Sarah: I probably would have believed you!

Dr Dryden: Mm-hm. Why is that?

Sarah: I don't know – but if you had reversed a lot of the things you've said, I probably would've believed you. If you'd said, 'Well, you *should* bow down and respect your mother, because that's the law of the land', I probably would have gone along with it.

But you didn't say that – and one of the most important things that you've taught me is to accept myself, and to accept other people as they are. Mother's not going to change at her time of life, so the best . . .

Dr Dryden: (humorously) Of course she is!

Sarah: (laughs) No, I don't believe you!

Dr Dryden: She's going to change! Look – *I'm* telling you this, and I've always been right in the past – you've got to listen to me! I've looked into my crystal ball, and I'm telling you she's going to change!

Sarah: (laughing) No, she won't change. The best I can do to cope with her is . . .

Dr Dryden: But look – I'm teaching you that she's going to change! Now, why aren't you agreeing with me?

Sarah: Well, if she does, I should just put up with her.

Dr Dryden: But why aren't you believing it just because I'm saying it? I'm the great Dr Dryden!

Sarah: (laughs) No, I don't believe it!

Dr Dryden: Why not!

Sarah: Because what you told me before was so true. It was so simple, I don't know why I couldn't see it myself!

Dr Dryden: You mean you're not going to accept everything as true just because I say it?

Sarah: Well, I'm not going to believe that mum's going to change at this point in her life.

Dr Dryden: Well, why not?

Sarah: Because after you told me that she wasn't, it was so clear. I don't know why I couldn't see it!

Dr Dryden: Well, did I actually tell you that she wasn't going to change, or did I ask you what the likelihood was?

Sarah: Well, you said the chances are she's not going to change. I mean, that made so much sense.

How am I going to change her at her time of life – and anyway, why should she change? And I've got to be honest – perhaps it's me, but she seems *nicer* now!

Maybe she's seen that I'm not going to put up with some of her nonsense – although some of it I *will* put up with, because that's her age . . .

Dr Dryden: But who told you to put up with some of it, and not stand for other parts of it?

Sarah: Well, you didn't say *that*, but you did tell me that I've got a choice. You didn't exactly say these words, but I think you wanted me to see that I can either stand up to her – and let her see that she's only going to get so far with me – or choose not to see her.

Dr Dryden: Who made the choice, there? I mean, I guess I *have* presented you with choices . . .

Sarah: Exactly – you've given me a lot of choices. They've *all* been choices!

Dr Dryden: Okay – can you now give *yourself* these choices? Have you learned a strategy of identifying choices?

Sarah: Yeah – I mean . . .

Dr Dryden: What do you need me for, then?

Sarah: Well, like I said – it's nice to have your rubber stamp upon it, sometimes.

Dr Dryden: Because . . .? If you don't have my rubber stamp on it, what?

Sarah: Well, you know, I'm not quite sure that . . . I was going to say that I'm not quite sure that I'm right. But I know you would say to me, 'Well, so what if you're not right every time? It doesn't matter that much. After all, you're going to make mistakes on occasion.'

Dr Dryden: Now, can you rethink that and actually take me out of the picture? Have the conversation with yourself again, but this time take me out of the picture.

Sarah: Well, I'm sort of saying that I *can* make decisions, and obviously I'm not always going to be right – I've got to accept that.

Whether you're there or not, I'm going to have to make decisions.

Dr Dryden: No, I think you need me! I think we'd better prepare to settle down and grow old together! Don't you think?

Sarah: (laughs) I'd probably be happy to think that – but I don't think your wife would appreciate it!

Dr Dryden: Mm-hm. In a sense, aren't we looking at some underlying belief that you *need* somebody to look up to, and upon whom to rely?

Sarah: Yeah, I think that *is* true.

Dr Dryden: Why do you *need* it?

Sarah: Well, I don't know – I think everybody needs somebody, don't they?

Dr Dryden: (humorously) Who is Dr Dryden's Dr Dryden?

Sarah: I can't imagine! I'd love to meet him!

Dr Dryden: Perhaps I have been helpful, but let me ask you: is it possible that you're underestimating the part that you've played, and overestimating the part that I've played?

Sarah: (sighs) No, I don't think so – because I think you're the only person that I could be so honest with. I've never been so honest with anybody, and although I may get a little bit nervous, I'm not *frightened* of you.

I mean, earlier on it was true and fair to say that I *hated* my mother! I'd never have told anybody that! I'd never say that to anybody!

Dr Dryden: Okay – so you've told me things that you haven't told anybody else, right?

Sarah: Mm. I might have gone in circles about it, but I've never been so straightforward.

Dr Dryden: Okay, fine. You've told me things that you haven't told anybody else, and I haven't thrown you out of the place. I've said, 'Yeah, okay – fair enough. So what else is new?' Right? But how does it then follow that you *need* me to look up to?

Sarah: Well, because you didn't say, 'Oh my God, you hate your mother? You've dared to marry twice and still find fault with your second husband?'

Dr Dryden: But do you think I'm the only person in the world who wouldn't respond in that way?

Sarah: Well, I haven't mixed that much outside of the family, and inside the family I would say yes, you are.

Dr Dryden: Right – but am I the only person in the world outside of your family?

Sarah: Well, I suppose not – but I haven't spoken to anybody like that, and I'm not likely to. You know, I didn't realize how good it was to be able to say these things . . .

Dr Dryden: So you start from, 'Because I've told Dr Dryden these things which I'm not likely to share with anybody else, and because he's given me a systematic hearing and has offered me some help, I therefore need his rubber stamp; I can't do anything else . . .'

Sarah: That's probably how I've been seeing it. But it's pretty obvious . . . I know our sessions have to come to an end, but I guess I don't want to think about that for now. I tell myself I'll worry about it when the time comes.

Dr Dryden: (humorously) Well, it's coming, so think about it!

Sarah: (laughs) Yeah, I know! I'll have to continue my conversations with you on my own, and then I'll probably be committed one day. They'll say, 'She walks down the street talking to this invisible bloke, you know!'

Dr Dryden: Yeah. 'Who *is* Dr Dryden?'

Sarah: I'll say, 'Ah, but he does exist!' Don't you ever move!

Dr Dryden: I'm suggesting that you might want to start phasing my image out, and start phasing *your* image in! In other words, can you imagine having a conversation with Sarah in the same way as you've had these conversations with me in your mind? Can you imagine that?

Sarah: Well, I suppose I'll *have* to, won't I?

Dr Dryden: You don't *have* to, but do you think it might be helpful to you?

Sarah: Well, yeah – I do think it would help.

Dr Dryden: Right, okay. Can you perhaps think in terms of testing out this hypothesis that you *need* my rubber stamp – that you really need me to say the same things that you've been saying to yourself, because I have some special power that makes them convincing? Would you like to do some work on that?

Sarah: Well, I should work on the theory that while you've been giving me choices, I'm the one who's been taking them – and the choices I've taken have obviously made me happy.

I've got to continue making my own choices, and be prepared that sometimes they won't be the right ones – but that's life, isn't it? Nobody always makes the right choices, the right decisions.

Up to now, the decisions I've made with your help have been good ones. I have to carry on making my own decisions and, most of all, be prepared to face the ones that *don't* work out.

Dr Dryden: And there's life after Dryden?

Sarah: (laughs) Could be!

Dr Dryden: Wow! Okay – so in a sense we really *have* dealt with the major item on your agenda, which was the premenstrual tension. And yet we've discussed it within the context of this other particular issue that I wanted to bring up. Last time I sort of felt that you were starting to put me up on a pedestal which, being human, I don't think I deserve.

So, can you see how we've actually been dealing with those two issues in one?

Sarah: Yeah.

Dr Dryden: How have you felt about my bringing this up? 'Look, I don't want to be your great rubber-stamping therapist.' How have you felt about that?

Sarah: Well, I can understand why you're saying it – but given how I've felt over the years, and being able to get some of it off my chest – I'm pretty sure *you'd* be putting somebody on a pedestal, too. I mean, to say 'thank you' really isn't enough – you *do* put people on a pedestal when they've made you feel that you're going to be . . .

Dr Dryden: Okay – so you're saying that if I was in a similar situation, I would have that tendency, too . . .

Sarah: Yeah – it's as if I was on trial and you got me off! Do you know what I mean? Honestly, people are grateful when they've been helped.

Dr Dryden: Right – but again, I would just urge you to be aware of not attributing enough to yourself. I have, if you like, asked you certain questions and made a few points here and there – but you're the one who's been out there, doing all the work.

Sarah: Mm.

Dr Dryden: I haven't actually been materializing! You've materialized me – and now I'm asking you to test the hypothesis that you can materialize *yourself*.

Sarah: Yeah – I do believe I can, really. I just have to keep reminding myself that I don't *have* to be anything special. People have got to take me the way I take them – it's as simple as that.

Dr Dryden: That's interesting, because it sounds like we're talking about the same attitudes. I mean, you're now saying that you don't want to be anything special, and I'm saying the same thing to you – I don't want to be anything special for you.

Sarah: Mm.

Dr Dryden: . . . In that 'looking up' sense. I may have been helpful, but I prefer to be sitting face to face with you, rather than having you look up to me.

Sarah: Yeah . . . well, I think that was one of my biggest problems. I thought that I had to be somebody special; there was this standard that I *had* to keep. And each time I reached the standard, it got higher! I think that's the way it was – I don't have any big standards now.

Dr Dryden: Okay – how would you feel about meeting in a month?

Sarah: Yeah.

Dr Dryden: That'll give you time to practise materializing yourself and . . .

Sarah: (humorously) If I don't turn up, you'll know I forgot who you are!

Dr Dryden: Yeah, that's right! Who is *he*? Never heard of him!

(End of recording)

By adopting a humorous stance, Dr Dryden attempts to help Sarah see that she doesn't have to regard all of his statements as representing indisputable truth, and that ultimately, she *chooses* what she will believe. Sarah recognizes that in attempting to guide herself and make choices, it is not an absolute necessity that she always be right.

Dr Dryden suggests that Sarah harbours the irrational belief that 'I *must* have somebody upon whom to depend', and attempts to engage her in disputing this notion. He reinforces the idea that Sarah can begin to work on fading out his image between sessions, and emphasizes that while he might have served in the role of facilitator, it was she who actually accomplished the work which led to her improvements. The session draws to a close with agreement to extend the time between meetings an additional week.

Within a time-limited approach to therapy, it can be particularly important for the therapist to be sensitive to the client's attitudes regarding treatment termination. It can be fairly easy for the client to develop a dependent relationship with the therapist, particularly when improvements in problem areas have been experienced. Frequently, clients will attribute these improvements to the therapist's skill and expertise, rather than to their own efforts. Hence, therapists are wise to take steps which help to ensure that the client leaves therapy with confidence in personal coping skills.

Compared to more passive approaches to psychotherapy, RET offers several significant advantages in this regard. First, it attempts to teach clients tools and techniques which can be independently utilized to deal with emotional upsets and problematic situations. Through use of these tools, clients can eventually learn to become 'their own therapists', and realize that they don't require on-going contacts with a supervising professional. Second, RET makes use of inter-session homework assignments, which require expenditures of time and effort on the part of the client. By making reference to successfully enacted homework assignments, therapists can make a strong case for attributing therapeutic gains to clients' work. Finally, rational-emotive therapists work with clients explicitly to identify and dispute self-defeating irrational beliefs such as 'I *need* somebody more powerful than myself upon whom to depend', and 'I *must* always make the right choices'. Replacing these beliefs with their more rational counterparts can further assist clients in developing a sense of independence and personal efficacy.

6 The later sessions

The eighth session: dealing with approval anxiety

In the previous session, Dr Dryden explicitly broached the issue of therapy termination, and attempted to help Sarah identify and deal with obstacles to independent coping. They agreed to let a month elapse prior to meeting again; this lengthier period between sessions can be viewed as providing Sarah with an opportunity to start adjusting to the challenge of being 'her own therapist'.

In initiating discussion of termination issues during the seventh session, Dr Dryden has allowed for the possibility that this area might remain problematic. If it turned out to be the case that Sarah did indeed continue to have difficulty with the notion of functioning without a therapist, additional time could be devoted to troubleshooting during the remaining three sessions. In this, the eighth session, Dr Dryden conducts follow-up on a number of issues, including Sarah's current attitudes concerning the approaching end of treatment. As will be seen, a good portion of the session is devoted to work on approval issues.

Dr Dryden: Okay, let's get our agenda together. I'd like to check up on two things: the premenstrual tension, and the issue of dependency that we discussed. What would you like to put on the agenda?

Sarah: Well, the premenstrual tension was a lot better this month – I remembered the things you told me to remember, and it was a lot better.

Dr Dryden: Yeah . . .

Sarah: And as for being independent about not coming here any more – well, I know that I've got to do that and I'm quite looking forward to having a go at it. Do you know what I mean?

I watched a programme on television the other night, and it was about people who abuse drugs and smoke and all of that. They were saying the same sorts of things that I suppose you would say to *me* . . .

Dr Dryden: What was that?

Sarah: That you've got to learn to face things yourself and do them without drugs and cigarettes. The programme showed what these people were like before they kicked their habits, and told how they had given up taking any type of drugs . . .

Dr Dryden: So, seeing that programme reinforced the notion of . . . what?

Sarah: Of the sorts of conversations *we've* been having – mainly the last one, where you said it wouldn't be wise to depend on coming to you to talk things over every month. I've got to face things – whether they're good or bad – and start to accept them for what they are.

Dr Dryden: Okay – perhaps we can come back to that a little later when we focus on the issue of dependency.

Is there any particular problem you'd like to cover tonight?

Sarah: Well, my ulcer really gets me down. I'm controlling it up *here* now (gestures to head), in the way that we've talked about controlling things – but it doesn't stop what happens down *there*.

Dr Dryden: Let's come back to that, okay? We'll call it your 'acidy stomach'. Is there anything else?

Sarah: Hm – not really, no. I know now that I *want* to face things. I've told you that the silliest things can upset me, but that's the sort of person I am – I'm going to have to accept that!

I've got to face the fact that just because something might not upset you, or Art, or Peter, it still might upset *me*. But I want to be able to let it upset me in a *reasonable* manner – so that I don't get things completely out of hand.

Dr Dryden: Okay – 'reasonable upsets' – we'll come back to that, too.

Sarah: Am I explaining myself properly? Do you know what I mean?

Dr Dryden: It sounds like you're saying that you recognize that you still get upset, and that you want to keep it within reasonable bounds.

Sarah: Yeah – I'm doing that to some extent now, and I hope to get even better with it.

Dr Dryden: Right – now, let's go back to the premenstrual tension. You said that it was better this month.

Sarah: Well, I could hardly believe it. My period had actually started, and I hadn't gotten the tension. I thought it was impossible, that I must have come on early or something – but I looked back over the days, and I saw that I had just been a little bit weepy and a bit touchy. If that's the worst I ever have, I'll get on my knees and thank God!

Dr Dryden: Yeah . . .

Sarah: Perhaps it was the talk I had with you, but my premenstrual period just seemed to slip by.

Dr Dryden: Right – but let's not *just* attribute it to that, because it could have resulted from a number of factors. We'll sort of keep an eye on it . . .

Sarah: Well, anyway – it probably had something to do with the fact that I'm more relaxed.

Dr Dryden: Okay – let's go to the notion I raised last time about dependency. Have you had any thoughts on that after our session?

Sarah: Up until last month, I was only sort of halfway facing any problems that would come up. I would think, 'Well, I can talk to the doctor about that – he's bound to give me some suggestions that will help me.'

I've got to give *myself* those suggestions. I have to make up my mind that if something doesn't suit me, it's just hard luck.

Dr Dryden and Sarah have established their agenda for the session, and have conducted a brief review regarding her premenstrual tension. They then turn attention to the issue of dependency, and Sarah states her recognition that it is important for her to work on giving herself the types of 'suggestions' that Dr Dryden has been providing her. Her statement here seems to imply that she not only recognizes the desirability of this; she also sees that she is *capable* of doing it – provided she chooses to make the effort.

Dr Dryden: Have you been doing that in the past month?
Sarah: Oh, yes.
Dr Dryden: So – you're seeing that since our time together is limited, it makes sense to try and solve problems on your own. Rather than postponing it until you come here, you can actually . . .
Sarah: Start there and then . . .
Dr Dryden: Right!
Sarah: I don't want to be dependent on anybody, really. I want to be able to get up in the morning and be myself – and if things don't go right, well . . .
Dr Dryden: But what's the current status on that? How do you feel about coping on your own in terms of working through problems yourself?
Sarah: Well, it's as simple as this – if I have premenstrual tension and I talk with you about it, you're not going to take it away.
    I realize that talking with you has been a great help to me, but I can't go on the rest of my life having somebody to talk with and hold my hand. That's not being myself – that's trying to be part of you!
Dr Dryden: Well, I see my role in therapy as this: I try to help you identify your problems, and then give you a way of looking at them that you can actually put into practice *yourself*.
Sarah: That's what I've been trying to do, you know. If I wake up depressed, I'd like to be able to tackle it myself.
    In these last two weeks, I definitely have found an improvement in myself. I am *freely* happy, and not just *forcing* myself to be happy. But in the first two weeks since I last saw you, I was waking up feeling a bit depressed – then, it was more a matter of forcing myself to get my jobs done.
Dr Dryden: Did you know what you were depressed about?
Sarah: I think I was physically and mentally tired – I don't know why.
    It makes me tired after I've been here! (laughs)
Dr Dryden: Yeah.
Sarah: I really feel tired after I've been here – and some mornings I wake up like that. I think it's the sort of person I am – I *do* drain myself of energy . . .
Dr Dryden: How?
Sarah: Well, I never sort of let my mind rest – I haven't been able to do that.
Dr Dryden: Mm-hm. When you say you haven't been capable of letting your mind rest, what does your mind tend to dwell on?
Sarah: Anything – I always find something to keep my mind ticking on. I don't look for it – it just happens.

Dr Dryden: But – what would be the flavour of the thoughts?
Sarah: If I'm truthful, I suppose it usually boils down to, 'What on earth are they thinking of me?'
Dr Dryden: Mm-hm.
Sarah: I wish I wasn't thinking that, but I guess that's what it amounts to.

In response to Sarah's statement that she never lets her mind rest, Dr Dryden makes an inquiry intended to identify the specific content of her cognitions. Here, Sarah's report indicates that she continues to worry over others' opinions of her. Dr Dryden next asks her whether she is making attempts to counter her upset-provoking thoughts.

Dr Dryden: Okay – do you respond to that thought, or do you just stay with it?
Sarah: Well, if something were to happen today, and I thought that somebody might be thinking something about me, I could worry about it all tonight. But since I know that by tomorrow it won't seem so important, I'd think, 'Well, don't worry so much – you know very well tomorrow you're going to feel a lot better about it'.
Dr Dryden: Mm-hm.
Sarah: That helps me not to feel so anxious about it.
Dr Dryden: But are you able to identify what you're worried about? Give me a typical example, so that I can understand it better.
Sarah: Well, I can tend to talk too quickly. I start to speak loudly and to get excited, and if I happen to be talking to somebody with whom I'm not particularly friendly, I'll later think, 'Oh God, I'll bet I was getting all excited and speaking too quickly – what do they think of me?'
Dr Dryden: Okay. How would you – using what you've learned here – talk back to yourself in order to be able to let that one go?
Sarah: They probably haven't been thinking anything bad, anyway. That *is* the truth – they probably *haven't* been thinking it . . .
Dr Dryden: Mm-hm, yeah.
Sarah: But anyway, I know that's what I do – it's no good saying that I don't.
Dr Dryden: So you tell yourself that they probably haven't been thinking poorly of you, and that that's the way you speak. Anything else?
Sarah: Well, that I'm capable of *not* speaking like that. If I'm going to meet somebody, I think, 'There's no need to get excited like that – the reason you're doing it is because you're worrying what they're thinking about you before you even get there!' Do you know what I mean?

Dr Dryden asks Sarah to provide an example of a situation in which she experiences approval anxiety. She relates her perception that she tends to talk too quickly and loudly when speaking with acquaintances, and describes how she then worries over the possibility that they might be thinking negatively about her.

Dr Dryden then asks her to consider how she might 'talk back to herself' in order to counter her anxiety-provoking thoughts. Here, it is noted that he chooses not to employ a didactic approach which could simply consist of providing her with a complement of rational self-statements. Instead, he asks her to exercise the skills and insights she has acquired in therapy by generating her own responses. This strategy can be viewed as promoting independent functioning, and also allows Dr Dryden to identify aspects of Sarah's cognitive coping responses that might require further refinement.

Sarah is able to generate two responses that could help her to deal with her anxiety. The first of these can be viewed as a form of empirical disputing, as it involves consideration of the probability that others will respond negatively. The second appears to be somewhat self-instructional in nature, since it seems to imply a directive to try and speak more calmly.

While these responses do represent potentially helpful vehicles for countering approval anxiety, they fail to take into account the possibility that some individuals may indeed think poorly of a person who speaks in an overly excited fashion. Noting this, Dr Dryden next asks Sarah how she might respond to this 'worst case' scenario.

Dr Dryden: Right, okay – but what if they *do* think badly of you for talking quickly? How could you respond to that thought?

Sarah: It's not so much that they're thinking badly – I don't think they're thinking badly of me. They probably think, 'Oh, she's just got bad news or something – she sort of gets carried away or excited . . .'

Dr Dryden: What if they do think that? How could you respond to that thought?

Sarah: Well, I'd rather they didn't think it, but if they do, there's nothing I can do about it.

Dr Dryden: But how would you feel about *you* if that were true – that they *were* thinking that you were a bit troubled?

Sarah: (pause) Um . . . it doesn't *really* upset me, but . . . I don't know – I'd just prefer not to be thought of like that.

Dr Dryden: But if they do . . . what?

Sarah: Well, it makes me feel a bit ashamed, I suppose.

Dr Dryden: Do you remember what we said about shame? What sorts of thoughts go along with shame?

Sarah: I'm not sure . . .

Dr Dryden: Can you see any difference between saying, 'I talk too quickly; that just means I've got a weakness', and 'I'm a lousy person for having that weakness?'

Sarah: Well, like you said before, a person is all made up of little parts – and that's just *one* part of me.

Dr Dryden: Mm-hm. Now, if you accepted yourself as a complex human being with both good and bad points, would you tend to feel ashamed about that one particular part?

Sarah: Not ashamed, but I'd just wish that I didn't do it. That's not as bad as being ashamed, I know.

Dr Dryden: Right. So, shame is thoughts about what?

Sarah: Thoughts about things you don't like about yourself.

Dr Dryden: Thoughts about *you*! Are they good thoughts or bad thoughts?

Sarah: Well, they're bad thoughts if you're ashamed.

Dr Dryden: Now, if you reminded yourself about being made up of both good and bad parts, do you think that would help you not to feel ashamed?

Sarah: Yeah – but if I go that deeply into it, I'm going to think, 'Well, they don't know the other good parts about me; they've just heard me getting sort of hysterical over a normal conversation'. I mean, they're not going to . . .

Dr Dryden: Mm-hm. But when you're feeling ashamed, you're having bad thoughts about *you* because you're treating yourself as what?

Sarah: Oh – a bad person.

Dr Dryden: Now, are you a bad person, a good person, or a person made up of good and bad?

Sarah: Yeah – a person made up of good and bad.

Dr Dryden: Okay – 'I do have this bad aspect, but I'm made up of both good and bad'. Can you imagine yourself using those thoughts?

Sarah has indicated that although she would prefer people not to regard her as 'troubled', she recognizes that she cannot control the manner in which other individuals think about her. Dr Dryden then shifts the focus to how *she* thinks about *herself* with respect to her self-perceived tendency to speak too loudly and quickly. Sarah makes reference to the 'Big I/Little i' model presented in the sixth session, and Dr Dryden attempts to emphasize that she can use this model to accept herself *with* this possibly negative characteristic.

Sarah: Well, thinking about it now . . . earlier, you said I didn't have to feel ashamed about admitting I'm upset, or a nervous type of person or something. With certain people, I find that I *am* better able to tell them such things about myself.

At work the other day, we were talking about smoking – and they couldn't believe how much I used to smoke, because they hardly ever see me with a cigarette. I told them that a lot of it had to do with nerves, because occasionally I *do* have bouts when I suffer with my nerves. I wasn't ashamed to tell them that!

Dr Dryden: Right, right.

Sarah: I think that was a good thing that you put into my head – I don't have to be ashamed to . . .

Dr Dryden: Oh . . . with my magic lamp!

Sarah: (laughs) Yeah! Without that conversation I had with you, I would never have dreamed of telling them.

Dr Dryden: Right – but *you* decided that. I never told you to go out and do it, did I?

Sarah has related the current discussion concerning shame and negative self-rating to material covered in earlier sessions. She refers to Dr Dryden's message that she can engage in self-disclosure concerning her upsets without feeling ashamed, and cites an instance in which she was successfully able to do so. She describes this message, however, as something that Dr Dryden 'put into my head'. He responds to this statement by making reference to the 'magic lamp' device utilized in the seventh session, and emphasizes that it was *her* decision to engage in self-disclosure. Here, he is again reinforcing the idea that Sarah doesn't 'need' him in order to function effectively in her interpersonal environment.

Sarah: No . . . but once before when I told you I start crying when I'm fussed over, you said something like, 'Well, what's so wrong about that? Why can't you tell people if you're upset?' At the time, I thought, 'Well, that sounds so simple to say – but you can't admit you're upset . . .'

Dr Dryden: Okay . . .

Sarah: But you can! And people just don't take any notice!

Dr Dryden: You can remind yourself that people probably *aren't* thinking anything negative about you, but even if they are, you can still accept yourself as a person who might have acted badly. If you practised that, do you think you would then stop worrying?

Sarah: Not completely, no. I don't think so.

Dr Dryden: What would you worry about, then?

Sarah: Deep down, I *really* think I would still be a little bit anxious about it. But now – as compared to when I first started coming here – I think I can *control* that worry.

You're not going to change me as a person. I don't believe that anybody can *really* change my personality – so I've got to learn to accept the way I am. And if I can accept the way I am, I can *control* the way I am.

Dr Dryden: So, you seem to be saying, 'If I go through some of the things we've just discussed, I'm still going to be a little bit anxious, but that would be an acceptable thing.'

Sarah: Yeah – I think most things are acceptable if they're kept under control. It's only if you let them get completely out of hand and start doing what I wanted to do – take tablets, go to sleep, not answer the phone . . .

Dr Dryden: Okay – if you want to go beyond that, then I'd suggest going over some of the things we've discussed *repeatedly* – you can really convince yourself that, 'Yes, I don't like others thinking certain things about me, but if they do, they do – that may be sad, but *I* can still accept me.'

If you do that, you may find that you're able to get rid of the anxiety – and free your mind to focus on things that you enjoy.

Sarah: Mm, yeah. I think that's the way I'm going to be, because you can't really change what I am – and I'm an anxious person. I've got to face that fact . . .

Dr Dryden: But . . . you don't have to be.

Sarah: Well, I can't really see myself ever living a life where I'm never going to be anxious about . . .

Dr Dryden: I'm not saying that. I'm saying, 'Yes, you have the tendency to make yourself anxious – but if you take some of the things we've discussed and go over them with more frequency and *conviction*, you may find that you then don't tend to become anxious.' You will probably still be *concerned*, but again, there's a distinction between anxiety and concern.

Let me see if I'm making myself clear – can you feed back to me what you've understood me to be saying?

Sarah: Yes – you're saying that eventually, if I keep going over this attitude I'm starting to have, I might not experience *real* anxiety. There will still be a slight concern, but that's normal in everybody.

We've all got concerns, but when it gets out of hand it becomes anxiety. That's when you start to need doctors and pills, and all the rest of it.

Dr Dryden: You see, my theory is that if you label yourself as an 'anxious person', you then won't go on to do that work.

Sarah: I will, though – because I don't want to keep going to the doctor. I don't want to be dependent . . .

Dr Dryden: I do believe that you'll go and do the work, but you may have it in your mind that this is about as far as you can reach.

Sarah: No – I've just started, you know.

Dr Dryden: I see – okay . . .

Sarah's stated goal of being able to accept herself as an anxious person could conceivably have emotional benefits for her, as it might prevent her from rating herself negatively when she perceives that she feels anxious. It is, however, potentially problematic in that it constitutes a global self-labelling that could lead her to inadvertently impose limitations on the coping capacity she might achieve. Dr Dryden takes note of this possible cul-de-sac, and intervenes by emphasizing that Sarah can attain a fundamental modification in her tendency to make herself anxious by practising an alternative rational philosophy with frequency and conviction.

RET strongly advocates a philosophy of self-acceptance; however, it encourages individuals to try to identify and change modifiable aspects of self (such as irrational beliefs and their dysfunctional emotional and behavioural consequences) that create obstacles to emotional adjustment and goal attainment. Here, the message that rational-emotive therapists attempt to convey to clients is similar to that embodied in the famous *Serenity Prayer*: Grant me the serenity to accept the things I cannot change/ The ability to change the things I can change/ And the wisdom to know the difference.

Sarah: I *do* think I can go a bit further than this – but like you said, it is true that I've labelled myself an anxious person. I'm aiming so that I become anxious less often – I want to be able to control myself. Do you understand what I mean?

Dr Dryden: Right – I think you've been using some of the things we've discussed, and you can actually apply yourself so that you don't have to be at the mercy of your thoughts.

Sarah: I know what you're saying – that's what I've got to try and do . . .

Dr Dryden: I'm saying that if you label yourself as a person whose mind is full of thoughts that you can do nothing about, then the danger is that you may not even *attempt* to change them. You may say, 'Well, I'm just the type of person whose mind is going to worry over this or that – I can accept myself for it, but I can't really expect to change it.'

Sarah: Well, I didn't mean that – what I meant is that I'll continue to be one of those worrying types, but I'm not going to let it get out of hand so that I become an anxious person who has to go to the doctor and take medication. Being anxious causes you to be all of the things that I was, which amounts to the word 'depression'.

I swear to you, I'm never going back to that level. I think that with a little bit of will power and less self-pity, you can come out of it and help yourself. I believe that I am at that stage, where I can bring myself out of it.

Dr Dryden: Yeah.

Sarah: So – I don't consider myself to be a really anxious person anymore. I can still have thoughts such as, 'Oh God, what if such and such happens?' – but now I can respond to them by saying, 'Well, so what if it happens – it won't be the end of the world'.

Dr Dryden: Right – I think what you're saying is that you might start off with that

worrying type of thought, but that you don't have to be at the mercy of it. You
can think it through so that you can get some resolution . . .

Sarah: Exactly! That's the way I wish I could have said it to you. That's the way I
hope to be, and I have been sort of using this therapy myself.

I've been practising the therapy myself, and it *does* work! I can't give you
really good examples, but . . .

Dr Dryden: Well, give me one.

Sarah: Um . . . Well, the week before the holidays I had my hair cut – and when I
got out of the shop and looked in the mirror, I wanted to take an overdose! I
thought, 'God, I can't go to parties looking like this!'

But then I thought, 'Well, number one, you'd better face the fact that they
can't put it back on – and number two, it's not going to be that bad – because
chances are, people are not going to be studying me!' That *is* true – do you
know what I mean?

So, I actually just accepted it, and stopped myself from being overly unhappy.

Dr Dryden: Right, yeah. You started off feeling anxious and depressed about it, but you
identified some of the things you were actually upset about and responded to them.

Sarah: Yeah – it was no good trying to kid myself that I *did* like it. I mean, I can't
say to myself . . .

Dr Dryden: Yeah – that's what I would call 'concern': you don't like it, but you can
accept you for it, and expose *you* to the world.

Sarah: I can honestly say to you that until I came here, I would have told Art that I
wasn't going to any parties. I probably wouldn't have admitted that it was
because of my hair, and I would've made a lot of silly stories up – and half
believed them, myself.

Dr Dryden: Right.

Sarah: But I went to the parties, I enjoyed myself, and we had a great time. I'm
sure nobody even noticed me, let alone my hair.

Dr Dryden: (chuckles) Right. Okay – let's go on to your 'acidy stomach'.

Sarah: Well, that example I've just given you would have caused my stomach to
go off. It only has to start off, and then the acid comes. That's it; it's too late
then. Now, I'm able to console myself afterward, but the damage there is done.

Dr Dryden: In a sense, I believe that no form of therapy is going to stop you from
becoming *aroused* about something initially – and that's the point at which you
say the acid comes. You can then talk yourself out of feeling anxious, but it's
too late for your stomach.

Sarah: It's too late, yeah. But the doctor told me that there are better drugs for that
sort of thing now, and that he'd prescribe them for me when I'd made progress
with my smoking.

Dr Dryden: Right, right. Now, what about 'reasonable upsets'? We've sort of covered that, haven't we?

Sarah: Yes, I think we covered it. There was an example today of what I would call
a reasonable upset.

I was at work, and who should walk in at lunchtime but Peter. I said, 'What
are you doing here? I thought you were at your school placement.' He said,
'Yes, but they don't give us a lunch – we have to get our own, you know.' I told
him, 'You'd better get in the back of the shop and have a cup of coffee, and a
bite to eat while you're at it.'

Six months ago, this would've given me a nervous breakdown! I would have thought, 'How wicked of that school not to give my son something to eat – the poor child is starving!' And with all that fussing, I would have started throwing up, you know.

But I didn't get that upset – I was *concerned* that he didn't have lunch, but – so what, he's a big lad and it won't hurt him to miss one meal. I just had the natural concern that any mother would have had.

Dr Dryden: Right.

Sarah: That was a good example. On the other hand, I recently went to visit a family that I've been dealing with through Social Services. Their little girl asked me to find out why she had to change schools, and I had to give her the bad news that she must move – Social Services could do nothing about it.

I really felt anxious about giving her that news, because I knew she was really going to be upset. I thought, 'Well, I've done all I can do, but she still has to be moved' – but nevertheless, the acid started.

Dr Dryden: You were saying before that you work on things in your head, but it doesn't seem to help your stomach. I'm wondering how you would have felt if you hadn't had the acid. Is it possible that the acid is exaggerating some of those feelings?

Sarah: Could be – I don't know. The ulcer is there, and once the acid comes up the ulcer starts giving me trouble. I believe that eventually I'll be able to control the acid, so that it won't affect the ulcer – but I think the ulcer itself needs drying up, for which I think they can give me tablets.

Dr Dryden: Okay – given the time, we'd better wrap things up for now. How would you feel about letting two months go by before we meet again?

(End of recording)

As the session approaches its end, Sarah states her intention to continue working at changing her tendency to make herself anxious. She acknowledges that when she experiences anxiety-provoking thoughts, she can respond to them in a manner that will help her not to feel anxious.

Brief review of the problems presented by her 'acidy stomach' leads Dr Dryden to make a statement concerning his view on one of the limitations of psychotherapy. He indicates that psychotherapy (particularly a cognitive-behavioural therapy such as RET) can assist individuals in modifying the upset-producing interpretations and meanings they may attach to aversive and noxious events, but that it is unlikely it can change a person's basic tendency to experience physiological arousal in the face of such stimuli. Thus, from the RET perspective, it is possible to replace inappropriate negative feelings with appropriate negative feelings. It may not be possible or practical, however, for clients to completely eradicate all forms of negative effect.

The session draws to a close with agreement to meet again in two months' time.

The ninth session: exposing one's humanness

Over the course of the preceding eight sessions, it seems evident that Sarah has made significant progress in overcoming her tendency to upset herself in response to particular issues and activating events. In particular, her realization that other people are probably not studying and judging her to the extent that she had believed has helped her to become less anxiety-prone in various inter-personal situations. It appears, however, that at times she still experiences feel-ings of shame and embarrassment when she perceives that she has behaved in a negative fashion or exposed a weakness. As such, a good portion of the current session is devoted to discussion of risk-taking exercises which entail purposely exposing one's 'humanness' to other individuals. The purpose of these particular exercises is to assist Sarah in creating opportunities to work on accepting herself with her negative aspects, such that she might become able to worry less about other people's opinions of her.

Dr Dryden: Okay – this is our ninth of the ten sessions, so this is the one before last. It's been two months since we last met – how have things been going since then?

Sarah: Um, great! I've been plugging along; not a lot of problems coming up. I still get my premenstrual tension – nobody can say that I don't get that.

Dr Dryden: Yeah.

Sarah: I was really bad with it this month, but most days are great. I still have my off days, but they don't upset me like they used to. I think, 'Oh, I'm having an off day – so what?'.

Dr Dryden: Right.

Sarah: Before, I used to really get depressed when I felt that I didn't have it in me to get anything done. Now, I just take every day as it comes – and if I don't feel like knocking the house over and going mad, I just do what's necessary.

I think that's more sensible – I'll just do the necessary things and then put my feet up, or go and visit a friend if that's what I feel like doing. I'm sort of helping myself, by *making* each day more pleasant. I think the fact that I can think like that is a big improvement in itself.

Dr Dryden: I think I've asked you this before, but have other people commented on the changes in you?

Sarah: Not so much my family, but then they wouldn't. I don't think I've got a particularly nice family, if you know what I mean. We're all a bit highly strung – so as you can imagine, they're probably too tied up with their own upsets to take notice of anybody else.

Dr Dryden: Right.

Sarah: I've noticed that I get on with the girls at work extremely well – I've been on three girls' outings with them, and I've only been at the job since Christmas. I mean, I couldn't have done that a few months ago – I would have had to make excuses and . . .

Dr Dryden: Because . . .?

Sarah: Because I would have thought, 'Oh, I can't go – I look horrible, I'll be miserable, and they'll talk about me.'

I'm not saying that none of those things entered my mind when they asked me to go, but I thought, 'Well, I'll look as good as they will'. When you get there you don't care who looks like what – you just have a drink and a chat. We went to a skittles place and had good fun – and I actually won, as well!

Dr Dryden: (chuckles) You won at skittles!

In the preceding portion of the transcript, Sarah has described the 'girls' outings' in which she participated. She recognizes these events as representing a positive deviation from her customary patterns of relating to others, as she was able to resist her usual urges to engage in avoidance behaviour and was actually able to enjoy herself within a social context.

As individuals with self-acceptance issues make progress in therapy, they are often able to take note of the beneficial consequences of becoming less approval-needy. This, in turn, can serve to increase their motivation to continue engaging in social risk-taking.

Sarah: I'm glad I made the effort to go – and it's given me something to talk about with Art and Peter. You know, I used to get stuck for something to talk about.

Dr Dryden: Right, yeah.

Sarah: So I talk about that, and I might even let Art come next time!

Dr Dryden: (humorously) Expose Art to the world, eh?

Sarah: Yeah – but I'm afraid that while I'm talking or playing skittles, he'll be watching me.

Dr Dryden: Yeah – and if he is?

Sarah: (laughs) I don't like it!

Dr Dryden: Because . . .?

Sarah: Well, I feel as if I might make mistakes, and I don't like making mistakes.

Dr Dryden: Okay – but can you see the difference between not *liking* making mistakes, and believing that you *mustn't* make mistakes?

Sarah: Oh, yeah.

Dr Dryden: What's the difference?

Sarah: Well, the fact is that if I make mistakes it really doesn't matter that much – I'm just a bit embarrassed about it, you know.

Dr Dryden: Right – it kind of proves what an incompetent person you are, doesn't it?

Sarah: Yeah – and Art would probably think the same way. As I've told you, he's just like me. (chuckles) That's probably why we got married!

Dr Dryden: Ohh! You would agree that if you make a mistake it proves you're incompetent?

Sarah: (chuckles) No, it doesn't now! It's just that I still can't get over being embarrassed about it. I will, I suppose – I mean, I was making a fool of myself with the girls, and it didn't bother me. They were making fools of *themselves* – it was all part of the fun. But I guess I have to build up gradually with what I feel comfortable doing in front of other people.

Dr Dryden: Is it mainly with Art that you're concerned?

Sarah: Um . . . I think it is, in a way – because I couldn't understand why he liked me in the first place . . .

Dr Dryden: Yeah.

Sarah: And I suppose I don't like to fall below any picture that he might have of me.

Dr Dryden: Because if you do . . .?

Sarah: Well, I feel sort of inferior.

Dr Dryden: Where does that feeling come from? What attitude does it come from?

Sarah: Thinking I'm not good enough, I suppose.

Dr Dryden: That's right! If you're thinking, 'I'm inferior', aren't you going to get those inferiority feelings?

Sarah: Yes, if I think that, I suppose I will . . .

Dr Dryden: Well, where's the evidence that you're inferior?

Sarah: There isn't any, really, I suppose . . .

Dr Dryden: (humorously) You don't sound too convinced about that!

Sarah: (laughs) I don't know if I set myself too high a standard to live up to . . .

Dr Dryden: Well, okay – let's assume that you *did* make a mistake and Art actually sees it and says, 'Right – I want a divorce! You're obviously an incompetent who can't hold a skittle ball correctly – I'm off!' Now, would that really prove that you were an incompetent?

Sarah: No . . .

Dr Dryden: What would that prove?

Sarah: (pause) It wouldn't prove anything – it would just prove that Art doesn't like a woman he thinks is incompetent. But that's not to say he's right!

Dr Dryden: Exactly, right. Now, how about risking that? How about showing Art that you actually make mistakes? My hunch is that if you risk that, you would wind up feeling freer. You wouldn't always be thinking, 'I've got to do this right for Art – otherwise, he'll be off!' And if he *were* to leave you, would you want to be married to somebody with such rigid high standards?

Sarah: No – but really . . . I'm blaming Art, but I don't know if it's *myself* that's set these high standards.

Dr Dryden: Well, that's often what happens – when we feel that we have to live up to this high standard, we come to think that other people share it, too.

Sarah: Yeah – it's not *really* Art. It's just that because I care about Art, I don't want to let myself down in front of him. He probably wouldn't really give a damn . . .

Dr Dryden: But let yourself down from what? I'm hearing from *angel-hood*!

Sarah: (chuckles)

Dr Dryden: 'I *should* be an angel, and I'm letting myself down when I make a mistake!'

Sarah: I don't know – I suppose I'm getting better at things and not caring . . .

Dr Dryden: Yeah – I think you *are* learning that other people aren't holding some of the views that you could think they would hold. For instance, you confronted your mother and asserted yourself with her. Have you continued to do that?

Sarah: Yes, I have.

Dr Dryden: Right. I guess the thing I would like to see you do more of is to show yourself what it means to be *human*, and not goddess-like. Do you know what I mean by that?

Sarah: You mean stop trying to appear perfect, I suppose.

Dr Dryden: Yeah – to yourself and to other people. What would you do differently if you worked on that? How could you expose your humanness to Art and to other people?

Sarah has disclosed her anxiety concerning the prospect of making a mistake in front of her husband. She is able to see that she is afraid of losing his approval, and that she would tend to feel inferior if this were to occur. Dr Dryden attempts to dispute the notion that committing an error makes one an inferior or incompetent human being, and initiates discussion of risk-taking exercises by asking Sarah to consider how she might go about exposing her humanness to other people.

Sarah: Well, with Art . . . I'm probably boasting when I say this, but without my going to work and managing the money, we couldn't afford any of the luxuries that we have.

Dr Dryden: Yeah . . .

Sarah: It's all because I manage money so well – I don't squander it, and I sort of manipulate it so that nobody goes short. But it's all behind the scenes – Art doesn't know that I'll sit home on my day off and work out the budget.

Dr Dryden: (humorous tone) Because you don't tell him!

Sarah: Because I don't tell him – exactly! So he just thinks . . .

Dr Dryden: That it gets done by magic.

Sarah: Yeah – he says, 'Oh, we do well for working-class people, don't we? It's great how we can afford a holiday abroad and still have a bit left for emergencies.'

Dr Dryden: And you bring this up because . . . what?

Sarah: Well, I never tell him that I do these things . . .

Dr Dryden: Because . . .? Why don't you tell him that?

Sarah: I like to think that Art doesn't have to have a lot of tension and worry – let him think that life's just good. I mean, that's the way I want him to feel.

Dr Dryden: Because if he thinks that's the way life is . . . what? I was wondering if you were thinking, 'If he feels that way, then he won't leave me'.

Sarah: Well, I'm not aware of thinking, 'Will he leave me if he thinks it's the other way?' He *knows* married life isn't a bed of roses, but . . . I don't want him to think it's a bed of nails, either!

Dr Dryden: No, but we're talking here about you really being able to accept yourself as a human being with both good and bad points, and the *value* of actually getting practice in showing people your humanness – while accepting *yourself* for that humanness.

Sarah: Oh – I mean . . . What I was trying to get at is that Art probably doesn't realize just how good I am with the housekeeping. If I told him about it, he'd probably think, 'Oh, she's got a bit of a brain!'

Dr Dryden: Would telling him that be a risk for you?

Sarah: Well, I would feel like I was showing off and asking for a reward like a kid.

Dr Dryden: That would really be telling him about something you're *good* at. How about showing him the *other* aspects of you – something that you're *not* too good at?

Sarah: (pause) Well, I could – by not being so thrifty. I mean, often I'll think, 'Let's go uptown and blow fifty or sixty quid on a nice dress'. I *could* go mad and do something like that, and then Art would say, 'My God, what have you done? I didn't think we could afford that, Sarah!' I could say, 'No, we can't – but I have!'

Then he would see another side of me, which is not *really* me – but I could do it to shock him, I suppose.

Dr Dryden: I was thinking more along the lines of what you described before – that you don't want to have Art come out with you because he might see you make a few errors.

Do you still doll up before he comes home?

Sarah: Yeah – I still get a shower and do my hair.

Dr Dryden: How about *not* doing that?

Sarah: Well, lately Art's been getting up and having breakfast with me – so he's seen me first thing in the morning as I really am, without a shower and my hair done. It doesn't seem to make a difference to him.

Dr Dryden: Right – this again is sort of challenging the notion that other people are going to take a lousy view of you. I think that's good, because it's an important learning.

What I'm really offering you is the opportunity to work on accepting *you* with your errors, which you can do by exposing them to others.

Sarah: Mm.

Dr Dryden: Even if other people *do* take offence, at least you've got your *own* acceptance – and won't be defining yourself as inferior. Do you know what I mean by that?

Sarah: Yeah . . . my one sister always expects me to be looking just so, and she comments on my appearance. She's always saying things like, 'Oh, your hair looks nice', and all of that.

Once, she came to the house when I'd got the 'flu, and had a bad period as well. I looked awful! Normally, I would have had a fit – but this time I remembered some of the things we've discussed. I thought, 'Well, if you feel poorly and look bad, you don't have to be ashamed. You can just tell them you're not feeling well!'

Dr Dryden: Right, right – that's it. But in a sense, it sounds like you were really attributing your appearance to the 'flu: 'It's not really me; if I was feeling okay I wouldn't look like this!'

How about showing yourself to them – warts and all – when you *haven't* got the 'flu! You could even invite them around, and kind of mess the place up a bit. I often suggest this assignment to women who run a home, because they worry, 'What if they think I'm a slob!'

Sarah: (laughs) Yeah – I know what you mean. My sister *did* pop in one Sunday morning, and I'd just got up and I *did* look like hell on earth. (Chuckles) And she *told* me as well! I thought, 'You bitch!' But it didn't bother me too much, to be honest.

Dr Dryden: Good, good. Now, I think that if you really work on that, you'll not only have your own self-acceptance at all times, but will also be better able to deal with those odd occasions when other people *are* going to think you're a lousy person. It seems you're learning that other people aren't as critical as you thought they might be . . .

Sarah: No, no – I don't think they are. I've been far too self-conscious. I still am to a point, but not *so* much . . .

Dr Dryden: Right. You see, you were kind of imagining that other people were holding the same attitudes that you were holding.

Sarah: Yeah – I thought they were *watching* me.

Dr Dryden: Right – and although you now know that most people won't be overly critical, some people *will*. But even so, you can still accept yourself with your faults.

Between now and the next time we meet, I'd like to see you embark on a series of experiments that will help to reinforce these ideas.

Sarah: Oh, yeah.

Dr Dryden: By *doing* the sorts of things I was suggesting earlier, you can effect a real *philosophical* change in yourself: *you* can accept you, and therefore not be dependent upon other people's acceptance.

In discussing risk-taking exercises, Dr Dryden suggests to Sarah that she take steps purposely to expose an error or weakness to her husband. She responds by indicating that she could choose to spend money imprudently, which would run counter to her usual efforts to run a tight budget.

Because enactment of this particular activity could be somewhat inconvenient in terms of the financial outlay it would require, Dr Dryden advances some specific suggestions regarding more practical (and less costly) risk-taking exercises that Sarah might choose to take on. He attempts to emphasize the point that strategically engaging in certain activities can facilitate the process of effecting beneficial changes in her personal philosophy.

As described in Chapter 2, individuals can dispute their irrational beliefs through both cognitive and behavioural channels. While cognitive disputing generally involves *verbally* challenging irrational beliefs (through the use of rational self-statements, internal dialogues, homework sheets, etc.), behavioural disputing requires the individual actually to engage in actions which run counter to these beliefs. Thus, a client such as Sarah – who adheres to the belief, 'I *must* maintain the approval of others' – might choose to take the risk of acting in ways which could conceivably provoke rejecting or disapproving responses in people. By doing so, she might provide herself with 'hard data' which support the notion that rejection is not *awful*. From the rational-emotive perspective, behavioural disputing represents a powerful vehicle for accomplishing deep-seated and enduring philosophical change.

Sarah: Yeah – because if I go on depending on *other* people, I'll be upset the rest of my life. The world *is* a bit cruel, I know . . .

Dr Dryden: Right – but it isn't as cruel as you had been thinking.

Sarah: No, no. Before, I thought it was so cruel that at times I wanted to go and kill myself – but I don't think that way any more.

By being a little bit tougher and sticking up for myself more – and by lowering my standards a bit – the world becomes a more pleasant place to live in.

Dr Dryden: Right.

Sarah: I'm glad to say that as Peter's getting older, he's becoming less like me every day. *He* doesn't care what other people think, and I think that's great!

Dr Dryden: Okay – but if you don't care at all, you're at risk for becoming like some of those people to whom you've made reference: those who cynically go about hurting people without giving a damn.

As far as other people's opinions are concerned, we've talked before about the differences between *over*-caring, being appropriately concerned, and not caring at all.

Sarah: Yeah – well, Peter seems to have the medium attitude. He's definitely not the type to go out and hurt people intentionally.

I was more referring to his attitudes about clothing and appearance – he doesn't get himself hung up on what other people might be thinking about him.

Dr Dryden: Right.

Sarah: I find myself thinking a bit more like that, now. When I first got my job, I used to get myself panicked. I'd think, 'I've got to look nice for work; then I've got to get back home, do the housework, and get myself looking nice again!'

It seemed that I was always worrying about trying to look nice and get my jobs done. But now, I'll just have a wash and get tidy for work, and leave it at that. And when I get home again, I don't have a nervous breakdown if I'm running late and can't take my evening shower.

Dr Dryden: Okay – you'll tell me if this seems a little bit extreme, but let me make a suggestion to you: how about having what we could call a 'dirty week'?

Sarah: Where I wouldn't shower?

Dr Dryden: Yeah!

Sarah: Oh, I couldn't do that!

Dr Dryden: You couldn't do that! Why couldn't you?

Sarah: (laughs) I just couldn't!

Dr Dryden: Because . . .?

Sarah: I'd feel so dirty!

Dr Dryden: But what would you be thinking about yourself being dirty?

Sarah: I'd be saying, 'I'm not nice!'

Dr Dryden: Uh-huh, right! You would *feel* dirty, but can you see the difference between saying 'Therefore, I'm not a nice human being' and 'I'm merely a human being who hasn't washed for a week'? Can you see that difference?

Sarah: Yeah.

Dr Dryden: In your own words, how would you describe the difference?

Sarah: (laughs) Well, I could be dirty for that week, and still be a nice person!

Dr Dryden: Yeah – now, do you think you would find that a challenge?

Sarah: Yeah, I would! A very big one! I'd find it a challenge not to wash for a couple of days, as long as I'm in normal, good health – but I'll definitely have a go at it. I didn't wash my hair yesterday, if that means anything!

Dr Dryden: Right – what I'm suggesting is that you go for a whole week without having a shower and washing your hair.

Sarah: If I did that . . . honestly, it would be a miracle! (Laughs) I'll bet you've had to say a lot of unusual things to people, but never that one!

Dr Dryden: Again, you're not going to feel clean, you're going to feel dirty – but the important thing here is to work on breaking the connection between feeling dirty and thinking of yourself as 'not nice'.

Sarah: Yeah – but I mean, isn't it normal to want to shower every day? I'll often shower as much as twice a day.

Dr Dryden: Right – that's okay. But I'm putting this to you as an experiment that will enable you to work at breaking the connection between the Big I and the Little i's. One of those Little i's will be for you to go a week without having a shower . . .

Sarah: (laughs) So I've still got my nice ways, but I'm just . . . mucky for a week!

Dr Dryden: That's right!

Sarah: It all has to do with standards I've set for myself – I'm allowed to look dirty when I'm working in the garden, but I'm not *supposed* to look dirty in the house.

Dr Dryden: Yeah – and the reason I'm suggesting this experiment is because it will help to give you some flexibility.

Sarah: Mm.

Dr Dryden: The phrase 'I'm supposed to' probably really means 'I *have* to!'

'I don't just *want* to be clean, I *have to* be clean – and if I can't have a shower, I'll feel anxious. It's okay to be mucky when I'm ill, because then I can attribute it to the 'flu . . .'

Sarah: Yeah . . .

Dr Dryden: '. . . and I really haven't fallen from my standards.' By having a mucky week, you can practise falling from your standards – and acknowledge that you're a human being, and not a fallen angel.

Sarah: Do you understand why I've got all of these standards? I mean, they're out of proportion, aren't they?

Dr Dryden: I think the reason you have them is because you're *human*, and humans do tend to create high standards for themselves. But the standards themselves aren't the problem – the problem is the belief that, 'I *have to* live up to my standards!'

Sarah: Mm – and that's when it becomes what you would call 'out of proportion'?

Dr Dryden: That's right – because once we believe we *have to*, how are we going to feel when we fall short?

Sarah: Mm . . . We feel that we're no good any more.

Here, Dr Dryden has explained RET's philosophy regarding the place of personal standards in either promoting or compromising one's emotional health. Establishing high standards can serve as a source of motivation to achieve goals which are of importance to the individual. Escalating these standards to the level of absolute *musts* and *have tos*, however, will put the individual at risk for significant emotional upsets. Negative self-rating, depression and anxiety may be likely to follow when the person fails to attain a standard which has been deemed an essential prerequisite for self-worth and happiness. Thus, rational-emotive therapists will frequently encourage clients to maintain their high standards (as these reflect a person's wants and preferences), but will try to help them learn how to refrain from transforming them into absolutistic, self-imposed demands.

Dr Dryden: Right. Now, the reason I suggested this exercise is because it can actually give you the experience of accepting yourself as a complex person with both good and bad points. In this case, being mucky for a week will be one of the bad points.

Sarah: So then I'll be able to become more flexible about what I do.

Dr Dryden: Yeah!

Sarah: Yeah – it *is* a good idea!

Dr Dryden: It's important that you realize you're putting your mind to accepting the Big I, and making the distinction between the Big I and the Little i's. Being dirty for a week is just one aspect of you.

Sarah: Mm . . . But you know, I sometimes get this funny feeling. I do my jobs and get through the day, and then I think, 'Well, what do I do now?'

I had similar sorts of feelings when Peter was a baby, and I first brought him home from the hospital. Just like the perfect mother I wanted to be, I would bathe him and tuck him up nicely in his crib – and then I'd think, 'Oh my God, now what do I do?' I can't explain exactly what I mean – it was just a feeling of being lost and not knowing what to do.

Dr Dryden: Yeah . . .

Sarah: I feel like that now, at the end of the day. I don't feel miserable or depressed . . .

Dr Dryden: No – you kind of feel lost . . .

Sarah: I do . . . Even in the mornings, after Art and Peter have had breakfast and gone off, I'll think, 'Now what do I do?' I know I've got to do the housework, but that's just part of normal routine.

Dr Dryden: (humorously) There's a new word I'd like to teach you – it may be rather foreign sounding, because I suspect you haven't used it much. It's called 'enjoyment'. Ever heard that word before?

Sarah: (chuckles) Oh, yeah. (Wistful tone) But what would I do on my own, anyway? What would I do?

Dr Dryden: Well, I guess you can look at it in two ways. The first way is to say, 'I don't know what to do; therefore, I'm lost'. The second way is to say, 'Okay, I don't have anything that I particularly enjoy doing. Let's experiment – let's see if I can *discover* things that I might find enjoyable.'

Sarah: I wonder if it has anything to do with not having any kiddies. I mean, I've got Peter, but he's no kid. When he was a baby I knew that even if I'd finished the housework and was idle, pretty soon he'd wake up and there would be plenty to do. But now, I haven't got that.

Dr Dryden: Right – so now you can actually discover things that you can do on your own for enjoyment.

What do you think some of those things might be? What do you think *other* people do for enjoyment that you might want to try out?

Sarah: Well, honestly . . . Last week I had been giving some thought to, 'What do other people do?'. (Chuckles) I can't knit – I'm not very good at that!

Dr Dryden: Do you paint?

Sarah: No.

Dr Dryden: Have you ever painted?

Sarah: No . . . I like to do things *with* people – I don't paint, but I'd love discussing art . . .

Dr Dryden: Yeah, okay – but you were talking about when you're on your own, and Art might be glued to the tube . . .

Sarah: The worst part is during the day, when Art and Peter are both out. I'll think, 'God, what do I do?'

Dr Dryden: When you've finished all your chores . . .

Sarah: Yeah – because I get sick of polishing. You can't keep polishing, can you?

Dr Dryden: (humorously) Well, you *could* – but how about finding out what other people do by either asking them or by going to the library and getting a book on hobbies? Do you enjoy reading? Do you read novels?

Sarah: Not really, no – I sometimes read Peter's sociology books, and I like that. Not that I intend to do anything with it, but I still enjoy reading them.

Dr Dryden: You do? Well, do you remember the library?

Sarah: (chuckles) Yes . . .

Dr Dryden: Do you ever go?

Sarah: No . . . I'm still restricted a bit, in the sense that I've got to go to work and do the housework – but then for the spare times I *do* have, I feel . . . well, 'lost' is the word, really.

Perhaps reading would be about the best thing for me . . .

Dr Dryden: But the point is, you can experiment! You could actually go to the library, find a book on hobbies, and try some of them out. See how they fit! Try a week on this and a week on that, until you hit on a number of things that you can really get into.

What would stop you from doing that?

Sarah: I just can't imagine what I can do – but like you said, I can start by going to the library.

When I get this lost, 'What should I do?' feeling, that tends to start me off. If I'm going to go down, that's when it happens.

Dr Dryden: Right – but you could actually discover some things that you like doing – couldn't you?

Sarah: Yeah, but I don't really know what. I'd like to say I can think of something, but I can't.

Dr Dryden: Well, look – I think I can prove to you that that's not true.

Let's suppose that we had Peter here, right? He's standing right here, and I have a gun in my hand. I say to you, 'Sarah, if you don't *immediately* come up with five things you can try out, I'm going to blow your son's brains out!'

Sarah: (laughs) Oh, I'd think of lots of things, then!

Dr Dryden has here employed with Sarah what he refers to as the 'terrorist dispute', a technique that is generally best used with clients only after some degree of rapport has been established. The purpose of a terrorist dispute is to demonstrate to clients that they are capable of undertaking activities or accomplishing goals that they may regard as 'too dangerous' or 'too difficult'. Sarah has indicated that she is unable to think of enjoyable things to do on her own; Dr Dryden quickly dispels this notion by asking her to imagine that her son's survival is contingent upon her generating a list of alternatives. As the session continues, she begins to put her mind to the task of identifying potentially enjoyable activities.

Dr Dryden: Right – now where does that take you?

Sarah: I suppose I could get one of those fitness records and do the exercises – I like that sort of thing.

It's just that I never think of doing things on my own – I always think in terms of having one of my sisters there, or a friend.

Dr Dryden: Yeah – it sounds as if you haven't yet learned that you can be the source of entertainment yourself – as opposed to relying on other people.

Sarah: Yeah . . . I like those fitness records because they're pleasant to listen to, and they say it's good to keep fit even if you're skinny. I enjoyed it when I went to an exercise group with the girls, but I know you can buy the record and play it at home. I could do that on my own.

Dr Dryden: So you see, you *can* think of things to try. If you put some more thought into it, you could probably develop a good-sized list – couldn't you?

Sarah: I suppose I could, yeah – and you think I'd find it enjoyable to do things on my own?

Dr Dryden: Well, that's part of the experiment! You might find it strange at first, because you're not used to it.

Sarah: Mm . . . I don't think I've lived a very normal kind of life.

Dr Dryden: Perhaps we can look at it like this: here's a woman who sees herself in terms of being a housewife, or mother, or wife – and she really hasn't yet discovered that she's a person in her own right who can enjoy herself in her own ways. Would it be valid to put it like that?

Sarah: Yeah, I suppose it would . . . But I can't say that I regret all of it.

Dr Dryden: Oh, no – I'm not saying you should regret it; I'm saying that you could experiment with adding a new dimension to your life. 'Sarah's not only housewife, wife, and mother – she's also a person in her own right.'

Sarah: I *do* like gardening – I don't really know what I'm doing, but that doesn't matter.

Dr Dryden: Okay, fine – but when it's winter and things aren't growing, you won't have that option. We're talking about developing options here.

Sarah: I think I'll start with the fitness record – in fact, I might be able to invite my niece to join me. She's a teenager, and she'd probably enjoy doing it . . .

Dr Dryden: Oh, yeah – but isn't that doing something with other people again?

Sarah: Yeah – but I think that I'd prefer to get into hobbies or activities where I can involve other people.

Dr Dryden: All right – but I'm suggesting that you might first get accustomed to the notion of doing things on your own. At least try it out!

Sarah: Right . . . Now, don't you dare tell anybody this . . .

Dr Dryden: (humorously) No, I wouldn't dream of it!

Sarah: (laughs) Um . . . I do the Social Services voluntary work, and I *really* like doing it – but I have to write notes on the people I visit, and hand them in to the probation office. I *dread* doing those notes, because I can't spell very well! So I sit there with Peter's dictionary . . .

Dr Dryden: Okay – but here, we're going back to the other issue we discussed: revealing your *humanness*.

Sarah: But you *can't* hand in a load of notes all badly spelled! I feel so terrible!

Dr Dryden: But would that be a good assignment for you? What attitude would you be working on?

Sarah: (laughs) *I'm-no-good*!

Dr Dryden: That's right, you see!

Sarah: What makes it worse is that this probation officer thinks I'm really good. He's pleased with the work I'm doing, but when he gets my notes he'll have a shock!

Dr Dryden: And he'll throw you out, right?

Sarah: No, he won't throw me out – because I use Peter's dictionary! (Laughs)

Dr Dryden: But would he throw you out for poor spelling?

Sarah: No, I don't think he would.

Dr Dryden: Want to test that out?

Sarah: Well, I have to – because I handed my notes in last night.

Dr Dryden: Oh, you did!

Sarah: I thought, 'Dear God, I hope they're understandable!' It took some of the joy out of it . . .

Dr Dryden: Right – that's exactly the point! Once you feel that you *have to* do something right, you tend to take the enjoyment out of it.

Sarah: I mean, all I have to do is call on people and have a chat, and perhaps give them some help and advice. I like doing that, and I like going to the volunteers' meetings – but when they say, 'Can you hand your work in?' I think, 'Oh, my God!' (Laughs)

Dr Dryden: 'Oh, my God . . .' what?

Sarah: Oh, my God – I'm ashamed I can't spell!

Dr Dryden: But again, what does shame really mean? If you hand in your spelling, what will you be revealing about yourself?

Sarah: I'll be thinking that they think I'm barmy: 'Look at this – she can't spell!'

Dr Dryden: And if they do, what would that mean?

Sarah: Well, it doesn't mean I'm barmy.

Dr Dryden: Right – now if you really wanted to work at it, that's the connection that you could break down. You could experiment by having a non-spelling week, a mucky week, and a week where you leave the house a mess and invite people around.

Sarah: (laughs) And the whole family would have me put in an asylum – they'd say, 'She's gone funny!'

Dr Dryden: Would they?

Sarah: No, but I'm sure they'd think it – but I won't care. That's something that you've taught me – I don't care what my family thinks any more. That is true.

Dr Dryden: Right.

Sarah: I mean, I don't want to hurt them – far from it. But I don't allow them to run my life any more, or my feelings.

Sarah relates her embarrassment about revealing her poor spelling to the probation officer, and Dr Dryden suggests that she might turn this into yet another opportunity for exposing her humanness. Sarah indicates that she has already submitted the work she was asked to complete, but reports that her anxiety interfered with her ability to enjoy the task of writing the notes. As it appears that she is worrying about maintaining the probation officer's approval, Dr Dryden asks her to consider what it would really mean about her if others were to regard her as 'barmy'. Sarah appears to recognize that she can choose not to let their opinions affect the way she thinks about herself.

Dr Dryden: So now there's a gap and you feel kind of lost because you're having difficulty filling it – because you haven't taught yourself that you can be the source of your own entertainment!

Sarah: Mm . . . I mean, sometimes at night if I'm bored, I'll do what I suppose many women do: paint my nails. I'll sort of take hours over each one, and when I'm finished I'll think, 'Well, that wasn't very satisfying – I could have done that in five minutes in the morning'. And I sometimes get the feeling that I'm being vain!

Dr Dryden: You sort of trap yourself into that position by believing that you can't think of other options. We have to threaten you with Peter's early demise . . .

Sarah: (laughs)

Dr Dryden: . . . in order to get you to come up with things. You sort of get trapped into the role and routine you've created for yourself, which is, 'Oh, I'm bored – I'll wash my hair yet again!'

Sarah: (laughs) Yeah, yeah!

Dr Dryden: So you can actually experiment with adding a new dimension to yourself – one that's *there*, but hasn't been released yet.

Sarah: Well, as I said – I'd really enjoy doing those notes if I could spell, but perhaps if I just sit down and do them without worrying about the spelling, I'll enjoy it more.

Dr Dryden: That's right!

Sarah: Like you said, the probation officer isn't going to sit there questioning my spelling. He might think, 'Well, she doesn't spell very good', but by the time I see him again, he's probably forgotten about it. (Laughs) *Hasn't* he? That's what I'll be asking myself when I next meet him!

Dr Dryden: Okay, but think that one through – if he hasn't forgotten it, that would mean . . . what?

Sarah: That would mean . . . I'd be thinking that *he* thinks, 'She can't spell – she's useless!'

Dr Dryden: And if he thinks you're useless . . .?

Sarah: No, *I* don't think I'm useless – I'm just embarrassed that I can't spell . . .

Dr Dryden: But embarrassment means, 'I'm revealing a weakness, and I *shouldn't* have this weakness'. Now, why shouldn't you have a weakness in spelling?

Sarah: (pause) Well, I was very bright at school, and I could spell up until the last few years. But I've had no reason to write anything, and now suddenly when I put pen to paper I realize that I can't remember how to spell this or that.

Dr Dryden: But I asked you a question – I asked you why you *shouldn't* have this weakness, not why it's undesirable.

Sarah: Well, I suppose there's no reason why I shouldn't.

Dr Dryden: That's right! For whatever reason, you've got the weakness – you can choose to either damn yourself for it, or to accept yourself with it. Now, which do you think would be in your best interest?

Sarah: Well, it's better to accept it, isn't it?

Dr Dryden: Not necessarily to accept *it*, but to accept *you* – as a person who . . .

Sarah: Can't spell.

Dr Dryden: Or, who can't spell *presently* – because you could teach yourself how to spell better.

Sarah: I've thought about that, yeah. I could use Peter's dictionary and give myself little tests.

Dr Dryden: That's right – now, would you find that enjoyable?

Sarah: Yeah – if I were able to find out that I could once again use this up here (gestures to head). Sometimes I *do* feel as if half my brain has gone to sleep, you know.

Dr Dryden: That's what I'm hearing – you're saying you've neglected a part of you that's enjoyable and perhaps curious – but if you want to, you can unleash it!

(End of recording)

The session ends with Dr Dryden's attempt to dispute Sarah's belief, 'I *shouldn't* have a weakness in spelling'. In responding to his disputing questions, Sarah makes a statement indicating that she sees it as preferable to accept her weakness in this area. Dr Dryden points out to her that while she doesn't have to accept the weakness, she can choose to accept *herself* with it. RET teaches clients that rating particular traits or behaviours as bad (and therefore as 'unacceptable') is not likely to result in emotional disturbance, as long as one abstains from applying a global negative rating to one's self.

The tenth session: treatment's end

As per prior agreement, Dr Dryden and Sarah have allowed three months to pass before meeting for their last session together. As this session begins, Dr Dryden makes reference to a written description of their therapy which he has prepared for publication as a chapter in a book entitled *Individual Therapy in Britain* (Dryden 1984b). He had sent Sarah a copy of the chapter to read between sessions, with the hope that it would enable her to take a broad overview of her therapy experience.

Dr Dryden: So, did you have an opportunity to read that?

Sarah: Yes, I did. I'd need A levels to understand a lot of it, but I understood the description you wrote about me because it's in plain English.

Dr Dryden: Yeah – and what did you make of it?

Sarah: I'm quite pleased if it's the truth – it shows there's an improvement!

Dr Dryden: Well, the best person to know the truth is you!

Sarah: Well, I felt a lot better after I'd read it. I thought, 'Well, it *is* true' – but I hadn't realized how true it was until I'd read it.

Dr Dryden: In what way?

Sarah: Well, the fact that I'm starting to cope on my own, you know. Even when I'm feeling down, it's not the end of the world – everyone feels down, sometimes.

Dr Dryden: Did you show the article to anybody else?

Sarah: (laughs) I showed it to Peter, but not to Art!

Dr Dryden: What was Peter's reaction to it?

Sarah: He thought a lot of it was true. He didn't really understand why I got depressed, but I wouldn't expect him to. He was better able to understand the beginning of it, because he's studying psychology and sociology. He thought it was funny that you said I shouldn't make him the centre of my universe . . .

Dr Dryden: Well, you *could*.

Sarah: Yeah, but I wouldn't be happy doing that – and it wasn't fair to him, anyway. I think that's the most important thing to me – that's the best thing that's come out of this . . .

Dr Dryden: What's that?

Sarah: That I won't focus everything around Peter – I've got to admit, that's mainly because I'm sure it wouldn't have done *him* any good. It wouldn't have been fair to him – he would have been terrified of failing in anything!

We definitely are better together since I've been coming to you. I noticed that in the early days, but I realize it more than ever, now.

Dr Dryden: I indicated in there that you've really yet to expose yourself and your weaknesses to the world, and that I'm not quite sure how you'll take it if you do and other people put you down. What are your thoughts on that?

Sarah: Well, I find myself *thinking* a lot more before I speak – which I never used to do before because I'd be too wound up. You might perhaps think that's not a good idea, but I find it's good for me. When I think before I speak, I don't always expect that other people will think badly of me.

I really think I've been very selfish in the past – you know, a bit self-pitying and . . .

Dr Dryden: 'Selfish' could be a good word for it. It may *appear* that you're very concerned with others, but you're mainly preoccupied with *yourself.* You're really thinking, 'I wonder what their opinion is of *me*? I wonder how *I'm* coming over? I wonder how *I'm* doing?'

By practising the attitude, 'If I come over badly, it's unfortunate, but hardly the end of the world', you'll tend to become less preoccupied with yourself. Then, you can focus more effectively on other people.

Sarah: Right – I think I'll give that a try.

Here, Dr Dryden has described one of the undesirable consequences of subscribing to the irrational belief, 'I *must* always maintain the approval of other people'. Individuals who hold this belief will often tend to be overly focused on the impression they are making within social situations, such that they may actually be rather insensitive to others' true intentions and motivations. They can tend to be hypervigilant for signs of rejection or disapproval, with the result that they may misinterpret the outcomes of particular interpersonal exchanges. To cite an example, a young man attending a party may perceive himself to be rejected when a woman he has been speaking with excuses herself in order to mingle with other partygoers. While her behaviour may have been largely appropriate to the circumstances at hand, the young man in question may draw the conclusion that he is unlikeable and spend the balance of the evening as a wallflower. Surrendering one's approval-related *musts* and *shoulds* can represent a route to greater emotional comfort and more appropriate behaviour within social situations.

The session continues with a brief review of issues covered previously.

Dr Dryden: You can keep that copy of the article, by the way.

Did you have your 'mucky week'?

Sarah: (laughs) I haven't had my hair cut in weeks! That may sound funny – but for me, it's good. It used to be that I had to have every hair in place!

Dr Dryden: What about a list of enjoyable things to do? Did you write that out?

Sarah: I didn't make a list, but I do what I feel like doing at the time.

Dr Dryden: Now, what about Art? Have you shown him some of your imperfections?

Sarah: (laughs) Oh, yeah! Well, just around last week I started wearing skirts again. I used to hate for Art to see my skinny legs, but now I don't care any more.

I've always liked skirts, but I was frightened to wear them. But I wear them now – and it's a big deal for me, you see.

Dr Dryden: Yeah, okay . . .

Sarah: And I'm having a try at growing my hair, even though I know it's a mess when it's grown. I've never done that before.

If I get fed up and cut it, it'll be for me – not for Art, that's for sure. I'll cut it if

I get fed up with it, not because I'm thinking, 'Does *he* think I look a mess?' That won't come into it.

Dr Dryden: Right! How are you doing with your spelling?

Sarah: Oh, well – I've overcome that, haven't I?

Dr Dryden: Have you?

Sarah: Yeah! I couldn't believe it when Social Services told me I had to write notes and hand them in, and that they'd be typed up and kept in the record department. I thought, 'Oh, I *can't* do that!'

(Laughs) Well, at first I was hiding in the kitchen and doing the notes with a dictionary, so that Art wouldn't see. But then, after we had our last talk, I sat doing some notes with a dictionary *at* my side, *in* front of Art – and he never even questioned it!

Dr Dryden: Yeah.

Sarah: I thought, 'Well, I'm not going to make a real issue of it – but if he asks, I'll say, "I just don't spell very well!" ' He'd probably just laugh and not say anything more about it. I mean, that's good!

Dr Dryden: Okay – and what's your fear about showing him the article?

Sarah: Um . . . Perhaps it was because I thought he'd say, 'Well, I never knew you felt all that'. I'd probably feel a bit ashamed.

I don't feel any shame whatsoever with Peter. I know that maybe it's not fair, as far as Art's concerned – but I just *don't* feel any shame with Peter, that's all.

Dr Dryden: Right. On that one, I suppose it all depends on what sort of relationship you want with your husband. You could take the risk of showing him the article, and even tell him that you were a bit ashamed because you didn't know how he would take it.

Sarah: Art knows that I have it – he sat nearby while Peter looked at it. I think he got the drift of what it was saying, because Peter made some comments on it while he was reading. Peter would say things like, 'Huh – your mum's not to blame for your behaviour' – that sort of thing.

I think a lot of people *do* tend to blame their parents, because they want an excuse for their behaviour. We have that notion run down our throats on television – if mummy doesn't do it right, you'll turn out badly.

Dr Dryden: The experiences you have with your parents certainly have an *effect* on your development, but a lot of theories fail to recognize that you bring your own *tendencies* to those experiences. Disturbing experiences don't necessarily *create* a disturbed person.

In the statement above, Dr Dryden makes reference to RET's position on the role played by childhood experiences in producing emotional disturbance. One's past history can certainly have an effect on one's current psychological adjustment; however, the unfortunate events and circumstances that may have been a part of that history do not in and of themselves *cause* present-day emotional problems. Rather, they may serve to influence the form that a particular individual's irrational beliefs may take, as well as the degree of conviction with which the individual subscribes to those beliefs.

The historical events of a person's life cannot be changed, but the irrational beliefs the person currently holds can (with effort and perseverance) be modified. Thus, RET regards the identification and disputation of irrational beliefs as probably representing the most effective means for remediating dysfunctional patterns of thinking, emoting and behaving.

Sarah: Mm, yeah. Well, I definitely have a better relationship with mum, now. I still have to be firm with her, though – because she'll dominate me if I let her. I had started asking her for dinner, and she was getting into the habit of coming every week. I told her nicely that I didn't want her to come any more than every three weeks, because I wanted the other two Sundays to do things with Art.

Dr Dryden: How did she take that?

Sarah: She was very nice about it. She said, 'That's all right – I understand that you've got to see Art's mum, too'.

Dr Dryden: Yeah – I had written in the article that you were afraid to assert yourself, because you might get a negative response from somebody.

Sarah: Yeah.

Dr Dryden: In a sense, it may have been better if you *had* received negative responses – that would have provided you with an opportunity to learn to cope with rejection.

Sarah: Mm.

Dr Dryden: But you didn't, and that's an interesting thing: often, people *won't* reject you when you assert yourself. Sometimes they will, but often they won't.

Sarah: My sister's been having some trouble with her mother-in-law, who's been ill. I genuinely wanted to help her there, so I offered – and I found that she said something that I'd never noticed in the past. She said, 'Oh, will it be too much for you?'

I wanted to help even more, then – because in the past I felt that they always thought, 'Oh, of course Sarah will do it – you don't even have to question whether she'll have time.'

Well, now I'm wondering if that was just *me*, or if I was offering too often and putting too much on myself. We all tend to take advantage of people – even the best of us will do that.

Dr Dryden: Okay, so – how do you feel about this being our last session?

Sarah: Um . . . I feel quite confident, actually. I'd like to think I could come back in six months or so and still tell you that I feel as strong as I do now.

Dr Dryden: That might be a good idea – why don't you call me in six months?

Sarah: Yeah.

Dr Dryden: You've got my phone number – and if there's any crisis that you think you *can't* handle, call me. But – try and cope on your own, first.

Are there any other areas that you'd like to go over tonight?

Sarah: I still find it difficult to handle a situation when I'm *sure* that somebody is purposely being nasty. I'm not quite sure how to respond – should I be nasty right back, or should I just pretend it never happened? People *are* nasty sometimes, and I'm not sure how to handle it.

Dr Dryden: You mean, you don't know what the right thing to do is?

Sarah: No.

Dr Dryden: How would you know what the right thing is?

Sarah: Well, I do think that sometimes people need to be put in place – if they're rude or unnecessarily nasty . . .

Dr Dryden: Yeah . . .

Sarah: I think you should answer them accordingly – but I find it pretty difficult to do that . . .

Dr Dryden: Because . . .?

Sarah: Because I get terribly embarrassed! I find I'll get my revenge in other ways, and it's usually a lot worse! The other person would've been better off if I'd answered them back!

Dr Dryden: If you told them off there and then, what would you be telling yourself to get embarrassed?

Sarah: Well, I don't know . . . I still find that some people tend to enjoy hurting your feelings. I don't know why that is . . .

Dr Dryden: That's right . . .

Sarah: I never know how to respond. If I answer them back I'm showing them that they've hurt me, which is what they set out to do – I'd be falling straight for the trap.

Dr Dryden: The way you've got things set up here, you can't really answer the question you've asked: 'What's the best thing to do so that they stop?'
    How will you know unless you experiment?

Sarah: Mm . . . Actually, I think putting them in their place *is* the right approach.

Dr Dryden: Okay – then what would stop you from doing that? When you say you're too terribly embarrassed, what do you mean?

Sarah: It's probably not embarrassment, now that you've put it like that. Perhaps I would feel annoyed because I'd let them see that I felt hurt, and that they had accomplished what they set out to do.

Dr Dryden: Would you be annoyed or angry? Do you remember the distinction between those two feelings?

Sarah: Yeah – I'd be annoyed.

Dr Dryden: But why would that stop you?

Sarah: Because I would hate to give them the satisfaction of knowing that they've hurt me.

Dr Dryden: Because if you give them the satisfaction, what?

Sarah: I'd just feel annoyed. I'd think, 'This is stupid to let them get their own way with something so spiteful or silly . . .'

Dr Dryden: But what's your purpose?

Sarah: To get them to stop.

Dr Dryden: You don't want to show them that you feel hurt – but if you don't speak up, how are you going to stop them?

Sarah: Mm, yeah. I suppose it depends partly on who it is, and how bad it is . . .

Dr Dryden: And it sounds as if you're saying, 'I *have to* do the right thing'. How will you know what the right thing is unless you experiment?

Sarah: Yeah, yeah – that's the only sort of thing that still tends to get me down a bit. I think, 'Why do people have to be unnecessarily hurtful?' But I suppose that's life . . .

Dr Dryden: That's exactly right. Some people may be emotionally disturbed, and have problems of their own – and that's the way they act!

In this portion of the transcript, Dr Dryden makes an inquiry concerning any additional problems or issues that Sarah might like to raise. She responds by describing her continuing difficulty with responding to people who 'purposely act nasty'. She states her belief that 'sometimes people need to be put in place', but gives indications that she blocks herself from acting assertively because she doesn't want to give others the satisfaction of seeing that she's upset. Dr Dryden points out this self-imposed obstacle, and encourages her to experiment with speaking her mind. He also suggests that she may be subscribing to the irrational belief, 'I *have to* do the right thing', and makes the observation that the nasty behaviour of some individuals may be a manifestation of their own emotional disturbance. This observation could be viewed as having the potential to provide Sarah with a useful insight concerning human behaviour, as it is possible that she neglects to consider the impact that psychological maladjustment may have on *others'* actions.

Sarah: Sometimes I think they just get jealous when they see other people happy – and as you can imagine, I've been doing a marvellous act all my life. I would never show anybody that I was unhappy – only Art and Peter.
Dr Dryden: Yeah.
Sarah: So, I'm probably the envy of everybody. I'll bet they think, 'Oh, she's never unhappy!' Little do they know I'm seeing a therapist.

I've always put this act on: 'Oh, I'm very happy – don't you dare think I'm sad!' I'm probably a prime target when *they're* feeling down.
Dr Dryden: We can't know exactly what's in their minds, but that could certainly be a component. Did you have anybody in particular in mind when you said that?
Sarah: Yeah – it always tends to be people at work. But no matter what's happened, or how bad I felt, I've always gone on pretending everything's fine.
Dr Dryden: Yeah.
Sarah: But as you've said, people *do* have normal everyday problems, and they don't have to be afraid to show it.
Dr Dryden: So unlike some people, you don't kind of go in and say, 'Oh, I had a lousy weekend'.
Sarah: Right.
Dr Dryden: Well, it's possible that some of them may dislike you for that. Disclosing some of your own problems might help you get on better with them . . .
Sarah: I think that's probably true. I used to work with a bigger crowd of people, and they'd all come into work talking about their problems – but I would never do that. I would just say very little, or talk about happy things. I suppose *I* would dislike somebody who never seemed to have a problem!
Dr Dryden: So you could actually tell them that you *do* have problems, and see how that affects them. At times, people who seem always to be looking on the bright side are resented by others.
Sarah: Yeah – I suppose it's understandable. I mean, at work I've been living a lie, to a point.

I find that the girls are much nicer at the job I have now, so sometimes I think, 'It must be *me* – I'm being oversensitive. I must be taking things the wrong way'.

But it doesn't have to be me. I *can* be oversensitive, but it still seems that some people are just unnecessarily hurtful.
Dr Dryden: Right.
Sarah: I won't say I never moan to the girls at work – I can complain about the job

just like everybody else does. But I never go in and say, 'Oh, what a weekend – Art and I had a fight and we're not talking'. I've never done anything like that.

Dr Dryden: Yeah – again, it all depends upon what your purpose is. If you wanted to, you could certainly tell them such things. But you also have the right to keep things private – *and* take the consequences!

Sarah: Yes!

Dr Dryden: One of those consequences may be that some people – not all, but some – may want to dent your armour.

Sarah: Mm. I mean, last week I went into work one day after I hadn't had a very good night's sleep. One of the girls said to me, 'You don't look very well – what's the matter?' I said, 'Honestly, nothing's the matter.' But I don't suppose it would have hurt to say, 'Oh God, I just couldn't sleep last night!'

Dr Dryden: So what stopped you?

Sarah: (laughs) I don't know!

Dr Dryden: What *would* stop you from saying that?

Sarah: Well, it would have meant telling them that I'd been up late, worrying about Peter and his exams . . .

Dr Dryden: Right.

Sarah: . . . and I didn't want to go into all of that.

Dr Dryden: Because . . .?

Sarah: Well, this isn't going to sound nice at all, but this particular girl is the type to turn around and say, 'Well, what the bloody hell were you worrying about that for?'

Dr Dryden: So you were thinking, 'If I told her the truth, I wouldn't get a very sympathetic response'.

Sarah: Right – far from it. So I felt that I didn't want to bother telling her.

Dr Dryden: Right – it may make sense not to share personal material with certain people. But with *other* people, you could. In the past, you haven't had the flexibility to freely make that choice.

It seems that you've thought, 'I have to keep things to myself, because it's shameful to admit that I have any problems'.

Sarah: Mm, yeah. But really, that issue is about the only thing that can really bother me.

I feel that I can handle most other things – I don't worry about them too much. I just carry on every day, and as things come up I cope with them.

Dr Dryden: Well, I want to wish you all the best, and you give me a call in about six months!

Sarah: I don't have to tell you how grateful I am! (Laughs) You *do* know, don't you?

(End of recording)

Sarah has described her tendency to shy away from self-disclosure concerning problems or upsets she experiences. Dr Dryden advances the hypothesis that this could serve to impair her relationships with certain of the people with whom she has contact, and again suggests an experimental approach with respect to observing the interpersonal consequences of sharing personal information of a more intimate nature. In addition, he indicates that she can also choose to give herself the *right* to keep certain material to herself.

This final session might be viewed by some readers as ending rather abruptly, as no time is spent on lengthy farewells or discussion of feelings that may have developed between client and therapist over the course of treatment. Dr Dryden simply extends his best wishes, and Sarah responds by expressing her gratitude for the help she has received. Such an ending is in consonance with RET's position on the place of the client–therapist relationship within psychotherapy.

As described in Chapter 2, a strong bond between client and therapist is considered an important element of the therapeutic process. When these two individuals have positive feelings toward each other and perceive that they are in agreement on basic tasks and goals, therapy may proceed more smoothly and perhaps achieve more successful outcomes. It is important to note, however, that RET is a psychoeducational approach to therapy, wherein the therapist attempts to teach the client (through a variety of strategies and techniques) the tenets of sound psychological health. Thus, the therapist can be viewed as mainly taking on the roles of teacher and consultant, rather than those of confidant and friend. With this approach, it is hoped that the client develops a greater sense of personal efficacy and becomes better able to independently cope with any problems that arise after therapy has ended.

Ellis (1982; Dryden and Ellis 1985) has described his positions concerning the issue of giving warmth or love to clients. Based on his own early experiences as a psychoanalytically oriented psychotherapist, he found that acting in a very warm manner toward his clients kept them coming for sessions and seemed to help them develop greater self-esteem. Eventually, however, he discovered that their self-esteem appeared to be *contingent* upon the approval he was conveying to them, and that they were experiencing little genuine improvement with respect to their emotional problems. He subsequently modified his approach such that it de-emphasized displays of warmth to clients, and began to experiment with the principles and techniques which resulted in his initial formulation of RET. As he shed the psychoanalytic approach and became increasingly active and directive as a therapist, he found that his clients appeared to benefit more from his therapy and less frequently formed dependent relationships with him.

What are Sarah's reactions to Dr Dryden's largely business-like approach to therapy? The following chapter, based on a follow-up session conducted nine months after the end of treatment, will provide some answers to this question.

7 The follow-up session

Over the course of the prior ten sessions, Dr Dryden and Sarah covered all of the areas described on her initial problem list, and identified and dealt with additional problem areas as well. The current follow-up session serves as an opportunity to review particular areas and issues, such that Sarah's maintenance of therapeutic gains can be assessed. It also allows Dr Dryden to make inquiries as to her response to the treatment he provided. He asks her to describe what she found to be the most important elements of therapy, and elicits her reactions to the rather business-like, problem-solving approach he has employed. Post-therapy interviews are relatively rare (except perhaps in empirical studies of treatment outcome), yet they can provide the practitioner with useful information which can be used for refining therapy skills.

In conducting a problem review, Dr Dryden ascertains that Sarah has maintained and even enhanced her gains in a number of the areas on which they focused attention. It becomes apparent, however, that she has been less successful in reducing her cigarette consumption. As such, a portion of this follow-up session is devoted to further treatment of this problem.

Dr Dryden: Okay – it's been nine months since you were last here, hasn't it?
Sarah: Yes, I think so. We had agreed that I'd come back in January, but I just never got around to ringing you.
Dr Dryden: Right. Since this is your proverbial check-up, let's go back to see where you were.

According to my notes, you were self-accepting in *certain* situations, but not in others. You were working on creating opportunities to expose your weaknesses in public, in order to be able to accept yourself in the face of public rejection and disapproval.

What's been happening on that score?
Sarah: I'm much more confident about *everything*. My life-style and circumstances really haven't changed – but I no longer tend to worry that something's wrong with me. If something is wrong with me, it's wrong with me.

I think *worrying* about being neurotic was actually worse than being neurotic, if you know what I mean.

Dr Dryden: Yeah, right.

Sarah: So, I just don't worry about things anymore. I still want to look nice and that sort of thing, but I don't *worry* about it.

I accept it for what it is – I'm a fussy person! I'm not going to worry about being a fussy person, because it takes some of the joy out of it. There *is* some joy in being a fussy person – from where I'm sitting, anyway.

Dr Dryden: Right! Do you still have your job?

Sarah: Yes, the same job.

Dr Dryden: Does it still place demands on your schedule?

Sarah: Yeah – they mess my hours about terribly.

Dr Dryden: And how do you cope with that?

Sarah: Great! I'll just think, 'Well, what I don't do now I'll do tomorrow. If it doesn't get done today, hopefully it will on another day.'

Dr Dryden: Right. Have you experienced any public disapproval or anything like that?

Sarah: Yeah, yeah, Quite a lot, actually – some with the family, and some at work.

At work the manager tends to be . . . I think she needs help, actually. She must be the centre of attention all the while, and she gets quite nasty if she can't be. I'll think, 'Well, to hell with it. At this precise moment you're not going to be the centre of attention, if I've decided that I'm going to be.'

Me and some of the girls went to a fancy dress party as the 'Three Degrees'. We mimed to some of their records, and because I knew the records I had to be the one in the middle. The manager didn't like that at all, because the one in the middle gets all the attention. She really seemed to disapprove, but I thoroughly enjoyed it.

Before I came to you, I might have backed down because I would've been thinking, 'Oh, she disapproves – I can't do it!' But instead I thought, 'To hell with you – I'm enjoying this!' The fact that she disapproved didn't bother me.

I just went into work on Monday as usual, and like all spoiled children she had gotten over it. But if she hadn't, it just would have been hard luck!

Dr Dryden: Okay, good! I don't know if you remember this, but toward the end of the therapy we discussed how you felt that you sort of *needed* me to look up to and seek help from. How are you faring with that?

Sarah: At first, I used to worry that I wasn't coming to see you. I used to think that I still needed you a bit – and I've really been looking forward to seeing you again, as well. But . . . I admire you, but I don't really *need* you any more.

Dr Dryden: That sounds good – but why not?

Sarah: Because I have to make it on my own. Even if you *wanted* to promise me you'd always be here, that really might not be possible.

Dr Dryden: So when we stopped our sessions, you realized that you had to rely on your own resources – is that what you're saying?

Sarah: Yeah.

Dr Dryden: Okay. How is Peter, by the way? How's he getting on?

Sarah: He's doing marvellously! He's so grown up and so confident in himself, he doesn't *need* me. He needs me in the sense that kids like to know their mothers are there, but he's doing great. He's just got an offer from a university, and he's doing well with his A levels.

Dr Dryden: What's he going to study?

Sarah: Um, sociology, psychology and social administration.

Dr Dryden: Is he going to take the offer?

Sarah: Yes, he's going! I'm so pleased about it, and I'm not even fretting that he'll be starving or something – he'll learn to cope!

Dr Dryden: Right. How about your mum? Do you still see her every week?

Sarah: Um, no – I don't. I go to see her when I feel like it – and to be honest, I sometimes go when my conscience pricks me a little bit. It's a combination of both.

I *do* have her 'round for dinner every third week, so I see her at least that often. That's enough for me, because I feel as if I'm doing my duty. I can't say it's more than that – it's just a duty I feel. But she enjoys it, and I'm glad for that.

Dr Dryden: What kinds of trouble have you had with your family?

Sarah: Well, I'm even more involved now with my social work, and I have to be a little bit firm with mum because she disapproves of anything you don't get paid for. I had to sort of put her in her place . . .

Dr Dryden: (humorously) Would she disapprove of me helping you?

Sarah: (laughs) Exactly! I'm just glad I'm one of the people who's able to contribute, rather than take for a change. I sort of put her in her place there, and she hasn't mentioned it since.

Dr Dryden: What about your sisters?

Sarah: My sisters? Well, they all seem to think I'm becoming some kind of do-gooder – but I don't care how they look at it. I'm doing what satisfies me – it gives *me* pleasure to be helping other people. When it no longer gives me pleasure, I shan't do it any more.

Dr Dryden: Okay – what about Art's family? Do they still make you feel like an outcast?

Sarah: No – I can hardly believe that I said that. I don't know if they really *did*, or if it was just something I felt.

Dr Dryden: Well, you thought that they didn't accept you because you were half-caste.

Sarah: Yeah, yeah. I used to get quite embarrassed when they would say things like, 'Oh, the dirty Paki up the road did such and such'. But that was probably something that I fetched on myself, because of being half-caste.

Now, I'm just pleasant with them and I enjoy the few times that I see them. I don't make any fuss about it – if they invite us to a family gathering, I'll go if I want to. If I don't want to, I'll just give them a polite excuse.

Dr Dryden: Right. What about rowing with Art?

Sarah: (laughs) Oh, God! That's one of the best things of all, because I really don't row with him any more. I may have an occasional tantrum, but that's probably because I can't have my own way.

Dr Dryden: Yeah – as you *should*!

Sarah: As I should! Art's still as soft as ever – he gives in to me. But now, when he gives in to me, I sit back and enjoy it instead of feeling guilty.

Dr Dryden: Right. And do you know how to make up with him now?

Sarah: Oh, yeah. In fact, I don't let anything between us get too out of hand, because I don't feel so miserable.

Dr Dryden: Yeah – what about the premenstrual tension?

Sarah: I still find that I get it – I'll feel sort of down. But it's rewarding and nice to know it isn't going to last – it's just something that's fetched on through chemical changes, and it'll go away.

I'll warn everybody around me when it's coming on, especially Art and Peter. But at least I can talk about it now, and I don't feel that it's going to go on and on. I don't dread its coming – in fact, to be honest, it's nowhere near as bad as it was.

Dr Dryden: What about your cigarette smoking?

Sarah: I'm still very naughty there. I don't smoke as much as I *did*, but obviously, I'm still smoking too much.

Dr Dryden: How much do you smoke?

Sarah: I'm back up to about fifteen a day – and I had cut it down to five or six. I still tend to get excited, but at least it's pleasant excitement.

Dr Dryden: Yeah, right – that's what I remember you saying. What about the old spelling?

Sarah: It's terrible – but it doesn't bother me at all! The probation office asked me to be the volunteer co-ordinator, and that means quite a bit of paperwork. I just do it on a Friday, because I don't work in the shop on that day.

Actually, I thought of you when they asked me to take the job. At first I thought, 'No, I can't do it because I can't spell!' But then I thought, 'Well, it doesn't matter that much. I'll just do my best.'

That's what I do, and nobody's complained. I hope they do, actually, because then I shall say, 'Well, I can't read half of the probation officers' writing!'

Dr Dryden: Right.

Sarah: I mean, it's absolutely appalling to think that they've got A levels in God knows what, and I can't read some of the notes they leave me. I have to go around saying, 'What the hell is this?' They'll start apologizing for their writing – but it doesn't matter all that much.

Dr Dryden quickly conducts a problem review in order to determine whether Sarah has been successfully coping with the problem areas covered over the course of therapy. He asks her how she is dealing with self-acceptance and approval issues, relationships with family members, disruptions to her routine, and cigarette smoking. It appears that she is doing well in all areas except the last; as such, attention is focused on her cigarette consumption.

Dr Dryden: Right. Getting back to what you were saying before – I think that one of the reasons you continue to smoke is because you enjoy it.

Sarah: Mm.

Dr Dryden: But do you know why you *don't* give it up?

Sarah: Hm . . . because I can't stand not having my own way, really.

Dr Dryden: 'I *must* have what I want! I run the universe, and I insist that . . .'

Sarah: (laughs) I'm very spoiled, actually!

Dr Dryden: Yeah! Now, if you really wanted to cut back down to about five, you could ask yourself, 'Well, why *must* I get what I want?' What's the answer to that question?

Sarah: Because it makes me feel comfortable – but I can't have everything that makes me feel comfortable, can I?

Dr Dryden: Well, *why* do you want to give up or cut down?

Sarah: Mainly because of the side-effects they say it has. It isn't the money, because I don't feel guilty about that.

Dr Dryden: Right – it's the side-effects. Now, if you continue with fifteen cigarettes a day, you realize that you increase your risk of certain diseases?

Sarah: Yeah.

Dr Dryden: Now, when you believe, 'I *must* have what I want', and you continue to smoke, what do you tend to think you *won't* get in the future?

Sarah: No – I don't believe that I won't get some disease in the future. I believe I'm going to get something, and it does worry me . . .

Dr Dryden: But . . .

Sarah: But . . . the need for the cigarette is greater, because I can't actually see any damage being done, or feel any pain . . .

Dr Dryden: 'And because I can't see it happening or feel any pain', what?

Sarah: I suppose I'm thinking it won't happen.

Dr Dryden: That's exactly right, you see. Now, it *may* not – but you're saying, 'Because I want it, I *must* have it' – and you're convincing yourself that the bad effects won't happen to you.

Sarah: Yes – that's what it really does amount to, doesn't it?

Dr Dryden: You don't *have to* cut down . . .

Sarah: No, I know I don't *have* to do anything . . .

Dr Dryden: That's right – you have every right to smoke yourself into an early grave.

Sarah: (humorously) I know – but I'm enjoying life too much now. I don't think I want to go into an early grave!

Dr Dryden: Right. And you may escape, even if you smoke fifteen a day . . .

Sarah: Yeah – but I don't *know* that. That's the chance I'll be taking, isn't it?

Dr Dryden: That's right – so if you're prepared for that chance, you'd better not whine and scream on your deathbed.

Sarah: That's right!

Dr Dryden: 'Why me, why me?' You'll *know* why, you see. So really, you'd better first ask yourself, 'Do I really *want* to cut down?' Do you?

Sarah: I really want to cut down . . .

Dr Dryden: To . . .

Sarah: About five a day.

Dr Dryden: Right. Well, you might then find it helpful to ask yourself, 'Why *must* I get what I want?' What's the answer to that?

Sarah: Because it makes me feel comfortable if I get what I want.

Dr Dryden: Yeah, but that's only why it's *desirable*. I didn't ask you why it's desirable, I asked you, 'Why *must* you?'

Sarah: I don't know why I must.

Dr Dryden: There *is* no evidence that you *must*. If that were true, it would imply that you run the universe!

You're really saying, 'I *must* have what I want – I *can't stand* being deprived!' Isn't that what you're saying at the time?

Sarah: (chuckles) I suppose I *am* saying that, yeah.

Dr Dryden: But you *can* stand being deprived, you see. Now, there's another technique you can use, as well. Let's say you want to stick to five – if you light up a sixth, just before you put the cigarette into your mouth, turn it around and put the *lighted* end in! I can almost guarantee you . . .

Sarah: (laughs) I guarantee you myself! I really will have a go at cutting down!

Dr Dryden: Yeah – but as I said, you don't *have* to. If you don't, you don't. But it does seem as if you're telling yourself, 'I *must* not be deprived of my pleasure!' Obviously, there's no law in the universe that states that!

Sarah: Mm-hm. But the consequences will be on my own head.

Dr Dryden: Right – if you stay at fifteen, you'll be taking more of a risk.

Sarah: I'd prefer to stick to five, because then there's a chance . . .

Dr Dryden: But you can monitor yourself, and you might find you look forward to them more. Do you *only* have a cigarette when you enjoy it? Do you enjoy all of them with equal pleasure?

Sarah: No, not really.

In discussing Sarah's continuing difficulty with reducing her cigarette consumption, Dr Dryden establishes that she still has the goal of smoking only five cigarettes per day. He suggests that she is subscribing to the irrational belief that 'I *must* have what I want when I want it; I *can't stand* being deprived', which contributes to low frustration tolerance and functions to sabotage her attempts to cut down. He attempts to dispute this belief, but reminds Sarah that she doesn't *have to* reduce the amount she smokes. He does, however, encourage her to take responsibility for the possible harm she may do to herself by choosing to continue her current level of smoking.

Dr Dryden: Okay – so you can choose to work again on cutting down. Have you had any new problems?

Sarah: New problems . . . Well, yes – taking on the co-ordinator's position was a bit of a problem, because of the responsibilities that go along with it. I've got to interview volunteer applicants, and I have to ask them a lot of questions – reversing *our* roles, you see. We're looking for reliable and honest people – genuine caring people – and they trusted that I'd have good judgement with that. I enjoy it very much, and I try and do my best . . .

Dr Dryden: Do you have to reject people?

Sarah: Yes – and that's one of the problems.

Dr Dryden: Do you write to them, or do you tell them face to face?

Sarah: Face to face.

Dr Dryden: How do you manage with that?

Sarah: I'm very pleasant and polite, but straight to the point. I don't try to hide what I'm saying, because I don't think that would be fair to them.

Dr Dryden: How do they take it?

Sarah: Well, they *seem* to take it very well – whether they go outside and cry like I might do, I don't know. But I think it's only fair that you're absolutely honest with them – but you must know yourself that there are nice ways of putting even the worst things.

Dr Dryden: That's exactly right, yeah.

Sarah: For example, quite often I'll have to tell some of the clients that I work with . . . Like today, I was dealing with one particular woman who frequently gets very, very drunk. I know it's a waste of time to go to her then, but it's always then that she rings me. So, I often have to say to her, 'Look, Elizabeth – call me tomorrow when you're feeling a little bit better.'

Even though I sort of feel a little pang of guilt, I know that I'm not going to ask Art to rush me off to meet someone who isn't going to take much notice of me or remember anything about it tomorrow.

Dr Dryden: Right.

Sarah: When I feel I *can't* go, I say, 'No, I can't go'. I couldn't have done that a long time ago! I would have put myself out, and then I would've gone home feeling irritable. Now, I sort of look at it in the right perspective – I know when I can help, and I know when it's better not to try.

Actually, Elizabeth once asked me to ring her mother and tell her that she hated her. I thought, 'God, that sounds familiar . . .'.

Dr Dryden: (humorously) And you said, 'Yes, but only if you ring mine, and say the same thing!'

Sarah: (laughs) That's right! I said, 'Elizabeth, I don't think your mother is going to appreciate my saying that. You save it up until tomorrow, and if you still feel the same way then *you* can ring her and tell her.'

I've remembered something you've been telling me all along: whatever I really want, it's up to *me* to get it. You're not going to do it for me. You'll help me and give me a bit of advice and some guidance, but you will not actually *do* anything for me.

Dr Dryden: That's right.

Sarah: This is something that I try to pass on to the clients I see – and it does work.

Dr Dryden asks Sarah if there are any new problems she would like to discuss. In responding to this, she makes reference to some of the interpersonal situations with which she has to deal as a volunteer co-ordinator. She reports that she has to interview (and occasionally reject) applicants for volunteer positions, and also describes her dealings with one of her clients. The content of Sarah's statements, however, suggests that these problems are really just interpersonal 'challenges' which she appears to be handling rather well.

It is interesting to note that in speaking about her client, Elizabeth, Sarah makes reference to the non-dependent, do-it-yourself philosophy she acquired in her own therapy. Apparently, she values this philosophy as important and useful for effective functioning, and she attempts to convey it to the individuals with whom she works.

Dr Dryden: Right – what else have we got here? How about dealing with Art's fussing and his desire to chat? Does he still fuss over you and want to chat?

Sarah: (laughs) Yeah, he does!

Dr Dryden: How are you coping with that?

Sarah: That's going okay – actually, I don't see so much of him nowadays with my job and my voluntary work.

Dr Dryden: How does he cope with your going out? Does he mind?

Sarah: No – because as I've said, he's so nice. I'm not saying that he never thinks, 'Oh God, another night on my own', but I've compensated for that a bit by getting him a video player for Christmas. He enjoys watching the videos, and it's great when I come home – the time we have together is good. Anyway, I want to be able to be what I am, and if he doesn't like it that way he'll have to say so.

Dr Dryden: Okay – you can correct me if I'm wrong, but my impression is that you've actually gone *beyond* what you had achieved at the end of therapy. It seems that you've actually made more gains – do you agree with that?

Sarah: Yes, I do.

Dr Dryden: Looking back over our work together, perhaps you can tell me what you see as the most important things that made the therapy successful.

Sarah: Thinking about the beginning . . . When I first came here, I was quite convinced that everybody else was wrong, and it was *such* a shame for me – how could they all keep picking on me and expecting so much of me?

Dr Dryden: Mm.

Sarah: But really, I think you made me see that *I* was expecting too much of *myself*. Because I couldn't achieve what I expected of myself, I was making myself miserable and depressed.

I'm not quite sure *how* you made me see it, but I came to realize that I didn't *have to* have all these great expectations of myself. I didn't *have to* be all this good! I could be what I was, and still be accepted by most people. Before, I wanted *everybody* to think I was just perfect – and how dare they put demands on me that I couldn't meet!

But *they* weren't really putting demands on me – I was putting the demands on myself. I suppose one of the nicest things that's happened is that I no longer put those demands on myself. I don't feel so pressurized any more.

Dr Dryden: (humorously) Except with respect to the cigarettes, which you *must* have!

Sarah: (laughs) Yes! You're not going to let me forget that!

Dr Dryden: That's right!

Sarah: But, you know – that was one of the nicest things that happened: I don't put demands on myself any more.

Another important thing was realizing that as much as Art and Peter love me, they can't *do* things for me. They can help by supporting me, but if I want to make any real changes, *I* have to make them. Like with cutting down on cigarettes – I *can* really do it when it comes to the crunch.

Dr Dryden: Yeah – the cigarette isn't going to fly out of your mouth on its own!

Sarah: No – and I can't expect Art to keep taking it off me. I'd only tell him off, anyway.

Dr Dryden: (chuckles) That's right! 'How dare you deprive me of what I *must* have!'

Sarah: That's what would happen! So, that's good in itself – I know that if I want any changes, I have to do them myself – or put up with the way things are.

Those are the two things that stand out most of all for me.

In describing what she regards to be the most important elements of her therapy, Sarah first makes reference to the insight she has gained concerning the manner in which her self-directed perfectionistic demands contribute to emotional up-sets. She apparently recognizes that these self-directed demands were tied to her approval neediness, and that they distorted her perceptions of other people's intentions and motivations. Whereas she once saw these others as placing unreasonable demands upon her, she now sees that *she* was placing demands upon *herself*. It is quite possible that this insight could serve to enhance her interpersonal relationships, as it could assist her in relating to others with less resentment and suspicion. Also, by refusing to adhere to rigid standards for personal conduct, she may be able to avoid recurring episodes of self-downing, guilt, anxiety and depression.

In addition to this insight concerning the harmful role played by her self-directed demands, Sarah indicates that she found it helpful to recognize that she bears the primary responsibility for enacting change in circumstances with which she is dissatisfied. Although not stated in the transcript, this principle could apply to Sarah's working toward greater emotional self-control, modifying unsatisfying aspects of her life situation, and trying to affect improvements in the interpersonal domain. In addition to seeing her responsibility for effecting desired changes, Sarah also sees that it may be best for her to simply accept particular circumstances when she is unwilling to put in the effort required to alter them.

Dr Dryden: Now, my approach to therapy differs from that of many other therapists. I very much tend to take a problem-solving approach – and although I certainly try to accept my clients the way they are, I don't try and give them excessive amounts of warmth and support.

Other types of therapists may think that I'm a bit too detached, and not warm enough to clients. Can you address yourself to that?

Sarah: Yeah – I can remember that when I first came here, I expected you to be very, very sympathetic. I *wanted* you to be very warm and sympathetic and say, 'Oh, what a shame – how *could* your mother do those things to you?'

I probably would have loved to have heard all that from you, but looking back it wouldn't have done me any good at all.

Dr Dryden: Why is that?

Sarah: Because you would have just been saying to me what I was saying to myself: 'What a shame for Sarah!'

At first, I used to leave here feeling *drained* – you would ask me so many questions, and you hardly ever *sided* with me. I would feel angry – but then I'd go home and think about our sessions, and the more I thought about them, the more I knew you were doing me good. You were making me face reality!

I distinctly remember you saying, 'You hate your mother – what's so unusual about that?' That meant a lot to me, but at the time I thought, 'God, that's a terrible thing to say – people *don't* hate their mums!' But many *do* – in fact, a lot of people are probably very false about their love for mummy.

I'm glad I can respect mum and be kind to her – but I'm not false to myself, and that's the thing that counts. I don't really love her, but I'd never go out of my way to hurt her. Sometimes I'd like to tell her a few things about the way she brought us up, but I know it wouldn't do any good – so I just don't bother with it.

Dr Dryden: If I *had* been more warm and sympathetic, what impact do you think that would have had on you?

Sarah: Well, I can only speak for myself – I don't know how that might affect other clients that you have. If you had been more warm and sympathetic, I don't think I'd be the person that I am today. I might have improved *slightly* – but I know the techniques you used with me were definitely right.

 If you were to get somebody else in here with the same sorts of symptoms that I had, I'd advise you that it couldn't hurt to add a bit of warmth here and there at appropriate times. But no – don't be *too* sympathetic.

Dr Dryden: Did you see me as being on your side, or as neutral, or what?

Sarah: I thought you were mainly neutral – although perhaps a *little* bit on my side, I must admit. But I knew that you were being totally honest with me, and that you weren't going to pamper me – so I thought, 'Well, I'd best help myself'. That's the best therapy you can give anybody!

Dr Dryden: Okay, good.

Sarah: Also, I sort of saw you as the last resort. I thought, 'This is one door from the nut house, so I'd better do something'. (Laughs)

Dr Dryden: (chuckles) That's an interesting way of looking at it! Well, I think we've reviewed most of the areas we worked on – haven't we?

Sarah: I think so.

Dr Dryden: So, I'll say to you as I say to all my clients: keep up the good work! And if you have a problem, try solving it yourself – if you run into difficulty, come back.

Sarah: That's fine, thanks – and *you* keep your good work up!

Dr Dryden: Right! I will.

(End of recording)

Dr Dryden views his approach to therapy as placing an emphasis upon problem-solving, rather than emphasizing provision of warmth and love to clients. He asks Sarah for her reactions to this approach, and she admits that she first entered his office with the expectation that he would cock an exceptionally sympathetic ear to her complaints and problems.

 Sarah indicates, however, that in retrospect she can see that such an approach would have been minimally beneficial to her, as it would have served only to reinforce her feelings of self-pity. This observation can be considered in consonance with the rational-emotive perspective on abreaction and catharsis techniques (Ellis 1982), which are viewed as vehicles by which individuals essentially *practise* (and thereby subscribe ever more strongly to) their irrational beliefs.

 Sarah also describes how she would leave early sessions feeling angry about Dr Dryden's seeming lack of sympathy and support. She indicates that as she thought about the sessions, however, she was able to see that their content was helpful. As Sarah states it to Dr Dryden, 'You were making me face reality!'

8 The post-therapy interviews

Dr Dryden

The second author (Joe Yankura) met with Dr Dryden in the book-lined study of his home in north-west London in order to obtain his reflections and observations on his therapy with Sarah. As approximately eight years had passed since the time of his sessions with her, he acknowledged that his recall of some of the fine details of the therapy was less than perfect. He was, however, able to provide considerable information concerning his initial impressions of Sarah, his conceptualization of her problems, and her response to the treatment he provided her.

Dr Dryden recounted that when Sarah first entered his office, she impressed him as a rather 'meek, subservient type of client, who in a sense wouldn't "say boo to a goose".' He did not, however, view her as being incapacitated by the problems she brought into therapy, and noted fairly early on that she seemed determined to make changes in the way she was living her life. In addition, he stated that 'I saw her as a person with potential, who wasn't realizing that potential nearly as much as she might'. Given his observations concerning her unrealized potential and the level of determination she appeared to manifest, he predicted that she would respond fairly well to treatment.

Dr Dryden reported that he and Sarah were readily able to establish rapport, and that there seemed to be no significant ruptures to their therapeutic alliance. He noted, however, that she may have had a somewhat negative reaction (in terms of feeling a bit irritated) with respect to the way he responded to her reports of her problems with her mother early on in the treatment:

> She really seemed to want me to say, 'Yes, your mother is an awful person', but I didn't offer that to her. Rather than blaming her mother for her problems, my approach was to say to her, 'Let's assume your mother *is* the way you describe her – now, how are *you* disturbing *yourself* about that?' She probably wasn't terribly thrilled by that approach, as it gave *her* the responsibility for the upsets she experienced with her mother – but given

that her reactions to me generally seemed positive, I sensed that she could take it.

Dr Dryden speculates that if Sarah had met with a therapist who tended to offer more sympathy and be less confrontative, she may still have made gains with respect to her problems – her therapy, however, may have been greatly prolonged.

Dr Dryden described the 'problem list' technique (suggested as a homework assignment in the first session) he used with Sarah as a strategy that facilitates fairly quick identification of therapeutic themes. By examining the items contained on a given client's problem list, the therapist can often begin generating hypotheses concerning the types of activating events likely to be problematic for the individual, the types of emotional and behavioural responses that may be manifested when these activating events are confronted, and the nature of the irrational beliefs to which the client may subscribe. Dr Dryden indicated that he attempts to refrain from getting locked into a particular conceptualization of a client's problems in the early stages of therapy, as this could lead to misinterpretations of subsequent data the client might provide and compromise the process of hypothesis revision. Nevertheless, he stated that Sarah's 'lack of self-acceptance and difficulty with asserting herself stood out like a beacon'. These issues, of course, became a focus of treatment as the therapy proceeded.

Given his observations concerning Sarah's seeming 'meekness' and non-assertiveness, Dr Dryden made several decisions concerning therapeutic style and strategy. First, he stated that he chose to adopt a fairly business-like stance with Sarah, as he predicted that an excessively warm and supportive approach would increase the possibility that she would form an intensely dependent relationship with him. A relationship of this sort may have proven quite counter-therapeutic, in terms of reducing Sarah's desire to stand on her own feet and work on developing her coping resources. Second, Dr Dryden largely allowed Sarah to prioritize the problems contained on her problem list, and intentionally shared the task of setting sessions' agendas with her. In doing so, he hoped to encourage her to become an active participant in her therapy and to take greater charge of her life. Finally, he adopted a relatively non-directive stance with respect to homework assignments, and generally left it to Sarah to think of ways in which she might put session content 'into practice'. Again, this was intended to foster her sense of personal efficacy and autonomy, and discourage the formation of a dependent relationship.

Sarah's response to these strategies generally appeared quite positive, as she did indeed become an active participant in the therapy with respect to agenda-setting and enactment of homework activities. In addition, Dr Dryden noted that she seemed to be 'actively thinking things through'. This made him fairly confident that she was not merely paying 'lip-service' to the ideas and techniques he was attempting to teach her. In fact, he often found that she would restate session content 'in her own terms'. He rarely discouraged her from doing so, given his recognition that clients probably derive greater benefit from therapeutic concepts that they are able to reformulate in a personally meaningful way.

Dr Dryden cited his use of a problem simulation technique – the 'pipe tobacco routine', introduced during the third session – as providing further evidence that

Sarah was not simply nodding at the ideas he was trying to convey to her. The reader will recall that within this routine, Dr Dryden asked Sarah to make a quick trip into town in order to buy him some pipe tobacco. She was able to refuse this (intentionally) unreasonable request, and subsequent inquiry revealed that her trust in her therapist enabled her to do so comfortably. In a way, this particular exchange between Dr Dryden and Sarah can be viewed as underscoring her approval issues: because she was confident that he had her best interest in mind and wouldn't reject her, she was able to say 'no' to him. This incident, however, also suggested to Dr Dryden that since she trusted him, she would probably not hesitate to disagree with him on points with which she took issue.

Psychotherapists often attempt to remain alert to the occurrence of *critical incidents* within therapy. While the phrase, 'critical incident', can be defined in a number of different ways (depending partly upon the therapeutic orientation of the individual offering the definition), it is generally used to refer to events taking place during a course of therapy which have a significant impact on the client and thus appear to influence therapeutic outcome. Identification of critical incidents *during* a given client's therapy can help the therapist to gain a better understanding of the types of strategies and techniques which are most likely to be meaningful for that particular individual, such that therapeutic effectiveness can be increased. Retrospectively, the study of critical incidents can facilitate therapists' understanding of human change processes (at least within the context of psychotherapy) in general.

With respect to identifying critical incidents occurring during Sarah's therapy, Dr Dryden first made reference to his utilization of vivid RET techniques. He readily acknowledged, however, that while the use of such techniques may stand out in the therapist's mind, this represents no guarantee that they have had a strong, beneficial impact on the client. While he believes that the vivid techniques he employed with Sarah were generally effective in conveying certain important rational-emotive concepts, he speculates that the interpersonal risks she took *between* sessions (such as acting more assertively with her mother) were perhaps even more instrumental in promoting her personal change process. He sees her risk-taking forays as genuinely representing critical incidents, as they allowed her to obtain hard evidence that severely adverse consequences rarely followed her attempts to act assertively. This evidence served to provide her with greater confidence, such that she was able to assume ever greater risks.

In addition to the impact of Sarah's attempts at interpersonal risk-taking, Dr Dryden views his handling of her dependency issues as having been highly important with respect to the outcome of her therapy. Somewhat past the midpoint of her treatment, he became alert to the possibility that she might have been tending to idealize him as a person she 'needed' to help her deal with difficult people and situations. As such, he directly broached this issue with her during the seventh session. As the reader will recall, he employed a strategy which involved asking her to imagine the sorts of things he might say to help her to cope with her premenstrual tension. In doing so, he assisted her in developing self-statements for dealing with this particular problem, and effectively demonstrated that she was capable of coping independently. As a result of this intervention, she appeared to acquire somewhat greater confidence in her own personal problem-solving skills.

The reader will also recall that as the therapy proceeded, Dr Dryden and Sarah agreed to space their sessions further and further apart. In his recollection of the therapy, Dr Dryden cited this as a deliberate ploy on his part which was intended to provide Sarah with increasing amounts of time to practise 'being her own therapist'. This rather indirect strategy, combined with the more direct intervention referred to above, probably helped Sarah to be better prepared to face the impending end of her therapy. As Dr Dryden worded it, 'She seemed to get the message that "Okay, maybe I really *can* make it on my own – and my therapist isn't giving me that message because he wants to get rid of me; he has faith in me." '

Dr Dryden views his work with Sarah as having been largely successful, given that she appeared to make progress with most of the problems she presented in therapy. While he credits himself with effective application of the principles and techniques of RET, he attributes a large measure of Sarah's success in therapy to a number of factors which stand apart from his skills as a therapist. In his own words:

> For me, this case underscored the fact that we therapists had better be humble, because it is probably the case that the major determinant of therapeutic outcome is what the *client* brings to therapy. I believe that the 'match' between Sarah and myself was a good one; however, I would also cite her determination and her tendency to think things through as being instrumental to the progress she was able to make.
>
> I would take some credit for the skilful application of technique, and for being astute enough to realize that this woman had potential and didn't need to have her hand held. One might say that I saw her potential and highlighted it, which helped her to get in touch with it herself.

In addition to her determination to make changes in her life and her apparent potential as a problem-solver, Dr Dryden also believes that Sarah's supportive home environment played a part in allowing her to benefit from therapy. Family members will sometimes overtly or covertly sabotage a client's efforts to become more assertive and handle problematic situations more effectively; as far as Dr Dryden was aware, Sarah's husband and son never engaged in sabotaging behaviour. In fact, Dr Dryden's occasional inquiries concerning family members' reactions to Sarah's 'changes' seemed to reveal that her husband viewed her therapy as beneficial.

As he and Sarah left her original problem list and began to focus on certain other issues (such as her premenstrual tension and cigarette smoking), Dr Dryden reported that he had a sense that they had accomplished most of the important work of her therapy. In his view, Sarah had not completely resolved her self-acceptance and approval issues, but seemed to have reached a point where she was much more capable of handling them on her own. He thus predicted that he would not hear from her again after their final meeting, even though he made it clear to her that she could contact him if she felt the need to do so. He believes that by treatment's end, Sarah was able to see that 'she was a more resourceful person than she had thought she was, and not the prisoner of her past that she had believed herself to be'.

She seemed ready – perhaps even eager – to face life's challenges on her own.

Sarah

In preparing the transcripts and commentary which form the basis for this book, careful review of the audiotapes which Dr Dryden recorded with Sarah was conducted. Through these tapes, Joe Yankura became acquainted with a woman who tended to be rather meek, non-assertive and approval-needy. As such, when he arrived at Sarah's home to conduct the interview for this chapter, he expected to be met at the door by much the same person. After all, Sarah's therapy had been quite brief, and conventional clinical wisdom holds that therapy clients frequently have difficulty in maintaining the gains they might have achieved by treatment's end.

The Sarah who sat for the interview, however, did not present herself as meek, non-assertive and approval-needy. Quite the contrary! Approximately eight years since the end of her therapy, Sarah has grown into a woman who is largely self-accepting, unafraid to voice her opinions, and passionately interested in the work which comprises her career. She has entered the human services field, and presently is employed as an administrator of a day centre for former psychiatric inpatients. She spoke openly and comfortably about her therapy experience, and provided updates on the problem areas which had been a focus of her treatment.

Problem review

The reader will recall that during her first session of therapy, Sarah spoke about her worries and overprotective stance with her son, Peter. During this interview, she was able to report that therapy helped her to view her son as an individual who is responsible for his own life. She was thus enabled to become a more relaxed parent, which in her view was beneficial for both herself and her son. In her own words, 'I learned to let go of Peter . . . Dr Dryden really helped *two* people, there!'

Peter has since completed his university studies, and also currently works within the human services field. Sarah stated that when he finished his schooling, he voiced his intentions to move back into her home with his girlfriend. She was able to put her foot down with respect to this issue, and told him in no uncertain terms that this arrangement was not going to occur. She recognized that giving her consent would have put her in conflict with her personal values concerning relationships and marriage, and also, as she stated, 'I had no intention of running the household with another female!' Sarah views this instance of being able to say 'no' to her son – whom she loves very much – as strong evidence that she no longer makes him 'the centre of her universe'.

In general, Sarah appears to have made great strides with respect to her ability to act in an appropriately assertive manner. She is more readily able to say 'no' to other people when it is called for, and finds it easier to act in ways which are in accordance with her own wants and values. She stated, for example, that her work often requires her to attend case conference meetings with a variety of mental health professionals. As per her report, these professionals frequently display a penchant for 'therapizing clients to death', as opposed to providing them with practical assistance in dealing with some of the immediate life stressors they are facing. Sarah describes herself as being very vocal at these meetings, in terms of emphasizing the desirability of initially helping clients to resolve some of these immediate stressors. As she put it, 'What good is therapy going to do the bloke who doesn't even know where he's going to sleep tonight?' Sarah believes that during the period of her life when she underwent therapy, she wouldn't have dared to disagree with 'experts' holding university degrees and professional certificates.

From the RET perspective, Sarah's capacity to act assertively probably increased as she continued to become more self-accepting and less approval-needy. As she began to take more interpersonal risks during therapy, she found that her expectations that others would react to her in a disapproving or rejecting manner were often unfounded. More importantly, however, she learned that she didn't have to place such extreme significance upon others' opinions of her: 'As long as I know I've put in my best, I don't give a damn what anybody else thinks any more. I like to be liked, but it's not the end of the world if I'm not.' Internalization of the self-accepting philosophy implied in the above statements very likely freed Sarah to pay closer attention to her own goals and preferences.

With respect to Sarah's improved ability to acknowledge and act on her goals and preferences, a therapeutically telling incident occurred while her interview was in progress. The phone rang, and Sarah left her seat to go and pick it up. From the living room, the interviewer was able to hear her say, 'No, he's still here. You'll have to call back later.' Sarah returned to the living room in short order, and reported that her husband had called, wanting to know if the interview had been completed. Rather than engaging in a lengthy conversation with him, she had decided to cut the call short in order to allow more time for the interview. 'Years ago,' she stated, 'I would have been asking myself, "Who do I please?" I decided that this interview was more important to me at the moment, so it was natural for me to say, "Sorry, you'll have to ring back." ' Sarah is better able to give consideration to what *she* wants, rather than constantly (and anxiously) trying to anticipate what *others* may want.

With regard to the issue of self-acceptance, Sarah is able to recount in detail the manner in which Dr Dryden would attempt to counter her tendency to engage in negative self-rating. She cited the following exchange as an illustration:

> Dr Dryden would say to me, 'If somebody calls you a nasty person, does that mean you're a nasty person?' I would say, 'Well, yes – if I did a nasty thing!'
>
> He'd then say, 'Okay – does that make you a *whole* nasty person? Do you do nasty things all the time? One moment you might act badly, the next moment you might not – what do you think that makes you?'
>
> If you think about it, it makes you a person who sometimes behaves badly, sometimes is pretty normal, and sometimes is absolutely lovely. I can be all those things! That's being human, isn't it?

It seems apparent from this quote that Sarah now views her 'self' as multi-faceted and ever-changing, and thus impossible to rate in a global, absolute sense.

In line with being less approval-needy, Sarah reported that she is no longer perfectionistic about her housekeeping, and worries less about her appearance. Here, it is noted that her former upsets about 'changing plans' probably stemmed from her self-created need to stay with routines (such as showering before her husband arrived home from work) which allowed her to present a 'perfect front' to the world. She stated that 'I'm still basically a person of routine, but I can adapt to change'.

Perhaps as a consequence of increased self-acceptance, Sarah views the behaviour of certain members of her family in a somewhat different light. She now believes, for instance, that her mother – who died several years ago – acted cruelly toward her children because *she* was rejected by her husband. Sarah notes that out of seven children, her mother was able to 'provide' her father with only one son, and that this may have been a significant source of conflict between them. As a result of this insight, Sarah states that she was able to become more tolerant and sympathetic toward her mother, such that during their last few years together 'we were probably more friendly than we'd ever been in our lives'.

Sarah recalls that during the therapy, Dr Dryden made a statement to the effect that 'Many people hate their mothers'. At that time, she found this observation to be particularly helpful in terms of overcoming her guilt concerning her hateful feelings toward her own mother. Sarah stated that the 'Invitations' analogy (employed by Dr Dryden during the second session) was also quite useful, in so far as it helped her not to take her mother's opinions too seriously. She realized she was making progress in dealing with her mother's criticisms when she found she was able to 'just forget about them, rather than mulling over them'.

With respect to her husband's family, Sarah now realizes that she was probably misinterpreting much of their behaviour toward her. Whereas she once regarded them as purposely being cold and rejecting (because she was half-caste, non-Catholic and previously divorced), she now accepts that they simply tend to be more aloof than her own family had been. Her beliefs concerning the manner in which family members *should* relate to one another, combined with her self-created need for approval, led her to view standard operating procedures within Art's family as evidence that she wasn't accepted.

During their sessions together, Dr Dryden and Sarah also focused attention on problems related to her premenstrual tension. Sarah reported that therapy helped her to become better able to accept the fact that she regularly experiences premenstrual tension, such that she doesn't tend to upset herself with thoughts that she's 'going crazy'. In addition, she related that she has learned to distinguish premenstrual symptoms from 'usual' upsets, with the result that she refrains from using the former to excuse the latter. This distinction is important to her, as it allows her to identify those aspects of her emotional life over which she can exercise some degree of cognitive control.

In comparison to her other problem areas, Sarah has been less successful in modifying her cigarette smoking habit. She seems to have decided that she is unwilling to endure the feelings of discomfort and deprivation that would accompany efforts to reduce cigarette consumption, but stated that she is able to accept her continued smoking as 'one of my flaws'. She refrains from negative self-rating in connection with her smoking, and expressed her recognition that she will be responsible for any adverse health effects it causes. At the time of this interview, she reported that she was smoking a pack of cigarettes per day.

Critique of the therapy

When Sarah was asked to describe the parts of her therapy which she found most memorable, she replied by first making reference to the Big I/Little i diagram which Dr Dryden presented to her in the sixth session. She indicated that this device was most helpful in terms of teaching her the illogical aspects of global self-rating, and stated that she has even utilized it successfully with some of the clients with whom she works. She also has a clear memory of the session when 'Dr Dryden went stupid, got down on all fours, and acted like a donkey'. The intended message of this bit of therapeutic theatricality (enacted during their second contact) was not lost on her, as she was able to describe its purpose as 'pointing out that although sometimes we may do mad things, that doesn't make us mad people'. It is interesting to note that the use of visual aids and the 'donkey routine' both can be considered to fall within the category of vivid techniques in RET; as noted in Chapter 2, Dr Dryden employs such techniques as means to increase therapy's impact on the client. It seems evident that the techniques described here had considerable utility in terms of disputing Sarah's global negative ratings of herself.

Sarah also made reference to other aspects of the therapy which she found particularly helpful. She indicated, for instance, that she learned that it is preferable 'to acknowledge and deal with upsets, rather than hide from them'. In addition, she stated that Dr Dryden would frequently encourage her 'to look at things from another angle', such that she was led to re-examine some of the upset-provoking meanings and evaluations she tended to attach to problematic activating events. She cited the use of 'what if' questions as representing an especially useful tool, which she has been able to employ on her own: '*What if* somebody said you don't look nice today? Is it really the end of the world? Is it necessarily *true* that you look horrible just because they said you look horrible?' By continuing to acknowledge her upsets and critically question her thinking, it appears that Sarah has met with considerable success in 'acting as her own therapist'.

In response to an inquiry concerning features of the therapy which she found unhelpful, Sarah made reference only to the fact that she had entered therapy thinking that her therapist would be very sympathetic, and Dr Dryden's approach had failed to meet this expectation. As she had previously done in the follow-up session, however, she stated her recognition that an excess of sympathy might only have reinforced her feelings of self-pity. As she put it, 'If he'd said, "Yes, isn't the world awful", I probably would have gone away thinking, "There you go – that *proves* it!" ' Sarah was able to recall that Dr Dryden consistently refrained from blaming others for her problems; over time, this stance served to encourage her to take responsibility for the emotional upsets she experienced.

Sarah does not regard her therapy as having resulted in fundamental modifications in her basic personality structure. Rather, she views it as having been instrumental in removing the factors which stood as obstacles to full expression of the personality she believes she always had. In her words, 'The therapy didn't *change* me; it allowed me to find myself and be myself. It encouraged me to take risks, which in turn gave me the confidence to become who I really am.'

It appears that Sarah has made very good use of her therapy.

She is daring to be herself.

References

Adler, A. (1927). *Understanding Human Nature*. New York: Garden City.

Beck, A.T., Rush, A.J., Shaw, B.F. and Emery, G. (1979). *Cognitive Therapy of Depression: A Treatment Manual*. New York: Guilford.

Bordin, E.S. (1979). The generalizability of the psychoanalytic concept of the working alliance. *Psychotherapy: Theory, Research, and Practice, 16*: 252–60.

DiGiuseppe, R. (1991). Comprehensive cognitive disputing in rational-emotive therapy. In M.E. Bernard (ed.) *Using Rational-Emotive Therapy Effectively*. New York: Plenum.

Dryden, W. (1984a). *Rational-Emotive Therapy: Fundamentals and Innovations*. London: Croom Helm.

Dryden, W. (ed.) (1984b). *Individual Therapy in Britain*. Milton Keynes: Open University Press.

Dryden, W. (1987a). *Current Issues in Rational-Emotive Therapy*. London: Croom Helm.

Dryden, W. (1987b). *Counselling Individuals: The Rational-Emotive Approach*. London: Whurr.

Dryden, W. and Ellis, A. (1985). Dilemmas in giving warmth or love to clients (interview). In W. Dryden (ed.) *Therapists' Dilemmas*. London: Harper & Row.

Dryden, W. and Ellis, A. (1987). Rational-emotive therapy: an update. In W. Dryden, *Current Issues in Rational-Emotive Therapy*. London: Croom Helm.

Dryden, W. and Ellis, A. (1989). Albert Ellis: an efficient and passionate life (interview). *Journal of Counseling and Development 67*: 539–46.

Ellis, A. (1957). Outcome of employing three techniques of psychotherapy. *Journal of Clinical Psychology 13*(4): 344–50.

Ellis, A. (1962). *Reason and Emotion in Psychotherapy*. New York: Lyle Stuart.

Ellis, A. (1969). A weekend of rational encounter. In A. Burton (ed.) *Encounter: The Theory and Practice of Encounter Groups*. San Francisco: Jossey-Bass.

Ellis, A. (1973). *Humanistic Psychotherapy: The Rational-Emotive Approach*. New York: Julian Press (paperback edn, New York: McGraw-Hill).

Ellis, A. (1976). The biological basis of human irrationality. *Journal of Individual Psychology 32*: 145–68 (reprinted, New York: Institute for Rational-Emotive Therapy).

Ellis, A. (1977). The basic clinical theory of rational-emotive therapy. In A. Ellis and R. Grieger (eds) *Handbook of Rational-Emotive Therapy*. New York: Springer.

Ellis, A. (1979). The biological basis of human irrationality: a reply to McBurnett and LaPointe. *Journal of Individual Psychology 35*(1): 111–16.

Ellis, A. (1980). Rational-emotive therapy and cognitive-behavior therapy: similarities and differences. *Cognitive Therapy and Research* 4(4): 325–40.

Ellis, A. (1982). Must most psychotherapists remain as incompetent as they now are? *Journal of Contemporary Psychotherapy* 13(1): 17–28.

Ellis, A. (1983) with P. Krassner and R.A. Wilson. *An Impolite Interview with Albert Ellis* (rev. edn). New York: Institute for Rational-Emotive Therapy.

Ellis, A. (1985a). Expanding the ABC's of rational-emotive therapy. In M.J. Mahoney and A. Freeman (eds) *Cognition and Psychotherapy*. New York: Plenum.

Ellis, A. (1985b). *Overcoming Resistance: Rational-Emotive Therapy with Difficult Clients.* New York: Springer.

Epictetus (1956). *Enchiridion* (G. Long, trans.). South Bend, IN: Regenery-Gateway (original work undated).

Garner, A. (1981). *Conversationally Speaking.* New York: McGraw-Hill.

Horney, K. (1950). *Neurosis and Human Growth.* New York: Norton.

Johnson, N. (1980). Must the rational-emotive therapist be like Albert Ellis? *Personnel and Guidance Journal* 59: 49–51.

Jones, M.C. (1924). A laboratory study of fear: the case of Peter. *Journal of Genetic Psychology* 31: 308–15.

Knaus, W. and Wessler, R.L. (1976). Rational-emotive problem simulation. *Rational Living* 11(2): 8–11.

Lazarus, A.A. (1977). Toward an egoless state of being. In A. Ellis and R. Grieger (eds) *Handbook of Rational-Emotive Therapy*. New York: Springer.

Maultsby, M.C. and Ellis, A. (1974). *Technique for Using Rational-Emotive Imagery.* New York: Institute for Rational-Emotive Therapy.

Moore, R.H. (1983). Inference as 'A' in rational-emotive therapy. *British Journal of Cognitive Psychotherapy* 1(2): 17–23.

Sichel, J. and Ellis, A. (1984). *Self-Help Report Form.* New York: Institute for Rational-Emotive Therapy.

Walen, S.R., DiGiuseppe, R. and Wessler, R.L. (1980). *A Practitioner's Guide to Rational-Emotive Therapy.* New York: Oxford University Press.

Watson, J.B. and Rayner, R. (1920). Conditioned emotional reactions. *Journal of Experimental Psychology* 3: 1–14.

Yankura, J. and Dryden, W. (1990). *Doing RET: Albert Ellis in Action.* New York: Springer.

Index